# INTRODUCTION

The formal assessment for GP entry has undergone several successive changes, firstly with the addition of extended matching questions (EMQs) and secondly with the replacement of the 'True/False' multiple choice questions (MCQs) with the single best answer (SBA) or 'best of many' format. This new format is deemed to be a better test of applied knowledge, since it lends itself to assessing problem solving/diagnostics and choice of investigations and management rather than pure factual recall. This is possibly why it has been adopted by many Royal Colleges.

Having to choose one option out of five may seem more difficult since there is no longer the 50:50 chance for a guess being right; however, the problem solving nature of the questions makes them much easier to 'work-out', provided you have had enough practice with your revision of basic medicine. Although there may be some questions where the true answer jumps right at you, I would suggest that you still consider each other option before settling on your choice. In many cases however, you may find that your reach an answer by a process of elimination, which is a good technique to use.

We have reproduced the case-based style of modern MCQ questions, where candidates are confronted with a long passage of useful and useless information to process in each case. This is time consuming and you should use this book to practice sifting through the facts carefully yet with speed. One useful tip is to highlight or underline the useful facts in the text as you read them or write a list of clinical features in the margin to avoid having to reread the case several times. Preparation is key because, in the absence of negative marking, you must try to ANSWER ALL THE QUESTIONS.

A final tip is to think of the context of each scenario especially when asked for the 'next best', 'most appropriate' or 'best' diagnostic test or treatment option. Depending on the time, place and urgency of the case, the correct answer may vary greatly depending on which of these questions is asked.

You will find that some questions contain several parts. Make sure that you attempt all parts of the question before reaching out for the answer.

Good Luck
D.R.P

# CONTENT

# SECTION 1

# Cardiovascular

**Q.1 - Part 1**

Mr Jaye is a 72-year-old retired carpenter. His brother recently died of a heart attack at the age of 75 and Mr Jaye comes to see you to request a check-up. He claims to be fit and well, and walks his puppy dog for an hour every day on the Moors. He denies any chest pain or shortness of breath and is on no medication. On examination, he has a good volume pulse at 78 beats per minute and blood pressure is 122/68 mmHg. You hear an ejection systolic murmur at the left sternal edge. There are no murmurs at the carotids.

What is the most likely diagnosis?

1. Aortic stenosis
2. Aortic sclerosis
3. Pulmonary valve stenosis
4. 'Flow' murmur
5. Hypertrophic obstructive cardiomyopathy

**Q.1 - Part 2**

Which is the most appropriate investigation to arrange next?

1. Echocardiogram
2. Ambulatory blood pressure monitoring
3. Exercise tolerance test
4. 24-hour ECG monitoring
5. None of the above

**Q.2**

Mr Kunganathan is a 63-year-old corporate lawyer. He has a 6-month history of intermittent chest pain on running to catch his train. He smoked over 20 cigarettes a day between the ages of 20 and 50 and lost both of his parents due to heart attacks at the ages of 56 and 59. His blood pressure averages 142/96 mmHg and his BMI is 32 kg/m$^2$. Fasting blood tests reveal a glucose of 6.8 mmol/L and cholesterol of 8.7 mmol/L.

You need to discuss his coronary risk factors and primary prevention of a serious cardiac event. Which of the following is the most important factor to discuss with him?

1. Blood pressure
2. Smoking
3. Work stress
4. Diet
5. Family history

**Q.3**

A 38-year-old intravenous drug user presents with sudden onset chest pain, radiating to the neck, jaw and back. He collapses, with a blood pressure of 70/20 mmHg in the right arm and unrecordable in the left. His ECG shows atrial fibrillation and hyperacute T waves in leads II and III. You hear a faint diastolic murmur at lower left sternal edge.

What is the most likely diagnosis?

1. Acute infective endocarditis with valve rupture
2. Acute inferior myocardial infarction
3. Acute dissection of thoracic aorta
4. Coronary artery spasm secondary to narcotic use
5. Supraventricular tachycardia secondary to narcotic overdose

**Q.4 - Part 1**

Mrs Gatter is a 45-year-old woman who has a 3-week history of worsening central 'throbbing' chest pain. It radiates all over the surface of the chest wall and is worse when lying on her front in bed at night, but is better when lying flat on her back.

Which of the following features is the most useful to discriminate non-cardiac from cardiac chest pain?

1. Triggering of pain by pressure points
2. Response to GTN spray
3. Presence of tachycardia
4. Pain at rest
5. Shortness of breath

**Q.4 - Part 2**

Which is the most likely diagnosis?

1. Somatisation
2. Costochondritis
3. Pericarditis
4. Pancreatitis
5. Gastro-oesophagitis

**Q.5**

Your registrar hands you an ECG of a patient in the emergency assessment unit and points out that there is right axis deviation.

Which of the following is unlikely to cause this type of ECG abnormality?

1. Systemic hypertension
2. Atrial septal defect
3. Chronic obstructive pulmonary disease
4. Right bundle branch block
5. Pulmonary embolus

**Q.6**

Which of the following statements is not true regarding percutaneous coronary angioplasty (PTCA) ?

1. NICE recommends that the majority of PTCAs involve stenting
2. It has been shown that PTCA improves morbidity but at present there is not clear evidence of a positive overall effect on mortality
3. Drug-coated stents reduce the risk of restenosis
4. Up to 3% of PTCA procedures will run into complications necessitating an emergency bypass graft
5. PTCA is more likely to be the method of treating for coronary stenosis in diabetic patients than bypass grafting

**Q.7**

Mr Lake is a 52-year-old man who presents to Accident and Emergency with central crushing chest pain radiating to his jaw, sweatiness and shortness of breath. His only past medical history is paroxysmal atrial fibrillation for which he is on warfarin. The nurses give him oxygen and prepare an ECG.

What is the next immediate medical management?

1. Aspirin 300mg PO, morphine 5-10mg IV and metoclopramide 10mg IM
2. Aspirin 75mg PO, morphine 5-10mg IV and metoclopramide 10mg IV
3. Aspirin 300mg PO, morphine 5-10mg IV and metoclopramide 10mg IV
4. Aspirin 300mg PO, morphine 10-20mg IM and metoclopramide 10mg IM
5. Morphine 5-10mg IV and metoclopramide10 mg IV

**Q.8**

Which of the following options is not an indicator of a positive exercise tolerance test?

1. Tachycardia
2. ST segment elevation
3. Ventricular dysrhythmia
4. Angina pectoris
5. Failure to increase the blood pressure with exercise

**Q.9**

Mr Terrebilini is a 57-year-old pharmacist who is admitted with an acute anterior myocardial infarction. He is transferred to the Coronary Care Unit, where he is promptly thrombolysed. Within 30 minutes, he becomes acutely short of breath, hypotensive and loses consciousness.

Which of the following is the least likely cause of his deterioration?

1. Complete heart block
2. Pulmonary embolus from mural thrombus.
3. Acute left ventricular failure
4. Ventricular tachyarrhythmia
5. Anaphylaxis

**Q.10**

Mrs Rothstein had a myocardial infarction 5 days ago for which she was promptly thrombolysed. On day 2, she developed complete heart block and a temporary pacing wire was placed. She has experienced some further transient chest pain over the last few days. Ten minutes ago she complained of increasing shortness of breath and just now she has become suddenly hypotensive and the medical emergency team have been called.

Which is the least likely cause for this deterioration?

1. A new myocardial infarction
2. Ventricular arrhythmia
3. Left ventricular aneurysm
4. Mitral regurgitation
5. Ventricular septal defect

**Q.11**

Which of the following is NOT an absolute contraindication to thrombolysis?

1. Heavy vaginal bleeding
2. Severe hypertension controlled with nitrates
3. Oesophageal varices
4. 3 months post-partum
5. Acute pancreatitis

**Q.12**

Mrs Ubrinitsky had a myocardial infarction 3 weeks ago. She was taken straight to her local hospital where she had an emergency angioplasty and stenting to a proximal lesion in the left anterior descending coronary artery. She was discharged a week later on aspirin, clopidogrel, bisoprolol, ramipril and simvastatin. She comes to you today with a 5-day history of increasing shortness of breath and sharp chest pain, worse at night. On examination, she has a weak pulse of 68 beats per minute and quiet heart sounds with no appreciable murmurs. She has crepitations in her lung bases which are both dull to percussion and she is warm to the touch.

What is the most likely diagnosis?

1. Infected coronary stent
2. Idiosyncratic intolerance to angiotensin converting enzyme inhibitor
3. Infective endocarditis
4. Rheumatic fever
5. Dressler's syndrome

**Q.13**

Mr Allard is an 82-year-old man with occasional stable angina. He is currently taking aspirin, multivitamins, salbutamol, quinine sulphate, simvastatin and occasional GTN sublingual tablets.

Which of the following medications is most likely to increase his life expectancy?

1. Carvedilol
2. Isosorbide mononitrate
3. Clopidogrel
4. Bendrofluazide
5. Ramipril

**Q.14**

You are examining a 60-year-old man in Accident and Emergency who has presented with acute-on-chronic shortness of breath and chest pain. On auscultation you can barely make out any heart sounds, with the exception of the upper sternal edge and carotid regions.

What is the least likely cause?

1. Dilated cardiomyopathy
2. Pneumothorax
3. Obesity
4. Pericardial effusion
5. Emphysema

**Q.15**

Mrs Piquet had a non-ST elevation inferior myocardial infarction yesterday and was treated according to local guidelines with a low molecular weight heparin. Today she has become bradycardic with a pulse of 48 beats per minute and a blood pressure of 110/60 mmHg. She is pain-free and wants to go home. Her ECG shows P waves with every QRS complex but the P-R interval increases with each complex until a QRS is missed; then the cycle starts again.

What is the best management option?

1. Give her 0.6 - 1.2 mg of atropine iv
2. Call the Cardiology registrar and request that she be placed on the urgent angiography list
3. Place temporary pacing wires and pace her
4. Observe her with telemetry ECG monitoring
5. Cardiovert her with a synchronised DC shock

**Q.16 - Part 1**

A patient's ECG shows the following:

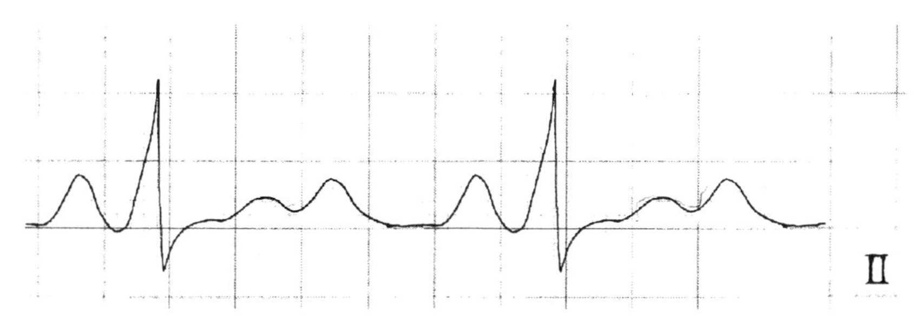


What is the likely diagnosis?

1. Hypokalaemia
2. Hyperkalaemia
3. Hypomagnesemia
4. Hypercalcaemia
5. Hypothermia

**Q.16 - Part 2**

What is the most likely underlying cause for this abnormality?

1. Total parenteral nutrition (TPN)
2. Hypothyroidism
3. Furosemide
4. Spironolactone
5. Small cell carcinoma of the lung

**Q.17**

A 40-year-old librarian presents with a 2-hour history of fast and regular palpitations. His ECG is shown below. He quickly becomes confused and short of breath. His pulse is now 220 beats per minute and his blood pressure is dropping. He came to Accident and Emergency alone and in his pocket you find a becotide inhaler and a packet of omeprazole.

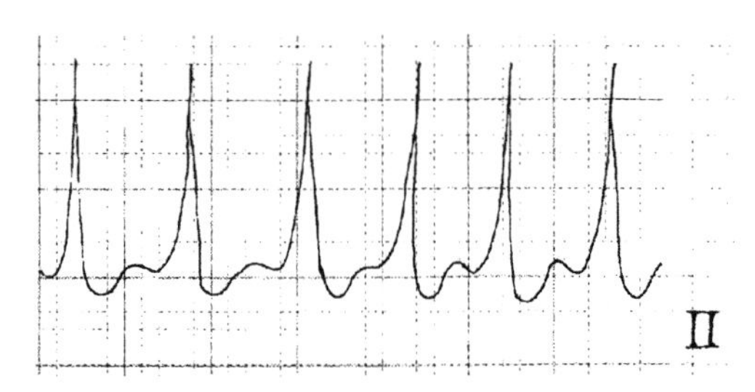


Which is the best management option?

1. Try vagal manoeuvres such as the valsava manoeuvre
2. Check Mg, K and Ca and correct any deficiencies with iv supplementation
3. Give verapamil 5-10mg iv over 2 minutes
4. Give adenosine at 6mg then 12mg boluses according to response
5. Prepare for synchronised DC cardioversion under sedation

**Q.18**

John had an inferior myocardial infarction yesterday. His ECG shows complete heart block and he has a heart rate of 46 beats per minute with narrow QRS complexes. His blood pressure is 108/68 mmHg.

Which of the following statements regarding pacemakers is correct?

1. Most pacemakers sense only in the atria and then pace only in the ventricles
2. A 'demand' of 60 beats per minute means that the maximum rate that the pacemaker will pace at is 60 beats per minute
3. If Mr Giorgio had a temporary pacemaker placed and set to a normal heart rate, a pacing spike would only be seen on the ECG if or when he became haemodynamically compromised and the pacemaker 'cuts in'.
4. Mr Giorgio currently does not require a pacemaker
5. If he had a pacemaker inserted today, Mr Giorgio could be allowed to drive again in a week's time

**Q.19**

Mrs Testa is a 60-year-old woman who has felt so unwell that she had to take time off work in the past few days. She has had a cough productive of yellow sputum and has felt 'a little feverish'. On examination her temperature is 37.7 degrees Celsius. She has an irregularly irregular pulse at 90 beats per minute and her blood pressure is 136/82 mmHg. She has a respiratory rate of 24 breaths per minute and saturations of 96% on room air. Her apex beat is displaced laterally and she has a pansystolic murmur radiating to the axilla. She has a few coarse crepitations in the upper zones that clear on coughing. She had a heart attack 2 years ago and has since been taking aspirin, atenolol, atorvastatin and lisinopril.

You give antibiotics for the bronchitis, but what else would you wish to do?

1. Arrange to start warfarin, and organise an ECG and echocardiogram with outpatient review
2. Arrange to start warfarin, load her with digoxin and organise an ECG and echocardiogram with outpatient review
3. Admit her to the ward and commence amiodarone infusion
4. Admit her to the ward and commence flecainide infusion
5. Admit her to the ward and prepare her for emergency DC cardioversion

**Q.20**

Daniela is 66 and is admitted with shortness of breath. She has had no chest pain but has had worsening shortness of breath over a few months, more so in bed in the middle of the night, with a little wheezing. She had moderate sounding crepitations in both lung bases, but she is obese and her heart sounds are difficult to determine.

Which of the following features or findings in conjunction with an ECG is the most specific to diagnose heart failure?

1. Raised serum angiotensin convertin enzyme (ACE)
2. Raised serum b-type natriuretic peptide (BNP)
3. Ground glass shadowing on high resolution chest CT
4. S3 heart sound
5. Raised serum renin

**Q.21**

Mr Jacob is a 47-year-old gardener. He presents with blurred vision and headache. He is thin, with a tanned appearance, flame haemorrhages on fundoscopy and blurred disc margins. His blood pressure is 180/110 mmHg. His blood tests show: Hb 17g/dL, WBC 6 $x10^9$/L plts 386 $x10^9$, Na 138, K 3.1, Urea 6.9, Creatinine 112 µmol/L. His urine dipstick shows protein+, blood - glucose - and leukocytes -.

Which is the most likely diagnosis?

1. Chronic glomerulonephritis
2. Addison's disease
3. Haemochromatosis
4. Conn's syndrome
5. Cushing's disease

**Q.22**

Myriam is a 22-year-old student who has just returned from an expedition in Nepal. Whilst travelling, she sustained multiple lacerations from a road traffic accident and spent several days in a local hospital there. She now presents with a 5-day history of fevers and shortness of breath. Examination reveals a regular pulse of 120 beats per minute, an ejection systolic murmur and splenomegaly. She has ++ blood on urine dipstick and an ECG shows a prolonged P-R interval.

What is the most likely diagnosis?

1. Rheumatic fever
2. Lyme disease
3. Acute bacterial endocarditis
4. Schistosomiasis
5. Typhoid fever

**Q.23**

Annie is a 70-year-old woman who has experienced episodes of dizziness and palpitations over the last few months. They occur at any time of day or night. Her past medical history includes a cholecystectomy at 45, hysterectomy at 60 and osteoarthritis. She is taking aspirin, codydramol and senna. Ausculatation reveals normal heart sounds and no murmurs. A 12-lead ECG reveals sinus rhythm at 90 beats per minute, normal axis and a couple of atrial ectopic beats.

Which investigation would you choose next to aid your diagnosis?

1. Exercise tolerance test
2. Ambulatory ECG
3. Echocardiogram
4. Tilt test
5. Electrophysiological studies (EPS)

**Q.24**

Mr Gabriel is a 68-year-old man who has had a prosthetic heart valve fitted. He is aware that he has to take antibiotics before medical procedures.

Which of the following does not require prophylactic antibiotics?

1. Oesophageal-gastro-duodenoscopy
2. Cystoscopy
3. Root canal treatment
4. Oseophageal dilatation
5. Sclerotherapy to oesophageal varices

**Q.25**

For which one of the following circumstances must a patient inform the DVLA?

1. Hypertension requiring medications to be controlled
2. Angina while driving
3. Myocardial infarction
4. Uncomplicated atrial fibrillation
5. Angioplasty with stenting

**Q.26**

Mrs Button is a 35-year-old woman with Type 1 diabetes mellitus resulting in nephropathy and retinopathy. She has end stage renal failure and has an indwelling central venous catheter in situ. She has a two-day history of fevers, nausea and vomiting after attending a barbeque yesterday. She is brought in by ambulance after collapsing at home. She is now drowsy, and complains of sharp chest pains. She has evidence of pulmonary oedema and her ECG shows a sloping ST elevation with large T waves.

What is the most likely diagnosis?

1. Diabetic ketoacidosis
2. Acute myocardial infarction
3. Acute pericarditis
4. Salmonella endocarditis
5. Staphylococcal endocarditis

**Q.27**

Mr Frederick is a 68-year-old retired solicitor. He has had angina for 6 years, but has never had a heart attack. He stopped smoking five years ago and since retirement he manages to play golf most weekdays. His symptoms had been moderately well controlled on medications, but a few months ago his nitrate was increased to get better control. Over the last month however he has found that he has had to take his GTN several times a day particularly when walking the hilly part of the golf course. This often makes him feel a little dizzy. He has no pain at rest, nor breathlessness.

He is currently taking: aspirin 75mg OD, atenolol 50mg OD, ramipril 5mg OD, Imdur ® 30mg BD and simvastatin 20mg OD.
On examination, he has a good volume regular pulse of 64 beats per minute. His blood pressure is 108/62 mmHg. Auscultation is unremarkable. He has moderate varicose veins on both legs and mild swelling of his ankles.

Which option is the best next step to take?

1. Alter the dose and timing of the Imdur ®
2. Add in nifedipine
3. Add in diltiazem
4. Add in nicorandil
5. Refer for angiography

# SECTION 2

# Dermatology

# ENT

# Eyes

**Q.28**

You have just seen Mrs Percy in your practice, who showed you an interesting rash that she has developed on her arm. She describes it as a ring-like group of itchy bumps. She shows you that some of the skin has thickened with increased markings where she has scratched but not broken the skin.

Which of the following descriptions would best fit in your referral letter?

1. Annular cluster of pruritic papules with local excoriation
2. Annular cluster of pruritic papules with local lichenification
3. Planar cluster of pruritic papules with local lichenification
4. Annular cluster of purpuric papules with local induration
5. Macular cluster of pruritic papules with local excoriation

**Q.29**

Bernard is a 48-year-old architect. He comes to you for advice about a few mildly itchy areas of depigmentation that he has noticed around the neck line. On examination you see several defined macules of subtle hypopigmentation measuring 1 to 2 cm in diameter. Close up, they have a very subtle scale. He hasn't used any new detergents or cosmetics of late, nor has he taken any new medications. His regular medications include thyroxine and metformin.

What is the most likely diagnosis?

1. Discoid eczema
2. Vitiligo
3. Chloasma
4. Pityriasis versicolor
5. Pityriasis alba

**Q.30**

Catherine is a 32-year-old woman who has Crohn's disease. She has had a partial colectomy and ileostomy due to stricturing disease, as well as several courses of immunosuppressants and high dose steroids, which have rendered her glucose intolerant. She comes to you with a two-week history of nodular lesions that have appeared on her right shin. She says that "at first it was sore, then it became lumpy the size of a ten pence piece. Then it seemed to break down in the middle, letting out some pus".

What is the most likely diagnosis?

1. Dermatitis herpetiformis
2. Erythema multiforme
3. Pyoderma gangrenosum
4. Erythema nodosum
5. Necrobiosis lipoidica

**Q.31**

Mrs Tighlit is 82 and lives alone. She was persuaded to come to you by her niece who had been visiting from Australia. She shows you a skin lesion on the side of her face that "everyone has been fussing about.". You see a well-defined raised lesion measuring 1cm in diameter. It has a shiny opalescent border with visible capillaries around a central crater with broken skin.

What is the most likely diagnosis?

1. Actinic keratosis
2. Rodent ulcer
3. Bowen's disease
4. Squamous cell carcinoma
5. Seborrhoeic keratosis

**Q.32**
Mr Sami is a 39-year-old roofer. He makes an appointment to show you a mole on his neck that he is worried about.

Which of the following features of this mole is the most significant regarding likely malignancy?

1. Itch
2. Erythema
3. Weeping of tissue fluid
4. Weeping of blood
5. Change in shape

**Q.33**
Samuel has been suffering from skin condition, which you believe to be pemphigus. He has multiple bullae on his trunk. When pressure is applied to the edge of a lesion it enlarges as the epidermis separates further from the dermis.

What other name is given to this phenomenon?

1. Pompholyx
2. Koebner phenomenon
3. Dermatographism
4. Auspitz sign
5. Nikolsky sign

**Q.34**

Simone is a 36-year-old laundry attendant who has noticed several skin rashes over her body. Your junior colleague suggests it might be a form of psoriasis but was unsure because there were some unusual features.

Which of the following features is uncommon to the diagnosis of psoriasis?

1. Pustular lesions on the soles or palms
2. Pitting lesions on the nails
3. Very itchy lesions
4. Scaly lesions in the groin crease
5. Symmetrical small joint polyarthritis

**Q.35**

Laetitia is a 29-year-old theatre manager. She has a long-standing skin condition for which she sees the dermatologists on a regular basis. They commented that she should take care of her skin since her condition exhibits the Koebner phenomenon.

Which of the following conditions is not associated with the Koebner phenomenon?

1. Vitiligo
2. Lichen planus
3. Bullous pemphigoid
4. Lichen simplex
5. Psoriasis

**Q.36**
Zack is a 27-year-old high-sea fisherman who complains of dry patches of skin on the sides of his face which occasionally itch. The rest of his medical history is unremarkable and he has had no allergies. On examination, you notice dry skin with a very subtle scale on the maxilary prominences of both cheeks. There is no erythema, excoriation, or dermal swelling.

Which is the best treatment option to try from the list below?

1. Hydrocortisone 1%
2. Aqueous cream
3. Benzoyl peroxide
4. Betnovate cream
5. Emulsifying ointment

**Q.37 - Part 1**
Mr Monzon is a 72-year-old retired market trader. He presents to your surgery with a troublesome rash around his left eye. He thinks it may have followed an incident when he scratched his face with a twig whilst gardening. It started as red and itchy skin with tingling a few days ago but the area quickly became swollen and broken down. On examination there is a warm and tender area of swelling and erythema around his left eye. On top of this, there are multiple islands of yellow crusts and a few tiny blisters.

What is the best management option?

1. Prescribe a course of high dose oral antibiotics and review in a few days
2. Prescride oral antivirals and topical fusidic acid and review in a few days
3. Prescribe topical antibiotics and antifungals
4. Refer to acute centre for intravenous antibiotics
5. Refer to acute centre for intravenous antibiotics and antivirals

**Q.37 - Part 2**

What further investigations, if any, may be necessary?

1. Tumour markers
2. Nuclear medicine white cell scan
3. Skull x-ray
4. CT of the head
5. None required

**Q.38**

Veronica is a young mother of two children, 2 and 4 years of age. Both children have eczema and are on treatment from the paediatric dermatologist. She is desperate to find out what else she can do to help reduce her children's itching.

Which of the following options may be the best help for her?

1. Change them to cotton free clothing
2. Turn down the central heating at home
3. Try them on an elimination diet
4. Change from dairy to soya milk
5. Towel dry them rather than air dry after bathing

**Q.39**

Marie is a 40-year-old receptionist who complains of an unusual rash on her body. She has multiple pink rounded macular lesions with a subtle scale to them, widely distributed over her back and chest, allthough she claims that the lesion on her shoulder appeared before all the rest.

What is the most likely diagnosis

1. Porphyria cutanea tarda
2. Guttate psoriasis
3. Seborrhoeic dermatitis
4. Pityriasis rosea
5. Rosacea

**Q.40**

Martyn is a 29-year-old fashion designer. He has experienced a number of itchy skin lesions that have evolved over a few weeks. On his wrists and neck, you see groups of irregularly shaped flat-topped purple lesions. You also notice a few raised lesions with overlying white streaks on the side of his tongue.

What is the most likely diagnosis?

1. Lichen simplex
2. Lichen sclerosus
3. Lichen planus
4. Plaque psoriasis with mucosal involvement
5. Leukoplakia

**Q.41 - Part 1**

Paula is a 52-year-old secretary who presents with a four-day history of bilateral hearing loss. She has had a 'bad cold' lately and a little dizziness and ringing in her ears but no pain.

Which option is the most informative test for classifying the type of hearing loss?

1. Imaging of the skull
2. Otoscopy
3. Pure tone audiometry
4. Weber's test
5. Valsalva manoeuvre

**Q.41 - Part 2**

You review Paula several weeks later. Otoscopy reveals a cloudy bulging drum in the left ear and a retracted drum in the right. Audiometry shows conductive deafness.

How would you manage the patient?

1. Reassurance that most cases resolve in few months with a follow up for a few months for consideration of grommets if she is no better
2. Bilateral grommet insertion and biopsy of the post nasal space
3. Co-amoxiclav orally for 14 days
4. High dose oral steroids
5. Trial of nasal decongestants and review in a week

**Q.42**
Terence is a 48-year-old traffic warden who complains of a painful swelling on his left ear. On examination there is an irregular subcutaneous nodularity of the upper tip of his left pinna.

What is the most likely diagnosis?

1. Exostoses
2. Basal cell carcinoma
3. Cauliflower ear
4. Cerumen
5. Chondrodermatitis nodularis chronica helicis

**Q.43**
David is a 38-year-old dentist who came to you a week ago complaining of deafness and pain in his right ear following a 'cold'. He returns today very unwell. Despite taking a week of co-amoxiclav and bed rest, over the last 48 hours he has developed high fevers, worsening pain, deafness and vertigo as well as a foul smelling discharge from the right ear. He looks systemically unwell and is febrile. On otoscopy, the drum appears perforated with a pearly white appearance behind it.

What is the most likely diagnosis?

1. Acute anaerobic otitis media
2. Chronic suppurative otitis media
3. Cholesteatoma
4. Otitis externa with retained foreign body
5. Labyrinthitis

**Q.44 - Part 1**
Mr Numida is a 76-year-old retired headmaster. He has been troubled by increasing tinnitus in both ears for the last few months which is starting to disturb his sleep. He denies any vertigo or headaches and does not believe that he is losing his hearing, although he admits he finds it difficult to hear people on the phone lately. He was treated for tuberculosis in his twenties, but since then has not seen a GP except for some travel vaccinations 5 years ago. He has lived alone for the past year since his wife died. He keep involved in the local community and he is looking forward to a trip he is organising to Belgium for a group of friends next month. On examination he appears to have some hearing loss in both ears and otoscopy is unremarkable.

What is the most likely diagnosis?

1. Presbyacusis
2. Acoustic neuroma
3. Ototoxicity from drugs
4. Meniere's disease
5. Depression

**Q.44 - Part 2**
What is the best management option?

1. Hearing aid
2. Referral for imaging of the brain then neurosurgical opinion
3. Carbamazepine
4. Betahistine
5. Counselling

**Q.45**

Martha is a 54-year-old hotel receptionist. She complains of a 3-month history of dizziness. She describes the sensation of the watching the room spin around her. It lasts for about a minute at a time, any time while she is awake and is worse if she has been startled. She denies any hearing loss or tinnitus. She has otherwise been previously well and is only taking multivitamins.

Which is the test best suited to identify the most likely diagnosis?

1. Tilt test
2. Hallpike test
3. Electroencephalogram
4. Calorimetry
5. Romberg's test

**Q.46**

Mr Plotski is a 42-year-old tennis coach. He has had a history of cough at night for the last 18 months, worse during the spring time. More recently he finds he is frequently needing to blow his nose. Over the last few weeks however, he has felt more blocked up and has lost the sense of smell and taste. On examination, his eyes are a little watery and he has rhinorrhoea. Just beyond the entrance of both nostrils there are smooth round mucosal projections. You graze one with a swab but Mr Carson doesn't flinch.

What is the most likely underlying cause?

1. Tumour of the cribriform plate
2. Foreign body
3. Allergic rhinitis
4. Hypertrophied turbinate
5. Cystic fibrosis

**Q.47 - Part 1**

Frances is a 32-year-old advertising executive who comes to Accident and Emergency with a nose bleed which, although only trickling, has not stopped after 2 hours. She had a skiing accident 1 month ago which resulted in an open fracture of her left femur. This was complicated by a post operative deep vein thrombosis. She is haemodynamically stable but is demanding that someone stops the bleeding immediately.

What is the best initial management option?

1. Sit her up in a chair with her head tilted downwards and get her to pinch the anterior portion of her nose
2. Lie her on a couch with her head down but turned to one side while she pinches the anterior portion of her nose
3. Lie her on a couch with her head down but turned to one side while she pinches the bridge of her nose
4. Sit her up in a chair with her head tilted downwards and get her to pinch the bridge of her nose.
5. Obtain venous access, cross match 2 units of blood, send blood for clotting studies and fast bleep the ENT on call.

**Q.47 - Part 2**

What is the most likely underlying cause for this epistaxis?

1. Hypertension
2. Nose picking
3. Cocaine abuse
4. Factor V leiden deficiency
5. Spontaneous bleed

**Q.48**

Emily is a 32-year-old waitress. You saw her 5 days ago when she came to request a sick note. She had already taken time off work due to a viral infection which most people had been experiencing. At that stage her cough had mostly cleared but she was still feeling generally weak with a blocked nose and sinus congestion. You prescribed some decongestants to go with her regular anti-inflammatories. She returns today saying that things have got worse. She feels more blocked up than ever, her nose is still watering, she has a tense headache over her eyebrows and a bad taste in her mouth.

Which is the best management option from the list below?

1. Reassure her that things will improve with time if she perseveres with her medications
2. Tell her to stop the decongestant, but reassure her that things will improve with time
3. Tell her to stop the decongestant and prescribe a course of co-amoxiclav
4. Add in a nasal steroid to reduce the swelling
5. Refer her to ENT for considering sinus wash out

**Q.49**

Mrs Nicholas brings her 8-year-old son James to see a doctor. She is concerned that his upper respiratory tract infection has caused him a sore throat as she believes his tonsils are inflammed.

Which of the following features would make you more likely to refer for a tonsillectomy?

1. High fevers and raised white cell count
2. Positive swab culture for group A streptococcus
3. Accumulation of saliva that is difficult to swallow
4. 6 episodes over the last 5 years
5. Having to take time off from school

**Q.50 - Part 1**

Agnes is a 68-year-old woman with diabetes and angina. She comes to you for her diabetic annual review which is 6 months overdue. She needs a lot of support with maintaining good glycaemic control. She agrees that her eyesight may have deteriorated since she met you last, but blames a lot of this on poor lighting at home. On fundoscopy, you note microaneurysms and blot haemorrhages at the periphery, with a ring of hard exudates at the fovea.

What term best describes her retinopathy?

1. Background diabetic retinopathy (BDR)
2. Preproliferative diabetic retinopathy (PPDR)
3. Proliferative diabetic retinopathy (PDR)
4. Diabetic maculopathy
5. Retinal haemorrhage

**Q.50 - Part 2**

What action would you take?

1. Reassure her that since there are no active bleeding points you just need to keep tight glycaemic control and monitor her regularly with retinal photography
2. Increase her oral antihypertensives, encourage tight glycaemic control and review her 6 monthly with retinal photography
3. Routine referral to the ophthalmologist
4. Urgent referral to the rapid access ophthalmology clinic
5. Urgent referral to today's emergency ophthalmology clinic

**Q.51**
Mr Oyele is a 48-year-old finance manager. He comes for a routine check up; however he does mention that he has noticed some blurred vision in the evenings and has had increased thirst. He also gets headaches at work when 'the stress gets to him'. He weighs 98 kg and is 1.65 m tall. His blood pressure is 160/98 mmHg. As part of his examination you perform a fundoscopy.

Which of the following findings on fundoscopy is suggestive of hypertensive rather than diabetic retinopathy?

1. Cotton wool spots
2. Microaneurysms
3. Hard exudates
4. Arteriolar narrowing
5. Haemorrhages

**Q.52**
Charlotte is a 23-year-old student. She has just returned from a 3-month expedition to South America. During her trip, she experienced a short episode of 'misting vision' whilst out trekking. This lasted most of the day but resolved after a night's rest. At that time she had a severe one-sided retro-orbital headache and felt generally weak. She is a smoker of 20 'roll-ups' a day and admits having smoked 'other substances' with the locals. She has a thin build and says that she has lost weight since an episode of food poisoning at the beginning of her trip, after which most of the group decided to avoid eating meat. Her past medical history is limited to an appendicectomy at age 10 and she is on no regular medications. On examination she has 6/5 acuity in both eyes. However the disc appears brighter on the left side compared to the right.

What is the most likely underlying cause for this presentation?

1. Vitamin B12 deficiency
2. Multiple sclerosis
3. Migraine
4. Toxic optic neuritis
5. Retinal artery occlusion

**Q.53**

Odette is a 48-year-old violinist who is brought in by ambulance to hospital one evening. She was on stage ready to perform a solo for the opening piece, but as the lights dimmed and she turned to focus on her music score she experienced excruciating pain in her left eye. The pain was so severe that she collapsed and vomited. She said that she could see a ring of light which she thought was from the stage lighting; she thought that she was going to die. Her left eye is red and watery with a misty cornea. Her pulse is 120 beats per minute and she is trembling and breathless at 28 breaths per minute.

What is the most likely diagnosis?

1. Acute episcleritis
2. Acute retrobulbar neuritis
3. Acute closed angle glaucoma
4. Acute panic attack
5. Acute scleritis

iscMEDICAL
Interview Skills Consulting

# SECTION 3

# Endocrinology

# Metabolic

**Q.54**

Simone is a 17-year-old student who is brought in by ambulance after having collapsed at a night club. She doesn't remember much about this episode except some tingling in her fingers which has now passed. She has type 1 diabetes and she tells you that the doctors are pleased with her control at the moment, although she had a 'rocky time' when doing her GCSEs. She has a GCS of 15 with normal pupils and no focal neurological signs. Her pulse is regular at 90 beats per minute with a blood pressure of 120/64 mmHg and no postural drop. Her capillary blood glucose is 6.2 mmol/L.

What is the most likely cause of this event?

1. Hyperventilation
2. Amphetamine abuse
3. Hypoglycaemic attack
4. Hyperglycaemic attack
5. Addisonian crisis

**Q.55**

Odette is a 68-year-old Jamaican in whom you diagnosed Type 2 diabetes 18 months ago. Despite lifestyle changes she had to start oral hypoglycaemics a year ago and is currently taking metformin and glipizide. You see her for a review of her diabetes and notice her HbA1c is 7.2% compared to 7.4% at diagnosis. However, looking at her home glucose chart, her glucose is very well controlled. She even shows you her record card from a local slimming club which shows slow but steady weight loss over the last 6 months. You calculate her BMI as 25 $kg/m^2$.

What is the best option?

1. Congratulate her on the weight loss and encourage her to continue good glycaemic control
2. Test her for a haemoglobinopathy
3. Take a fructosamine measurement
4. Try her with orlistat
5. Refer her to the specialist nurse for extra adherence and lifestyle support

**Q.56**

Allyson is an 18-year-old mathematics student. She is brought into Accident and Emergency after collapsing at family gathering. She is too weak to give a history but her older sister Mischa is a medical student and gives you a clear account. Mischa describes her sister as looking anxious and sweaty before becoming confused and passing out. Unlike Mischa who has diabetes, Allyson suffers from asthma but usually only requires occasional salbutamol. However, Allyson recently finished a short course of prednisolone after her breathing deteriorated following an upper respiratory tract infection.

On examination, she is very thin, with a GCS of 15 with normal pupils and no focal neurological signs. Her pulse is regular at 82 beats per minute with a blood pressure of 104/62 mmHg. Her electrolytes are normal but serum glucose is 1.8 mmol/L. She is promptly resuscitated and you manage to get urgent advice from the on call endocrinologist who suggests an immediate series of tests. These results come back in due course and the computerised comment on the report reads 'normal' for all the pituitary hormones except LH and FSH which are 'low', C-peptide reads 'low' and insulin is 'high'.

What is the most likely cause for this presentation?

1. Addisonian crisis from steroid withdrawal
2. Exogenous insulin
3. Insulinoma
4. Acute alcohol intoxication
5. Social phobia

**Q.57 - Part 1**

John is a 72-year-old retired postman. He was diagnosed with diabetes about 20 years ago and despite lifestyle changes he has had to take medications. He complains of increased pain in his legs, worse at night, feeling as if his feet were on fire. He still keeps active and his favourite pastime is walking his dog in the hills. On examination of his feet he has a prominent first metatarsal head projecting medially on both feet. There is thickened skin around these areas which has decreased sensation. Part of these areas are broken and weeping. You don't have access to neuropins or a tuning fork but his proprioception is intact. His toes are warm and he can feel you touching them. You find it difficult to examine distal pulses.

What is the most likely cause of his symptoms?

1. Charcot's joints
2. Diabetic arteriopathy
3. Sensory polyneuropathy
4. All of the above
5. None of the above

**Q.57 - Part 2**

What is the best next option to help John with his symptoms?

1. Bed rest and tighter glycaemic control
2. Refer to chiropodist for debridement and fitting of better footwear
3. Amitryptyline 10 to 25 mg nocte
4. Capsaicin 0.075% cream
5. Refer to vascular surgeon

**Q.58**

Mr Ngoyo is a 59-year-old managing director who comes to you for a check-up in order to apply for life insurance. He has previously been fit and well, requiring no regular medications and has no symptoms of note. He weighs 88 kg and is 1.7 m tall. His blood pressure is 130/70 mmHg. His full blood count and biochemistry are normal except a for fasting glucose of 6.8 mmol/L.

What is the best next step?

1. Reassure him that things are fine for now and review in 6 months
2. Send him to a dietician and recheck the glucose in a few months' time
3. Check his urine for glucose
4. Organise an oral glucose tolerance test (OGTT)
5. Request an HbA1c

**Q.59**

Mr Ellis is a 59-year-old IT engineer. He was diagnosed with diabetes 3 months ago when a fasting blood glucose taken at his GP practice came back high. At that time, he was reluctant to start medications and wished to try lifestyle changes to improve his health. Since then, he has increased his time spent on exercise and has given up smoking; however his BMI is still raised at 30 kg/m$^2$ and his glucose is still high. His creatinine is 110 μmol/L and there was glycosuria detected on urine dipstick.

Which of the following drugs would you consider to be the best first line drug?

1. Metformin
2. Gliclazide
3. Enalapril
4. Rosiglitazone
5. Acarbose

**Q.60**

Mr Lee is a 63-year-old accountant. You have recently diagnosed him with Type 2 diabetes. His blood pressure is 152/96 mmHg and his BMI is 31 $kg/m^2$. His HbA1c is 7.6% and his cholesterol is 7.2mmol/L.

Which is the most important factor in preventing macrovascular complications such as coronary heart disease?

1. Increasing exercise
2. Reducing weight
3. Reducing cholesterol
4. Strict blood pressure control
5. Strict glycaemic control

**Q.61 - Part 1**

Priscilla is a 26-year-old receptionist. She has been having trouble conceiving with her partner despite unprotected regular intercourse for almost a year and she thinks it is because she is overweight. She thought she had fallen pregnant a few months ago but it was just a missed period. However her periods have always been irregular and it is difficult to tell if it is late. On examination she has obvious abdominal obesity and a high BMI. She also has facial hair and acne.

What is the most likely diagnosis?

1. Polycystic ovarian syndrome
2. Cushing's disease
3. Prolactinoma
4. Hypothyroidism
5. Kallman's syndrome

**Q.61 - Part 2**

What is the most appropriate next management option?

1. Profile of pituitary hormones
2. Transsphenoidal tumour resection
3. Start metformin
4. 24-hour urinary free cortisol
5. Give bromocriptine

**Q.62**

Steve is a 28-year-old musician. He has noticed increased swelling under his nipples and thinks that he is growing breasts. Recently, he has noticed that he gets morning headaches more often, but not every day, and most often they are associated with heavy drinking and smoking 'weed' at a gig the night before. On examination he has bilateral gynaecomastia. He has a few tattoos but no other skin blemishes. His abdomen is soft and non-tender with no organomegaly.

What is the most likely cause for his symptoms?

1. Alcohol
2. Cannabis
3. Amphetamines
4. Chronic liver disease
5. Prolactinoma

**Q.63**

Mr Brooks is a 52-year-old estate agent. He comes to you because he feels generally unwell. He is low in mood and lethargic. In fact he is sleepy a lot of the day and loses his attention easily, even when engaged in conversation with a client. His wife says that it must be because "he keeps the whole street awake at night with his snoring". He is concerned about his weight gain, and he has had to buy new shirts because the collars were too tight. On examination he does have a large build and is overweight at 110 kg. When you take his pulse, his hands feel doughy and sweaty. His blood pressure is 148 / 96 mmHg. You also detect glucose on his urine dipstick.

Which of the following is the best next investigation?

1. Oral glucose tolerance test (OGTT)
2. 24-hour urinary cortisol
3. Dexamethasone suppression test
4. Insulin like growth factor 1 (IGF-1)
5. Serum growth hormone

**Q.64**

Lucy is a 22-year-old drama student. She has been feeling unwell for a few days with pain passing urine, increased urinary frequency and over the last day, increasing abdominal and loin pain that has become more intense on the right side. She has lost her appetite and has vomited this morning. While talking to you, she is retching. She has Type 1 diabetes, asthma and hayfever. She took her temperature at home and found it was 37.9 degrees Celsius. She tells you that she tried to take her blood glucose measurement at home but the machine didn't register it. It just said 'Hi'.

Which of the following options is the most important next step?

1. 4 - 8 units of subcutaneous insulin stat followed by an insulin sliding scale
2. 4 - 8 units of intravenous insulin stat followed by an insulin sliding scale
3. 1 litre of normal saline intravenous stat
4. Commence 3rd generation cephalosporin intravenously
5. 10 mg of metoclopramide intramuscularly stat with nasogastric tube insertion

**Q.65**

Nadia is a senior executive in a high-flying city PR and Media company. She has a very busy work and social life, often out late at night with friends or entertaining clients at short notice. She felt very unwell the other day when a client was late for dinner and she had already taken a pre meal dose of insulin. She loves her job and worked hard to get to where she is, but she also has Type 1 diabetes and glucose control is hard to manage with this lifestyle.

When considering her insulin formulations, which would be the best type to include in her regimen?

1. Glargine
2. Mixtard ®
3. Insulatard ®
4. Humalog ® or Novarapid ®
5. Actrapid ® or Humulin ®

**Q.66**

Sheila is a 46-year-old dinner lady. She has a 5-day history of flu-like symptoms including headaches, fevers, myalgia and diarrhoea and, like a few of her colleagues, she has had to take time off work. She felt so bad with headache that, at the weekend, she attended Accident and Emergency. A few tests were taken but she was discharged with simple pain killers and told to see you, her GP, in the week. The hospital test shows thyroid function as follows, with normal range in brackets:

TSH - 60 (70 - 140 mmol/L)
T4 - 0.3 (0.5 - 5.0 mu/L)

What is the most likely diagnosis?

1. Sick euthyroid syndrome
2. Subclinical hypothyroidism
3. Subclinical hyperthyroidism
4. Secondary hypothyroidism
5. Hashimoto's thyroiditis

**Q.67**

Mr Hawkins is a 53-year-old insurance broker. He has been non-specifically unwell for a number of months and blames it on work stress. He has lost two stones in weight over the last month without actively dieting. He is convinced that he has a cancer because he noticed a lump in his neck. He is very agitated and distressed about this. He was seen by a locum a few weeks ago who recorded finding a lump in Mr Hawkins' thyroid gland. The locum requested blood tests, including thyroid function profile, and a radio-isotope thyroid scan was organised. Mr Hawkins has returned today for the results. The report states '...diffuse uptake of isotope with a hot nodule on the lower pole of the right lobe...'.

What is the most likely diagnosis?

1. Papillary adenocarcinoma of the thyroid gland
2. Anaplastic adenocarcinoma of the thyroid gland
3. Medullary adenocarcinoma of the thyroid gland
4. Functional adenoma of the thyroid gland
5. Graves' disease

**Q.68**

Gergana is a 27-year-old dancer. She gave birth to her first child 6 weeks ago. It was a long labour and she wasn't able to have an epidural. She delivered vaginally, but had a heavy post-partum haemorrhage which required a 7-unit blood transfusion. She comes to you feeling non-specifically unwell. She has low mood, says she is extremely tired and feels dizzy a lot of the time. In particular, she feels light-headed when she gets up first thing in the mornings. She collapsed whilst out with her partner in the supermarket the other day and a passer-by who was diabetic took her blood sugar level because she thought Gergana looked as if she was having a 'hypo'. The reading was 'Lo' and a sugary drink made her feel a bit better.

What is the likely cause of these problems?

1. Post-natal depression
2. Sipple's syndrome
3. Waterhouse-Friederichsen's syndrome
4. Kallman's syndrome
5. Sheehan's syndrome

**Q.69 - Part 1**

Mrs Garcia is a 42-year-old bank clerk. Her eyes feel dry and gritty and she is experiencing some blurred vision at the end of the day. She otherwise feels very well and does not complain of any aches or pains elsewhere, nor tiredness or lethargy. On examination, she appears happy but with a startled expression. Her eyes are a little red and you notice the cornea visibly all around each iris. On testing her eye movements, she describes double vision on extremities of lateral vision.

What is the most likely underlying cause for her eye problems?

1. Graves' disease
2. Multinodular thyrotoxicosis
3. Myasthenia gravis
4. Myotonic dystrophy
5. Sjögren's syndrome

**Q.69 - Part 2**

Which step is most likely to help with these visual problems?

1. Viscotears ® eye drops
2. Orbital radiotherapy
3. Propranolol
4. Carbimazole
5. Referral to a neurologist

**Q.70**

Doris is a 72-year-old retired cleaner. She came to you a few weeks ago for a check-up because she had been feeling generally unwell with lethargy and shortness of breath. She lives in a ground floor flat close to her local shops. Despite this she felt that light activities were too much for her. You took a series of blood tests and discovered a raised TSH and low T4.

Which of the following complications is most likely to occur after initiating treatment?

1. Seizures
2. Atrial fibrillation
3. Confusion or psychosis
4. Angina
5. Hypertension

**Q.71**

Geeta is a 62-year-old housewife and grandmother. She fell whilst out shopping a few weeks ago and sustained a wrist fracture. The biochemistry results from her discharge summary, with normal values in brackets, are shown in the table below.

| | | | |
|---|---|---|---|
| Sodium | 141 | mmol/L | |
| Potassium | 4.6 | mmol/L | |
| Urea | 6.8 | mmol/L | |
| Creatinine | 70 | µmol/L | |
| Albumin | 36 | g/L | |
| Bilirubin | 8 | µmol/L | |
| Aspartate transaminase | 20 | iu/L | (7-40) |
| Alkaline phosphatase | 100 | iu/L | (25-115) |
| Adjusted calcium | 1.8 | mmol/L | (2.20-2.67) |
| Phosphate | 1.86 | mmol/L | (0.87-1.45) |

What is the most likely cause for this pattern of results?

1. Osteoporosis
2. Osteomalacia
3. Multiple myeloma
4. Hypoparathyroidism
5. Paraneoplastic disease

**Q.72**

Sartaj is 32-year-old marketing assistant recently diagnosed with chronic renal impairment. The renal specialist indicated in a recent clinic letter that Sartaj has low calcium levels and she has asked your help to remedy this.

Which of the following is the best option for you to try?

1. Increase his dietary dairy consumption
2. Oral calcium supplements
3. Oral alfacalcidol
4. Oral calciferol
5. Oral calcium and magnesium supplements

**Q.73**

Rajan is a 36-year-old surveyor. He has experienced several bizarre episodes whilst at work over the last few months. They include palpitations, sweats and tremors. He went to Accident and Emergency due to an episode a few weeks ago when he felt like he couldn't breathe. They commented he had a very high blood pressure and some glucose in his urine dipstick. One junior doctor also thought he had a goitre. His symptoms settled by the time he got his blood tests back, which were normal, so they let him go. On examination today, he seems well, with a regular pulse of 88 beats per minute and a blood pressure of 122/76 mmHg. He weighs 76kg and is 1.6m tall. His urine dipstick is normal and you can't palpate any neck masses.

What is the likely diagnosis?

1. Conn's syndrome
2. Phaeochromocytoma
3. Thyroid storm
4. Cushing's syndrome
5. Carcinoid syndrome

**Q.74**

Mr Cairns is found to have Cushing's syndrome due to a screening test that you ordered after he presented with symptoms suggestive of the condition.

Which is the best combination of tests to localise the cause of this syndrome?

1. High dose dexamethasone suppression test and low dose dexamethasone suppression test
2. High dose dexamethasone suppression test and MRI of the pituitary fossa
3. High dose dexamethasone suppression test and plasma ACTH level
4. High dose dexamethasone suppression test and corticotrophin releasing hormone (CRH) test
5. High dose dexamethasone suppression test and petrosal sinus monitoring

**Q.75**

Ricky is a 48-year-old man with manic depression. He is brought in by ambulance to hospital after a housemate found him unconscious on his bedroom floor. Ricky had locked himself in his room after an argument with his girlfriend 2 hours previously. 20 minutes later the housemate heard a thud and had to bash the door down to get into his room. There was an empty bottle of whisky on the floor and next to it was a paracetamol pack with 30 empty blisters.

What is the best management strategy?

1. Gastric lavage and start N-acetyl cystine immediately
2. Gastric lavage and give activated charcoal and start N-acetyl cystine immediately
3. Give activated charcoal and start N-acetyl cystine immediately
4. Gastric lavage, give activated charcoal and await the 4-hour plasma paracetamol level to guide you further
5. Give activated charcoal and await the 4-hour plasma paracetamol level to guide you further

**Q.76**

Tarina is a 16-year-old student. She is brought into Accident and Emergency by friends after collapsing in the street. She didn't lose consciousness for very long and there were no abnormal limb jerks noticed by the friends, nor did she lose urinary continence. She is weak and the history is taken via her friends. They claim that she hasn't got any known medical problems although she had seemed a little different over the last few days, particularly depressed and disappearing off to the toilet by herself. On examination she appears thin and pale. She has dry skin and wiry hair. Her nails are brittle and the skin is tough over thedistal interphalangeal joints of the index and middle fingers of her right hand. Her pulse is 80 beats per minute with a blood pressure of 88/42 mmHg. Her respiratory rate is 30 breaths per minute. Her arterial blood gas shows a pH of 7.25 and a base excess of -18 mmol/L. The analyser comments that the anion gap is normal.

From the following list, what is the most likely explanation of these findings?

1. Laxative abuse
2. Paracetamol overdose
3. Aspirin overdose
4. Carcinoid syndrome
5. Lactic acidosis

**Q.77**

Roshina is a 38-year-old beautician, who has an 8-month history of increased thirst and micturition. She gets through several litres of mineral water whilst at work each day. Her past medical history is unremarkable and she is taking no medications or herbal remedies. Examination is also unhelpful and you organise a few blood and urine tests. Both her plasma and urine osmolality tests come back as 'low'.

Which is the best management option?

1. Refer to endocrinologist for a water deprivation test
2. Refer to a neurologist to asses for cranial diabetes insipidis (CDI)
3. Refer to endocrinologist to treat nephrogenic diabetes insipidis (NDI)
4. Advise her on taking her employers to an industrial tribunal
5. Counsel her and discuss behavioural management strategies

**Q.78**

Cyril is a 57-year-old ex-army officer. He has recently been diagnosed with myeloma and has just started a course of chemotherapy. He soon becomes very unwell, nauseated and vomiting. He is dehydrated and his blood tests reveal renal failure with a raised potassium. One other substance is likely to be raised and contributing to the renal impairment.

You can give specific treatment for it. Which substance is it?

1. Lactate dehydrogenase
2. Urate
3. Calcium
4. Magnesium
5. Creatinine kinase

# SECTION 4

# Gastroenterology

# Nutrition

**Q.79 - Part 1**

Meena is a 22-year-old single mother. She has had soreness in the mouth for a few weeks, particularly on the tongue. On examination, you see that her tongue is red, smooth and mildly swollen. There are no breaks in the skin surface or exudates.

What is the most likely diagnosis?

1. Aphthous ulceration
2. Cheilitis
3. Glossitis
4. Oral thrush
5. Gingivitis

**Q.79 - Part 2**

What is the likely underlying cause?

1. Amyloid deposition
2. Vitamin C deficiency
3. Iron deficiency
4. Candida albicans
5. Anti-smooth muscle antibodies

**Q.80 - Part 1**

Ali is a 48-year-old postmaster. He complains of a 2-month history of difficulty swallowing.

Which of the following features would best distinguish between a malignant lesion and a neurological cause?

1. Regurgitation
2. Pain on swallowing
3. Intermittent versus constant symptoms
4. Weight loss
5. Difficulty with liquids from the start

**Q.80 - Part 2**

Ali has a barium swallow as an outpatient. The report states that there is corkscrew motion in the oesophagus.

What is the most likely diagnosis?

1. Achalasia
2. Oesophageal spasm
3. Normal peristalsis
4. Bulbar palsy
5. Pseudobulbar palsy

**Q.81**

Andrew is a 42-year-old finance manager. He complains of indigestion that has bothered him for the past few months. It is a sharp epigastric pain that is worse before eating and aggravated by alcohol and spicy foods. He doesn't think that he has lost any weight and denies any difficulty or pain on swallowing or acid brash. Symptoms are no worse before bed time or lying flat. Other than occasional hayfever, he has not had any other significant medical problems and is on no regular medication from a doctor or over the counter. His BMI is 22 kg/m$^2$ and examination is otherwise unremarkable.

Part a : Which of the following is your first management option?
Part b : Which option would you choose next if the first is unhelpful?

1. Treat with a proton pump inhibitor alone
2. Test for helicobacter pylori and treat with triple therapy if test is positive
3. Try simple antacids and cut down on rich and spicy foods
4. Refer for upper gastro-intestinal endoscopy
5. Treat with triple therapy (amoxycillin, clarithromycin and proton pump inhibtor)

**Q.82**

Malik is a 44-year-telephonist. He complains of heartburn and indigestion that has been going on relentlessly for several months. It is worse in bed at night or after a large meal. He has lost a little weight but put that down to a slimming programme that he is trying out. He doesn't smoke and drinks minimal alcohol at weekends. He has tried several over-the-counter indigestion remedies but they have also been unhelpful. He thought that his lifestyle was to blame but he still experienced symptoms on a recent two week 'detox' at a health spa. His only other medication is occasional paracetamol for headaches. He works long hours and doesn't find much time to eat at work. His BMI is 32 kg/m$^2$ and examination is otherwise unremarkable.

What is the best next management step?

1. Treat with a proton pump inhibitor alone
2. Test for helicobacter pylori and treat with triple therapy if test is positive
3. Try simple antacids and cut down on rich and spicy foods
4. Refer for upper gastro-intestinal endoscopy
5. Treat with triple therapy (amoxycillin, clarithromycin and proton pump inhibitor)

**Q.83**

Ahmed is a 37-year-old stockbroker. He has a 6-month history of intermittent heartburn that has become more constant over the last few months. He gets pain before and after meals, during the daytime and asleep at night. He has tried several over-the-counter remedies including Zantac ® but this has not really helped. He has recently given up smoking and he drinks no alcohol. He has a BMI of 28 $kg/m^2$. You suspect gasto-oesophageal reflux disease (GORD).

Which of the following is the most likely to clarify this diagnosis?

1. H. pylori serology
2. $^{13}$C-urea breath test
3. Barium swallow
4. Upper gastro-intestinal endoscopy
5. Oesophageal pH and manometry testing

**Q.84**

Eileen is a 57-year-old check-out assistant. A few days ago she was taken into hospital as an emergency after collapsing with abdominal pain. She was thought to have a perforated ulcer and was managed conservatively. An endoscopy revealed a large solitary ulcer in the lesser curvature of the stomach on a background of erythema and few other gastric erosions. She also has chronic obstructive pulmonary disease for which she takes regular inhalers. A week ago, her breathing deteriorated and she was given a 7-day course of 40 mg prednisolone daily. She is on no other medications nor has any allergies.

What is the most likely underlying cause of this presentation?

1. Helicobacter pylori
2. Corticosteroids
3. Cushing's ulcer
4. Curling's ulcer
5. Zollinger-Ellison syndrome

**Q.85**

Jake is a 24-year-old mechanic. He has had diarrhoea for 2 days. His stool frequency is 6 to 8 times per day, he has urgency and describes the stool as watery, but he has not noticed any blood. He has tried to keep drinking fluids but is now feeling a little dehydrated and generally unwell. The other day he noticed a little sharp pain around his anus on defecation and a small amount of fresh blood on the toilet paper after wiping. He is otherwise fit and well and on no medications. His girlfriend has had a similar illness. She doesn't work so she has gone to see her own doctor today. On examination his pulse is regular at 98 beats per minute, his blood pressure is 108/60 mmHg and he appears mildly dehydrated. His temperature is 37.7 degrees Celsius.

What is the best management option?

1. Arrange admission for intravenous therapy, inpatient investigations and notify the local consultant in communicable diseases about a possible outbreak of food poisoning
2. Reassure him, advise on oral rehydration therapy and give him a pot for stool sampling
3. Reassure him, advise on oral rehydration therapy and loperamide and give him a pot for stool sampling
4. Reassure him, advise on oral rehydration therapy and loperamide
5. Reassure him, advise on oral rehydration therapy. Give him a pot for stool sampling and notify the local consultant in communicable diseases about a possible outbreak of food poisoning

**Q.86**

Cheryl is a 36-year-old secretary. She come to you about changes in bowel habit that she has had for many months. She gets urgency and diarrhoea some times and at other times constipation and abdominal pain.

Which of the following would make diagnosis of inflammatory bowel syndrome (IBS) very unlikely?

1. Mucus on stool
2. Tenesmus
3. Pain waking her from sleep
4. Pain worsening during menstruation
5. Bloating

**Q.87**

Mrs Santos is a 76-year-old retired cook. She is brought into Accident and Emergency after collapsing following an episode of diarrhoea, which she describes as violent and looking as black as tar. She had been well over the last few weeks and the last time she saw her doctor was 2 months ago when she ran out of all her medications. Her medications comprise: cocodamol, naproxen, aspirin, atorvastatin, ramipril, frusemide, spironolactone, metoprolol, Imdur ® and GTN tablets.

She is a little pale, but alert and comfortable at rest on the trolley. Her pulse is regular at 62 beats per minute and her blood pressure is 98/58 mmHg. Her abdomen is diffusely tender but there is no rebound, guarding or masses to be found. Her urgent blood results are shown below.

| | | |
|---|---|---|
| Sodium | 137 | mmol/L |
| Potassium | 4.9 | mmol/L |
| Urea | 10.2 | mmol/L |
| Creatinine | 73 | μmol/L |
| Haemoglobin | 9.0 | g/dL |
| Mean cell volume | 68 | fL |
| Platelets | 428 | $x10^9/L$ |
| White cell count | 7 | $x10^9/L$ |
| APTT | 30 | secs |
| INR | 1.12 | |

Which is the best management option from the following list?

1. Transfuse 2 units of blood with frusemide according to protocol
2. Infuse 1 litre of normal saline stat
3. Infuse 1 litre of normal saline over 1 to 2 hours
4. Infuse 1 litre of normal saline over 1 to 2 hours and start ferrous sulphate tablets
5. Infuse 1 litre of normal saline over 1 to 2 hours, order some fresh frozen plasma and start ferrous sulphate tablets

**Q.88**
A colleague of yours is away and as a favour you are checking through her pile of laboratory results. You come across one which states:

| | |
|---|---|
| Name | John Jenkins |
| Sex | M |
| DOB | 23/12/1984 |
| Indication | Jaundice |
| *Bilirubin:* | *48 μmol/L (significantly unconjugated bilirubinaemia)* |

What is the most likely diagnosis?

1. Gilbert's syndrome
2. Gallstones
3. Hepatitis A
4. Hepatic congestion in cardiac failure
5. Haemolysis, elevated liver enzymes and low platelet count syndrome

**Q.89**
Michelle is a 32-year-old alcoholic with liver cirrhosis. Her recent endoscopy shows moderately-sized oesophageal varices.

Which of the following is the best management option to eradicate these varices?

1. Endoscopic sclerotherapy
2. Endoscopic balloon ligation
3. Isosorbide mononitrate
4. Propranolol
5. Transjugular Intrahepatic Portosystemic Shunt (TIPSS)

**Q.90**

Michael is a 38-year-old office assistant. He went out on a stag night with his friends last night and consumed a lot of alcohol. On waking this morning, he became nauseated and couldn't stop himself from vomiting. He vomited up to half a dozen times. In the last bout of vomit he noticed streaks of bright red blood, at which point he passed out and his friend called an ambulance. He has no past medical history of note and takes no medications or illicit drugs. He drinks about 2 pints of beer a day and about 15 units in the form of beer and spirits at the weekend. On examination his pulse is regular at 70 beats per minute with a blood pressure of 130/80 mmHg. His hands are a little trembly but there are no other peripheral signs. There is no abdominal distension or thoraco-abdominal skin changes. He is mildly tender in the epigastrium but there is no guarding, rebound tenderness or masses on palpation.

Which of the following options will form part of your management plan?

1. Control blood pressure with a beta blocker or a nitrate and alert endoscopist on call
2. Start glypressin infusion and alert endoscopist on call
3. Start octreotide infusion and alert endoscopist on call
4. Reassure and discharge after a short period of observation if baseline blood tests are normal
5. Refer to surgeons to consider a Nissen's fundoplication

**Q.91**

Harry is 42-year-old banker, who has cirrhosis secondary to autoimmune hepatitis. He is under long term follow-up with the liver unit. He was brought to you by his wife who noticed a change in his behaviour and conscious level. On examination he is drowsy and disoriented in place and time but not in person. He fails simple motor commands.

What is the most likely precipitant that has caused this complication?

1. Intake of high potassium foods (bananas, raisins etc)
2. Taking paracetamol for a headache for the past 24 hours
3. Constipation
4. Hypoglycaemia
5. Hayfever

**Q.92**

Celia is 42 and has alcoholic liver disease with cirrhosis. She presents to you with increased abdominal girth. On examination, she has peripheral signs of chronic liver disease. Her pulse and blood pressure are normal and she is afebrile. Her abdomen is a little distended and you elicit shifting dullness. You carefully tap some peritoneal fluid which is clear and straw-coloured. The laboratory report the white cell count as $10/mm^3$.

At this stage, what is likely to be the best therapeutic step?

1. Paracentesis with fluid restriction
2. Paracentesis with albumin replacement
3. Intravenous cefuroxime and metronidazole
4. Furosemide and fluid restriction
5. Spironolactone and fluid restriction

**Q.93 - Part 1**

Milton is a 49-year-old bus driver. He has been diagnosed with diabetes for 6 years and gets recurrent urinary tract infections. During one such episode requiring antibiotics, you discover that he has abnormal liver function tests. On review of his medical history, several other conditions lead you to suspect he has hereditary haemochromatosis (HH).

Which of the following would be most likely to occur as a complication of HH?

1. Atrial fibrillation
2. Emphysema
3. Premature ejaculation
4. Neuropsychiatric problems
5. Kyphoscoliosis

**Q.93 - Part 2**

What might be the most appropriate test at this time to substantiate your theory?

1. Serum ferritin
2. Transferrin saturation
3. Full blood count
4. Genotyping for the C282Y mutation
5. Liver biopsy with Perl's stain

**Q.94**

Maria is a 29-year-old pharmacist. She has a 6-month history of diarrhoea, weight loss, malaise and lethargy. Her stools have become pale and offensive, but there is no blood seen in them. More recently, she has been experiencing abdominal pain and bloating.

Which of the following would be the best option to confirm your diagnosis?

1. Positive anti-endomysial antibody
2. Positive anti-gliadin antibody
3. Positive anti-parietal cell antibody
4. Villous atrophy demonstrated on small bowel biopsy
5. Small bowel barium enema

**Q.95**

Patrick is a 43-year-old tiler who has been diagnosed with primary sclerosing cholangitis.

Which one of the following conditions would he most likely be expected to have?

1. Rheumatoid arthritis
2. Thyroid disease
3. Ulcerative colitis
4. Pernicious anaemia
5. Systemic sclerosis

**Q.96 - Part 1**

Mrs Millen is a 43-year-old counsellor. She has been non-specifically unwell for a several months with malaise, lethargy and intense itching. She has had no weight loss, fevers or night sweats. Her blood results are shown below.

| | | | |
|---|---|---|---|
| Sodium | 135 | mmol/L | |
| Potassium | 3.2 | mmol/L | |
| Urea | 3.4 | mmol/L | |
| Creatinine | 66 | µmol/L | |
| Albumin | 32 | g/L | |
| Bilirubin | 32 | µmol/L | |
| Aspartate transaminase | 48 | iu/L | (7-40) |
| Alkaline phosphatase | 280 | iu/L | (25-115) |
| Haemoglobin | 11.2 | g/dL | |
| Mean cell volume | 68 | fL | |
| Platelets | 320 | $x10^9/L$ | |
| White cell count | 5 | $x10^9/L$ | |

Which of the following is the most likely diagnosis?

1. Hodgkin's disease
2. Non-Hodgkin's lymphoma
3. Primary biliary cirrhosis
4. Autoimmune hepatitis
5. Generalised pruritis

**Q.96 - Part 2**

What other complication may you expect Mrs Millen to experience?

1. Osteoporosis
2. Osteopetrosis
3. Osteonecrosis
4. Osteoarthritis
5. Osteochondritis

**Q.97**

Lorna is a 56-year-old teacher. She had been fit and healthy most of her life until 5 years ago, when a number of symptoms, including jaundice, took her to the GP. Tests showed that she had liver disease and she has since been followed up regularly. Due to recent weight loss and abdominal pain, you ordered a repeat ultrasound which shows a single large lesion suggestive of hepatocellular carcinoma (HCC).

Which of the following is the most likely underlying diagnosis?

1. Primary biliary cirrhosis
2. Autoimmune hepatitis
3. Alpha-1anti-trypsin deficiency
4. Hepatitis B infection
5. Hepatitis C infection

**Q.98**

Doreen is a 54-year-old personal assistant. She has recently been unwell with weight loss, malaise and jaundice. You discovered hepatomegaly on examination and so organised a liver ultrasound. This revealed multiple lesions consistent with metastasis.

Which of the following is least likely to be the primary tumour?

1. Stomach
2. Colon
3. Pancreas
4. Uterus
5. Breast

**Q.99**
Suzie is a 34-year-old accounts clerk who has ulcerative colitis. She goes to Accident and Emergency due to increased stool frequency, fevers and abdominal pain that is the worst she has ever experienced. On examination she is tachycardic, mildly hypotensive and febrile. Her abdomen is rigid and diffusely tender.

Which of the following is the best investigation at this point?

1. ESR
2. Barium enema
3. Haemoglobin
4. Abdominal x-ray
5. Erect chest x-ray

**Q.100**
Adrian is a 23-year-old student. He is being investigated for inflammatory bowel disease.

Which of the following features is much more suggestive of Crohn's disease than ulcerative colitis?

1. Uveitis
2. Sacroilitis
3. Aphthous ulcers
4. Osteomalacia
5. Clubbing

**Q.101**

Bernard is a 64-year-old unemployed alcoholic. He comes to see you because he wanted you to recommend an NHS dentist. His teeth are in a bad state; you notice some bleeding on his gums and suspect gingivitis. He also shows you a rash. He is generally dishevelled and hasn't shaved, but you notice that there are tiny bleeding points at the hair follicles. The hairs themselves look ragged and unusual. This is widespread and you also notice some purpura.

What is the most likely cause of these features?

1. Scabies
2. Vitamin B complex deficiency
3. Vitamin C deficiency
4. Bleeding disorder secondary to alcoholic liver disease
5. Alcoholic bone marrow suppression

**Q.102**

Nabila is a 28-year-old refugee from Sudan. You are seeing her for her first medical check-up, and are using an interpreter. You gather that she has been experiencing loose stools for the past few months along with a diffuse itchy rash. She is a little confused in her history and her gait is a little unsteady. On examination you think that her coordination is poor and her peripheral sensation is possibly diminished.

Which of the following deficiencies is she likely to be suffering from?

1. Niacin
2. Riboflavin
3. Thiamine
4. Cyano-cobalamin
5. Pyridoxine

**Q.103 - Part 1**

Andrzej is a 38-year-old Polish builder. He comes to Accident and Emergency complaining of intense abdominal pain. At first, he thought it was indigestion, after having eaten some fish and chips in a hurry on the way home from work. He describes the pain as being like a dagger piercing his stomach and through to his back. He has had pain similar to this several times before and has been admitted to hospital in his home country for it. He often gets loose pale stools that are difficult to flush away but his urine is pale. A few years ago, he completely stopped drinking alcohol for fear of more pain. On examination, he is curled up with pain. He weighs 80kg, he is afebrile with a high pulse and blood pressure. His sclerae are white. Abdominal examination is difficult due to the tense contraction of his abdominal wall muscles, but you do not elicit any tenderness or masses specific to the right upper quadrant.

Which is of the following is the most likely underlying diagnosis?

1. Peptic ulcer
2. Chronic pancreatitis
3. Choledocholithiasis
4. Cholecystitis
5. Carcinoma of the pancreas

**Q.103 - Part 2**

Andrzej self-discharged before his investigations were completed in hospital and you are now seeing him several weeks later as a follow-up.

Which of the following is the most useful investigation to confirm your suspected diagnosis?

1. Endoscopic retrograde cholangio-pancreatography (ERCP)
2. Magnetic resonance cholangio-pancreatography (MRCP)
3. Serum amylase
4. Abdominal ultrasound
5. Faecal fat analysis

# SECTION 5

## Infectious Diseases

## Immunology

## Allergies

## Genetics

**Q.104**

Jane is 30-year-old mature student. She is pregnant and her antenatal HIV antibody test has come back as positive.

What is the best approach from the options below?

1. Reassure her that this is likely to be a biological false positive and order a repeat test
2. Break the HIV diagnosis. Explain that the risks of treating her with antiretrovirals (ARVs) during pregnancy outweigh the benefits of reducing HIV transmission to the fetus, and so ARVs should instead be started for both of them immediately after delivery
3. Break the HIV diagnosis. Explain that even with best available treatments, that vertical HIV transmission occurs in the majority of cases and a termination of pregnancy is an option
4. Break the HIV diagnosis. Explain that even with best available treatments, a still birth or miscarriage is likely and a termination of pregnancy is an option
5. Break the HIV diagnosis. Explain that most vertical HIV transmission is via breastfeeding, so a Caesarean and bottle feeding alone (without ARVs) would be recommended to minimise the risk to the fetus, although a termination of pregnancy is an option

**Q.105**

John is a 25-year-old FY1 doctor. It is midnight and John is rushing into Accident and Emergency after sustaining a needlestick injury after taking blood from a patient who is newly diagnosed as HIV seropositive. You decide to give John HIV post-exposure prophylaxis (PEP).

Which of the following actions is the most important at this time?

1. Offer John a Hepatitis C vaccine as well as the PEP
2. Offer John a Hepatitis B vaccine as well as the PEP
3. Give the PEP within one hour of the risky exposure
4. Advise John to use condoms with his partner until he gets a final negative HIV test at the end of follow-up
5. Advise John to go to Occupational Health the next working day.

**Q.106**
Liz and Steve are about to go travelling in Africa and are requesting some advice.

Which of the following statements is the best advice regarding water for drinking?

1. Bottled water is the safest you can drink
2. As long as you boil it first, the water will be safe from microbial hazards
3. Chlorination (e.g. with purifying tablets) is the best option
4. As long as you filter it first, the water will be fine
5. Only drink what the locals are happy to drink

**Q.107**
Sam and Lauren are both feeling unwell. They have had diarrhoea and vomiting since yesterday afternoon and are feeling very weak. They think it is down to some poorly cooked food they had at a barbeque the day before yesterday. They have spoken to some friends who were there and some of them are also unwell.

Which of the following is the most likely cause of this food poisoning?

1. Listeria
2. Salmonella
3. Campylobacter
4. Shigella
5. Cryptosporidium

**Q.108 - Part 1**

Joseph is a 25-year-old cleaner. He comes to Accident and Emergency with a 3-day history of fevers, myalgia and lethargy. He has returned to the UK a week ago after spending a few weeks with his family in Kenya. On examination, he appears mildly dehydrated, but fully alert, sitting up in bed. He has a temperature of 37.5 degrees Celsius, a regular heart rate of 96 beats per minute and a blood pressure of 98/62 mmHg. The rest of the examination is unremarkable except a urine dipstick showing a trace of blood and ketones. You send away a number of tests and the haematologist soon phones you back to say they found Plasmodium falciparum with a parasitaemia of 4%, of which <1% are schizonts. The rest of his blood results are shown below:

| | | |
|---|---|---|
| Sodium | 142 | mmol/L |
| Potassium | 4.3 | mmol/L |
| Urea | 4.1 | mmol/L |
| Creatinine | 98 | µmol/L |
| Haemoglobin | 10.1 | g/dL |
| Mean cell volume | 79 | fL |
| Platelets | 122 | $x10^9/L$ |
| White cell count | 7 | $x10^9/L$ |

Which of the following is the best management option?

1. Start intravenous quinine and arrange transfer to a high-dependency setting
2. Start intravenous quinine, arrange transfer to a high-dependency setting and prepare for exchange blood transfusion
3. Admit to a closely observed medical ward and start intravenous quinine therapy
4. Admit to a closely observed medical ward and start oral quinine
5. Admit to a closely observed medical ward, start oral quinine and set up a drip for rapid fluid rehydration

**Q.108 - Part 2**

12 hours later Joseph deteriorates. His sister, who was with him, noted that he was a little irritable with her and tried to get some sleep. A little later, she tried to rouse him but was unable to do so.

Which of the following is likely to be the most useful test for immediate management of this complication?

1. Arterial blood gas
2. Urine dipstick
3. ECG
4. Group & and cross-match of blood
5. Capillary blood glucose

**Q.109**

Mrs Dorkins comes to you for advice. She has recently given birth to her first child and she is concerned about the child's future vaccinations. She read somewhere that some vaccines are actually 'live micro-organisms' and in some cases can cause disease in the patient.

Which of the following vaccines are given in a 'live-attenuated' form?

1. Hepatitis B
2. Haemophilus influenzae
3. Rubella
4. Neisseria meningitidis
5. Pertussis

**Q.110**

Niraj is a 32-year-old shop assistant. He presents with a 5-day history of malaise and lethargy and gradually worsening headache. Today he has had a fever of over 38 degrees Celsius at home, accompanied by sweating. On examination, he is alert and has no focal neurology. He is obviously photophobic and Kernig's sign is positive. A CT scan of his head shows no contraindication to lumbar puncture and the CSF results are shown below.

| | | |
|---|---|---|
| Macroscopic appearance | cloudy | |
| Protein | 3.2 | g/L |
| Glucose | 1.2 | mmol/L |
| Red cell count | 108 | cells/mm$^3$ |
| White cell count (predominantly lymphocytes) | 2230 | cells/mm$^3$ |
| Organisms | none seen | |
| Opening pressure | 19 | cm water |
| (Plasma glucose) | 5.2 | mmol/L |

Which is the best treatment option from the following list?

1. Nimodipine and refer to neurosurgeons
2. Rifampacin, isoniazid, ethambutol, pyrazinamide and prednisolone
3. Benzylpenicillin
4. Ampicillin
5. Cefotaxime

**Q.111**

Anita and Ben are in their 30s. They have been unwell for the last 2 days with increasing lethargy, mylagia, fevers and a dry cough. They have just returned from a holiday in Tanzania. They did go into rural areas during the daytime but they spent their nights in a modern hotel complex that had a policy of sealing all windows and doors in the evening before spraying with insecticide so that mosquito-free air was cycled through the complex. Even so, they both took all their antimalarial tablets reliably and show you the blister packs as evidence. On examination, Ben has a mild pyrexia and saturations of 93% on room air. His right lung has poor air entry and is dull to percussion. His chest x-ray shows consolidation on that side. Anita has similar findings, although not so unwell, there is also consolidation on her chest x-ray.

Which one of the following investigations is the most appropriate to confirm the likely diagnosis and direct their treatment?

1. Urinary antigen testing
2. Thick and thin blood film for parasites
3. Blood cultures
4. Blood for atypical respiratory serology
5. Sputum for microscopy culture and sensitivities

**Q.112**

Brandon is a 32-year-old personal trainer. He has just returned from a 3-week holiday to South-East Asia. He presents with a 5-day history of fevers, myalgia, headache and rash. The rash started a few days ago as an erythema over his limbs, torso and face. On examination, you at first thought that it was sun-tanning. He tells you he sought travel advice from the London hospital for tropical medicine before travelling and adhered to this strictly.

What is the most likely diagnosis?

1. Photosensitivity reaction
2. Syphilis
3. Dengue fever
4. Yellow fever
5. Typhoid fever

**Q.113**
Barry is 38-year-old IT systems manager with Type 1 diabetes. He complains of a 'head cold' and today he was just not able to get out of bed due to weakness; as a result he has called you out for a home visit. He blames himself for having taken public transport for a change the day before yesterday and having sat next to a woman who was 'sneezing over everyone'. He was due to have an influenza vaccination a month ago but due to work commitments he wasn't able to keep his appointment with the nurse. You are aware of a number of identified cases of Influenza A in the local area in recent weeks.

What is the best management option?

1. Advise bed rest, analgesia and give him a dose of the influenza vaccine now
2. Advise bed rest, analgesia and prescribe oseltamvir (Tamiflu)
3. Advise bed rest, analgesia and prescribe amoxycillin
4. Advise bed rest and analgesia alone
5. Advise bed rest, analgesia and prescribe amantadine

**Q.114**
Karl is a 33-year-old bricklayer. He went to his doctor a week ago with 'flu-like' symptoms and a bad sore throat. He was given a sick note and a course of penicillin, and was asked to come back today for review. You see him today and he is no better. He said he thinks that he is allergic to penicillin because he developed a rash soon after starting the tablets and so stopped them immediately. His sore throat is no better and he has also developed chest pains. On examination, he looks pale and weak, with cervical and inguinal lymphadenopathy and a palpable spleen. You send off a few blood tests and the result show a raised white cell count (predominantly lymphocytes), heterophil antibody test is positive and EBV IgG negative.

What is the most likely diagnosis?

1. Hodgkin's lymphoma
2. Non-Hodgkin's lymphoma
3. Infectious mononucleosis
4. Influenza
5. Q fever

**Q.115**

Omara is a 24-year-old refugee, recently diagnosed as HIV-seropositive. She is very unwell, cachetic, with oral candida, sebhorroeic dermatitis, lymphadenopathy and skin lesions that look like Kaposi's sarcoma. She complains of a progressive visual disturbance that began as clouding in one eye then rapidly progressed so that she can only just perceive light. She has no headache, neck stiffness or fevers. On fundoscopy it is difficult to visualise the optic disc and vessel; they are blurred and obscured by what looks like white clouds and haemorrhage.

Which of the following infectious agents is most likely to be responsible?

1. Cryptococcus neoformans
2. Cytomegalovirus
3. Toxoplasma gondii
4. Mycobacterium tuberculosis
5. Epstein-Barr virus

**Q.116**

Annabel is a 37-year-old farmer. She has felt unwell for the last week with lethargy and myalgia, particularly in her hands and feet. She put this down to physical exertion at work, given the current harsh winter weather. Over the last few days, she has developed a non-productive cough and fevers. She has also noticed a rash develop on her thighs. On examination, she has a mild pyrexia and a regular heart rate of 98 beats per minute. She has bilateral poor air entry along with inspiratory crepitations in her chest. On her thighs, you note an irregular collection of macules with pale centres. On leaving the bedside you retrieve the blood samples that you left by the open window and you notice the blood has a gritty appearance as if a precipitate has formed.

Which of the following is the most likely infective agent?

1. Chlamydia spp.
2. Klebsiella pneumoniae
3. Mycoplasma pneumoniae
4. Haemophilus influenzae
5. Legionella pneumophilia

**Q.117**

Olivia is a 37-year-old carer who is applying for a job in a private nursing home. Their Occupational Health Department requests that she has a few preliminary tests prior to taking the post. One of her reports reads: Hep B cAb positive.

What does this result mean and what action is required?

1. Chronic Hepatitis B infection: You should advise her to get all household contacts tested and immunised and refer her to a liver unit
2. Immunity to Hepatitis B due to past infection: No further action is required
3. Chronic Hepatitis B infection: You should advise her to get all household contacts tested and immunised, refer her to a liver unit and notify the local consultant in public health
4. Acute Hepatitis B infection: You should advise her to get all household contacts tested and immunised, refer her to a liver unit and notify the local consultant in public health
5. Immunity to Hepatitis B due to vaccination: A further booster is required according to local protocols

**Q.118**

Ramesh is a 37-year-old driving instructor. 10 days ago, he returned home from a holiday visiting relatives in East Africa. For the last 5 days, he has been unwell with fevers, myalgia, lethargy and diarrhoea. He was a little constipated when he first returned to the UK. He put this down to a change in diet and so took some laxatives. He thinks this may have precipitated the diarrhoea. On examination his temperature is 39 degrees Celsius, his pulse is regular at 62 beats per minute, with a blood pressure of 102/64 mmHg, and his capillary refill time is 3 seconds.

Which of the following tests is most likely to confirm the diagnosis?

1. Thick and thin blood films for parasites
2. Rapid antigen test for Plasmodium falciparum
3. Blood cultures
4. Stool culture
5. Stool microscopy

**Q.119**

Matt is a 32-year-old bar manager, known to be HIV seropositive. He has been unwell for a few days with upper respiratory tract symptoms and a dry cough, which has now become productive. He has felt feverish and weak and has now come to hospital. From his last visit to the specialist a month ago, he recalls that his CD4 count was 290 (cells/mm$^3$) and his viral load was around 15,000 copies/ml. He is not currently taking any antiretroviral medications. On examination he has a temperature of 37.8 degrees Celsius, with a regular pulse of 92 beats per minute and a blood pressure of 128/82 mmHg. His oxygen saturations are 96% at rest and drop to 90% on exertion that gets his pulse to 120 beats per minute. His chest is normal on the right but there is decreased air entry with bronchial breath sounds on the left. This is confirmed when confluent consolidation is seen on that area on chest x-ray.

What is the likely cause of his respiratory illness?

1. Streptococcus pneumoniae
2. Pneumoncystis jirovecii
3. Mycobacterium tuberculosis
4. Pseudomonas aeruginosa
5. Chlamydia spp.

**Q.120**

Lucille is a 45-year-old pensions advisor who had recently been diagnosed with myotonic dystrophy. She was told by the specialist that this condition exhibits the phenomenon of 'anticipation'. She didn't get time to ask him what this meant.

Which of the following is the correct explanation of this term?

1. It is an inherited condition which may be silent for many years but will present in later life after a trigger of some kind
2. It is an inherited condition which often skips a generation
3. It is an inherited condition which is more severe in males
4. It is an inherited condition that presents at an earlier age in successive generations
5. It is an inherited condition in which all daughters of affected males will be carriers

**Q.121**
Timothy has haemophilia A and his wife Julie, who is pregnant, is found to be a carrier for haemophilia A.

What is the likelihood that they will have a child who expresses the condition?

1. 100%
2. 75%
3. 50%
4. 33%
5. 25%

**Q.122 - Part 1**
Roshan is a 28-year-old policeman who comes to Accident and Emergency after reacting to a bee sting. There is swelling around the areas of the bite and he develops rapidly-spreading urticaria. His breathing has worsened and he becomes hypotensive, so he is rushed into resus, where you meet him. He is tachycardic but conscious.

Which of the following options should be your first drug of choice?

1. Hydrocortisone 200 mg iv
2. Chlorpheniramine 10 mg iv
3. 0.5 mg of adrenaline 1:10,000 iv
4. 0.5 mg of adrenaline 1:1000 iv
5. 0.5 mg of adrenaline 1:1000 im

**Q.122 - Part 2**
Which is of the following is the best drug for Roshan to carry with him in the future?

1. Chlorpheniramine tablets
2. Adrenaline for self-injection
3. Hydrocortisone cream
4. Loratadine tablets
5. Chlorpheniramine ointment

**Q.123**

Philip is a 76-year-old retired carpenter. He came to you last week with a respiratory tract infection. He was not very unwell, but because of a few signs in his chest and because he seemed mildly anaemic on clinical examination, you took a few blood tests, gave him some oral antibiotics and planned to review him today. Apart from a few rubbery, discrete cervical lymph nodes, his examination was otherwise unremarkable. His full blood count report is shown below.

| | | |
|---|---|---|
| Haemoglobin | 10.5 | g/dL |
| Mean cell volume | 81 | fL |
| Platelets | 167 | $\times 10^9$/L |
| White cell count | 32 | $\times 10^9$/L |
| (predominantly lymphocytes) | | |

What is the most likely diagnosis?

1. Chronic myeloid leukaemia
2. Chronic lymphocytic leukaemia
3. Myelofibrosis
4. Acute lymphoblastic leukaemia
5. Reactive lymphocytosis

**Q.124**

Kevin is a 33-year-old graphic designer. He has just been admitted with mild jaundice, which has developed after several days of suffering fevers, diarrhoea and abdominal pains. After taking blood from him, you notice that it took a long time to stop the bleeding. He mentions his gums were bleeding when he rinsed his mouth earlier. He has no obvious bruises on his body.

Which of the following diagnoses best explains these findings?

1. Gastro-enteritis with haemolytic uraemic syndrome
2. Acute viral hepatitis with liver dysfunction
3. Gastro-enteritis in a patient with haemophilia A
4. Acute Crohn's colitis with malabsorption
5. Ascending cholangitis with cholestasis

**Q.125**

Martina is a 29-year-old nursery nurse who has an acute deep vein thrombosis. As a result, a thrombophilia screen is ordered.

Which of the following statements from a pathology report would indicate the cause for thrombosis?

1. Protein S high
2. Protein C high
3. Factor V leiden mutation detected
4. Antithrombin III detectable
5. Anticardiolipin antibody not detected

**Q.126**

Mary is a 42-year-old yoga instructor. She has been feeling non-specifically unwell for several months with lethargy and menstrual irregularities. She used to suffer from heartburn but this is controlled with medication. She has also had some bowel disturbance with black stools. Her medications include omeprazole, ferrous sulphate and evening primrose oil. You order a few tests and the results are shown below.

| | | |
|---|---|---|
| Haemoglobin | 9.1 | g/dL |
| Mean cell volume | 96 | fL |
| Platelets | 378 | $x10^9/L$ |
| White cell count | 4 | $x10^9/L$ |
| Total iron binding capacity | Low | |

Which is the single most likely cause of Mary's anaemia from the list below?

1. Iron-deficiency anaemia
2. Pernicous anaemia
3. Hypothyroidsim
4. Myelodysplasia
5. Sideroblastic anaemia

**Q.127**
Frank is a 68-year-old retired ship worker. He has a 6-month history of malaise, lethargy and back pain. A plain x-ray of his spine confirmed lytic lesions and you suspect he has myeloma.

Which of the following results would confirm this diagnosis?

1. Hypercalcaemia
2. Reed-Sternberg cells on bone marrow biopsy
3. Plasmacytoma on bone marrow biopsy
4. Auer rods in white cells
5. Teardrop cells on bone marrow biopsy

**Q.128**
Eleanor is 4 years old and has recently been diagnosed with acute lymphoblastic leaukaemia. Her parents come to you to request more information. Which of the following would indicate a particularly poor prognosis for Eleanor?

1. Female sex
2. Presence of the Philadelphia chromosome
3. Her age at diagnosis
4. Lymphadenopathy
5. Visible bruising

**Q.129**
Clare is a 23-year-old physicist. She has had an acute febrile illness with mild jaundice and splenomegaly. Her bloods show a normocytic anaemia with a slightly elevated bilirubin but other liver enzymes are normal. You suspect a haemolytic anaemia. Which of the following tests would substantiate this theory?

1. Rouleaux formation seen on peripheral blood film
2. Raised reticulocyte count
3. Haemoglobin electrophoresis
4. Bence-Jones protein detected in the urine
5. Howell-Jolly bodies seen on a peripheral blood film

**Q.130**

You are signing off a a pile of blood reports for a colleague who is currently on leave and you come across the following report.

Name: Winston Brown    Patient No.: 978245
Date of Birth: 13/07/79    Country of birth: Jamaica
Clinical Details: Application for health insurance

| | | | |
|---|---|---|---|
| Haemoglobin | 14.1 | g/dL | |
| Mean cell volume | 94 | fL | |
| Platelets | 278 | $x10^9/L$ | |
| White cell count | 2.5 | $x10^9/L$ | (4.0 -11.0) |
| Neutrophils | 0.6 | $x10^9/L$ | (2.0 - 7.5) |
| Lymphocytes | 1.5 | $x10^9/L$ | (1.4 - 4.0) |
| Eosinophils | 0.1 | $x10^9/L$ | (0.04 - 0.4) |

What is the most likely reason for this finding?

1. Benign ethnic neutropenia
2. Recent steroid therapy
3. Drugs or chemotherapy
4. HIV infection
5. Sickle cell disease

**Q.131**

You are coming to the end of a long shift in Accident and Emergency when Colin, a 26-year-old builder, comes in with a painful sickle crisis. You have been shadowed all day by an over-confident medical student who is freely giving his advice on everything you do, but you suspect that he knows very little. Which of the following suggestions should you definitely ignore?

1. High flow oxygen should be given, especially if the arterial oxygen is low
2. You should cross match blood urgently in case you need to exchange transfuse
3. Opiate analgesia must be given cautiously since respiratory depression will lead to further oxidative stress and sickling
4. If Colin is febrile you should give blind antibiotics once blood cultures have been sent
5. You should give active intravenous fluid replacement

# SECTION 6

# Musculoskeletal

**Q.132**

Amir is a 67-year-old grocer. He complains of an 8-month history of back pain. Which of the following features would be the most suggestive of a sinister underlying cause?

1. Pain present in just one direction of movement
2. Sciatica in both limbs
3. Pain worse after a period of rest
4. Spinal deformity
5. Presence of buttock pain

**Q.133**

Walter is a 71-year-old retired fireman. He has developed increasing problems walking due to knee pain. You take a thorough history and examination as well as ordering a plain x-ray of his knees.

In general, which of the following x-ray findings would suggest a diagnosis of gout rather than osteoarthritis?

1. Joint space narrowing
2. Bone cysts
3. Periarticular erosions
4. Subarticular sclerosis
5. Osteophytes

**Q.134 - Part 1**

Sophia is a 42-year-old hotel receptionist who has recently been diagnosed with rheumatoid arthritis. She has come to ask you a few questions.

Which of one the following factors is NOT associated with a worse prognosis?

1. Presence of rheumatoid nodules
2. Vasculitis
3. Acute oligoarticular onset
4. Rheumatoid factor positive
5. Presence of erosion early after diagnosis

**Q.134 - Part 2**

Sophia's mother, who has suffered from rheumatoid arthritis for 12 years, shows you her hands. Which of the following features would you not commonly expect to see?

1. Boutonnière deformity
2. Rheumatoid nodules
3. Ulnar deviation at the metacarpal-phalangeal joints
4. 'Z' deformity of the thumb
5. Swan neck deformity in the fingers

**Q.135**

Mrs Cooper is a 53-year-old bus driver. She has recently been unwell with lethargy, malaise and joint pains. You cannot clearly attribute her symptoms and signs to one rheumatological diagnosis yet, so you have requested a number of tests. Her rheumatoid factor comes back as being raised, but you know this is not specific to rheumatoid arthritis.

In which of the following conditions would you be very unlikely to find elevated rheumatoid factor?

1. Arthritis mutilans
2. Sjögren's syndrome
3. Sarcoidosis
4. Systemic lupus erythematosus (SLE)
5. Advancing age

**Q.136**

Oswald is a 36-year-old squash coach. He has noticed increasing wrist pain over the last few weeks. Aspiration of fluid from the wrist joint shows crystals that are weakly positively birifringent on polarised light microscopy. Which of the following is the most likely diagnosis?

1. Carpal tunnel syndrome
2. Gout
3. Pseudogout
4. Tenosynovitis
5. Rheumatoid arthritis

**Q.137**

Ted is a 53-year-old taxi driver. He has been troubled with gout for many years and comes to you with an acutely painful attack. He has already taken naproxen at home which has given minimal relief. Which of the following would be the best next option?

1. Diclofenac
2. Allopurinol
3. Hydrocortisone injection
4. Colchicine
5. Dihydrocodeine

**Q.138**

Mr Jenkins is a 42-year-old photographer. He has developed increasingly severe pains in his wrists and knees as well as a few other systemic problems. The pains are worse in the morning when the joints are very stiff, and they ease off as the day goes on. At this stage you find it difficult to tell whether this is rheumatoid arthritis (RA) or a seronegative spondyloarthropathy. Which of the following features is the strongest indicator that this is a spondyloarthropathy rather than RA?

1. Asymmetrical joint involvement
2. Rheumatoid factor negative
3. Enthesitis
4. Associated eye disease
5. Associated skin features

**Q.139**

Mr Salter is a 45-year-old marketing manager. He has been troubled with increasingly severe lower back pain for the last 6 months. An x-ray of his thoraco-lumbar spine showed squaring of the lumbar vertebrae and fusion at the sacro-illiac joints.Which of the following is the best therapy to prevent deterioration in mobility?

1. Rest and non-steroidal anti-inflammatory drugs
2. Non-steroidal anti-inflammatory drugs (NSAIDs)
3. Sulphasalazine or methotrexate
4. Osteotomy for ankylosis
5. Physiotherapy

**Q.140 - Part 1**

Mrs Dalton is a 38-year-old veterinary nurse. She has been feeling generally unwell for several months. She has noticed that her hands are very cold and 'go a funny colour sometimes'. She has also become wheezy in bed at night and particularly if she has a 'nap' after Sunday lunch. Other than a diuretic for hypertension, she is on no other medications. On examination, her chest is clear with no wheeze, you attempt to take her peak flow but she can't fit her lips around the mouthpiece of the meter. The results of her blood tests are shown below.

| | | |
|---|---|---|
| Sodium | 137 | mmol/L |
| Potassium | 3.6 | mmol/L |
| Urea | 4.1 | mmol/L |
| Creatinine | 129 | µmol/L |
| Haemoglobin | 9.7 | g/dL |
| Mean cell volume | 82 | fL |
| Platelets | 215 | $x10^9/L$ |
| White cell count | 6.8 | $x10^9/L$ |
| | | |
| Rheumatoid factor (RhF) | positive | |
| Anti-nuclear antibody (ANA) | positive | |

What is the most likely diagnosis?

1. Rheumatoid arthritis
2. Mixed connective tissue disease
3. Sjögren's syndrome
4. Systemic sclerosis
5. Systemic lupus erythrematosus

**Q.140 - Part 2**

Which of the following tests is most likely to support this diagnosis?

1. Extractable nuclear antigens (ENA)
2. Anti-neutrophil cytoplasmic antigens (ANCA)
3. Serum creatine kinase (CK)
4. Renal biopsy
5. 24-hour urine collection including microscopy for casts

**Q.141**

Paul is a 28-year-old journalist. He has a 2-day history of swollen and tender knees, shoulders and ankles. He also has itchy watery eyes and pain when passing urine. He has recently returned from a 2-month backpacking holiday in Malaysia and Indonesia with his girlfriend. They took all the holiday prophylaxis they were instructed to, although they did have several bouts of 'food poisoning' during their travels.

Which of the following statements is true regarding Paul's most likely diagnosis and management?

1. Once this episode has resolved, a recurrence is unlikely
2. Chlamydia trachomatis infection is the most likely underlying cause
3. Symptoms should start to resolve once the appropriate antibiotics are given
4. Steroid therapy is a recognised treatment option
5. This condition is associated with positivity for HLA-DR4

**Q.142**

Ms Anderson is a 33-year-old dentist who has systemic lupus erythematosus (SLE) with renal involvement. She has felt a little unwell over the last few days with fatigue and fevers. All but one of the following results are suggestive of a flare in her SLE as opposed to another intercurrent illness.

Which one is not specific to a flare in the SLE?

1. Raised erythrocyte sedimentation rate (ESR)
2. Raised C- reactive protein (CRP)
3. Raised anti-ds DNA titre
4. Decreased complement C3
5. Increased complement C3d

**Q.143**

Fiona is a 36-year-old travel agent. She comes to show you a rash on her legs that she has noticed for a few weeks. It is a macular erythematous rash that spreads out like a net over her calves. She suffers from migraines and 6 months ago was admitted overnight at the local hospital because they thought that she was having a 'mini-stroke', but nothing was proven. She has a history of poor fertility, with three miscarriages in the past and decided to adopt children rather than to pursue 'lengthy procedures'. She is a non-smoker and her only medications are for her migraines.

Which of the following options is most likely to be of help to her?

1. Long term warfarin therapy
2. Heparin and low-dose aspirin
3. Oral steroids
4. Long term low-dose aspirin
5. Hydroxychloroquine

**Q.144**

Alice is a 24-year-old software engineer. She has been non-specifically unwell for several months with joint, skin and soft tissue problems. You suspect that she may have systemic lupus erythematosus (SLE).

Which of the following features is most likely to suggest SLE over any other rheumatological condition?

1. Pericardial or pleural effusions
2. Erythematous malar rash spreading over the nasolabial folds
3. Articular subluxation and deformity due to capsular laxity
4. Painful arthropathy due to periarticular erosions
5. Uveitis

**Q.145 - Part 1**
Mrs Goodman is a 66-year-old retired traffic warden. She complains of malaise, lethargy and pain with weakness in her shoulders and thighs.
Her medications include aspirin, salmeterol, ipratropium bromide, bendroflumathiazide, ramipril, simvastatin, senna. On examination, it looks like she is wearing dark eye shadow but she is wearing no lipstick. Her proximal muscles are weak and she has a few raised red papules over the knuckles of her hands. Her initial blood tests are shown below:

| | | | |
|---|---|---|---|
| Sodium | 135 | mmol/L | |
| Potassium | 4.2 | mmol/L | |
| Urea | 4.6 | mmol/L | |
| Creatinine | 98 | µmol/L | |
| Creatine kinase | 895 | u/L | (20-195) |
| Haemoglobin | 8.5 | g/dL | |
| Mean cell volume | 86 | fL | |
| Platelets | 312 | $x10^9/L$ | |
| White cell count | 6.3 | $x10^9/L$ | (4.0 -11.0) |
| Erythrocyte Sed. Rate | 76 | mm/h | |

What is the most likely cause of this presentation?

1. Rhabdomyolysis
2. Dermatomyositis
3. Drug-induced lupus
4. Hypothyroidism
5. Polymyalgia rheumatica (PMR)

**Q.145 - Part 2**
Out of the following list, which is the most important to include in your management plan?

1. Chest x-ray
2. Thyroid function tests
3. Biopsy of the temporal artery
4. Physiotherapy
5. Hydrocortisone cream

**Q.146 - Part 1**

Mr Franklin is a 68-year-old retired carpet fitter. He complains of a long history of back pain which has recently become much worse. On examination, he has an unusual facial appearance. You think that perhaps his forehead is large. He has normal painless spinal movements; however on palpation you notice that his left iliac crest feels warm, and is bulkier than the right. You organise some blood tests and x-ray of his lumbar spine. The results are shown below.

| Test | Result | Unit | Range |
|---|---|---|---|
| Aspartate transaminase | 23 | iu/L | (7-40) |
| Alkaline phosphatase | 432 | iu/L | (25-115) |
| Adjusted calcium | 2.34 | mmol/L | (2.20-2.67) |
| Phosphate | 1.04 | mmol/L | (0.87-1.45) |

*x-ray – lumbar spine:* There is some joint space narrowing of the lower lumbar vertebrae with a few osteophytic spurs. The pelvic bones show areas with a mixture of lytic lesions and sclerosis. There is marked deformity and disturbance of the trabecular pattern with bony expansion within the left iliac rim.

Which of the following is the most likely diagnosis?

1. Ankylosing spondylitis
2. Acromegaly
3. Osteoarthritis
4. Bone metastasis
5. Paget's disease

**Q.146 - Part 2**

Since you saw him a month ago, he has downloaded a lot of information from the internet and has come across several complications associated with this condition. Which of the following is not a recognised complication?

1. Heart failure
2. Deafness in both ears
3. Spread to involve the skin
4. Cancer of the bone
5. Spontaneous bone fractures

**Q.147**

Mr Hatcher is a 60-year-old headteacher who has been troubled by a headache for the last few days. It is localised to the left side of his face from around his cheek bone to his temples and over his left ear. He says:"The pain was so bad today that it seemed to make my vision blurred". The pain is made worse when he is eating and at time when he touches the skin of the area e.g. shaving. Which is the most likely diagnosis?

1. Temporo-mandibular joint dysfunction
2. Herpes zoster
3. Trigeminal neuralgia
4. Migraine
5. Giant cell arteritis

**Q.148 - Part 1**

Ms Burlington is a 76-year-old retired surgeon. She sustains a fractured neck of femur after slipping on an icy pavement. Which of the following aspects of her history would be least likely to suggest underlying osteoporosis?

1. Anorexia nervosa
2. Alcoholism
3. Hyperthyroidism
4. Early menarche
5. Smoking

**Q.148 - Part 2**

You organise a DEXA scan to assess her bone mineral density (BMD). The result is a T-score of -1.2. Which of the following is the correct interpretation of this result?

1. BMD is above the reference range - treatment not required
2. BMD is in the top quartile for females, no evidence of osteoporosis - treatment not required
3. BMD is diagnostic of osteopenia - preventative measures should be considered
4. BMD is diagnostic of osteoporosis - treatment should be considered
5. Can't comment, need to calculate the 'z-score' to advise further

**Q.149**

Mr Daniels is a 52-year-old financial advisor. He was moving heavy furniture a week ago and a little while afterwards he developed pain in his left shoulder. The pain has gradually got worse. It restricts his shoulder movement and it is even painful when he lies on that side in bed. On inspection, there is a normal anatomical contour from every aspect of the shoulder with no obvious swelling or skin changes. He is unable to abduct his shoulder from the anatomical position due to pain which is present even on passive movement.

Which of the following is the most likely diagnosis?

1. Adhesive capsulitis
2. Injury to serratus anterior
3. Rupture of long head of biceps
4. Osteoarthritis of the shoulder
5. Rupture of supraspinatus

**Q.150**

Jason is a 27-year-old IT helpdesk assistant. He comes into Accident and Emergency with an injury to his left knee that he sustained while playing football. He was about to kick the ball with his right foot when he was tackled by another player. He slipped and twisted on his left leg and fell to the ground. He was unable to straighten his left leg or walk on it. On examination, there is negligible swelling and there is pain all around the joint.

Which of the following structure is the most likely to be injured?

1. Anterior cruciate ligament
2. Posterior cruciate ligament
3. Meniscal cartilage
4. Lateral collateral ligament
5. Medial collateral ligament

**Q.151**
Patrick is a 67-year-old retired Pastor. He is brought in by ambulance after falling down a flight of stairs at home. He is alert. On initial assessment, you suspect that he has sustained an acute spinal cord injury.

Which of the following features supports the impression of spinal shock?

1. Brisk tendon reflexes in lower limbs
2. Hypotension
3. Spastic paralysis of lower limbs
4. Urinary incontinence
5. Reduced tone in anal sphincter

**Q.152**
Mike is a 34-year-old window cleaner. He comes into hospital after falling off his ladder and injuring his right arm. On examination there is considerable bruising and lacerations and you suspect that he may have broken his arm in several places. The little and ring fingers of the right hand appear clawed, with flexion at the distal interphalangeal (DIP) joints and extension at the metacarpal-pahalangeal (MCP) joints. He cannot abduct his right little finger or adduct his right thumb. He has altered sensation over the medial aspect of his right hand.

Which of the following is the most likely site of the nerve lesion?

1. The lower roots of the brachial plexus in the axilla
2. The medial epicondyle of the humerus
3. The lateral epicondyle of the humerus
4. The distal ulna
5. The carpal tunnel

**Q.155 - Part 1**

Maria is a 17-year-old single mother to 7-w
bottle-fed but Maria is managing to breastfe
Leah has been crying for 4 hours solid almost
is very concerned that there is something s
Leah turning red in the face and drawing h
crying and grimacing. At present, Leah is se
obvious abnormalities on physical examinatio

Which of the following is the least appropriate

1. Plot her weight and head circumference
   to previous measurements
2. Refer for a paediatric opinion
3. Enquire about the feeding pattern and me
4. Enquire about the baby's sleep pattern
5. Establish what social support Maria has
   baby in general

**Q.155 - Part 2**

Maria has heard about this problem from oth
about it in magazines. She asks you which,
advice that she has heard, is the best thing to
her baby.

Which answer would you single out?

1. If she wants to continue breastfeeding, s
   from her diet for a trial period
2. She should change to a teat with slower f
3. She should try changing to a soya milk fo
4. She should either breastfeed or bottlef
   mixed feeding, as the baby is suffering fro
5. She should be given a prescription for Inf

# SECTION 7

# Paediatrics

**Q.153**

Jodie is 28 years old and has asthma. She is
first child. She does not know anyone wh
amongst her friends and is wondering whether

Which of the following is not a recognised a
Jodie's child?

1. Reduced risk of necrotising enterocolitis
2. Reduced risk of atopy
3. Reduced risk of insulin-dependent diabete
4. Reduced risk of ear infections
5. Reduced risk of Vitamin D deficiency

**Q.154**

Sarah is 18 and comes from a travelling famil
the last four months and did not know that
unbooked for antenatal care and presented t
Her baby was born at 32 weeks weighing 2.0
find out about any relevant past medical history

Which of the following pre-existing conditions is

1. Crohn's disease
2. Brittle asthma
3. Insulin-dependent diabetes mellitus
4. HIV
5. Systemic lupus erythematosus

**Q.156**

Harvey is 4 weeks old. His mother has brought him to see you as he has been vomiting over the past 3 days. The vomiting episodes have increased in frequency and severity over that time, and he now vomits shortly after every feed. He still appears hungry and keen to feed, though he is a little less alert than he was this morning. He has not had a wet nappy for 12 hours.

Which of the following options would you be least likely to carry out as part of your investigation of Harvey's condition?

1. Arrange an urgent abdominal ultrasound
2. Check urea and electrolytes
3. Ask the mother to feed Harvey whilst you palpate his abdomen
4. Abdominal x-ray
5. Perform a capillary blood gas

**Q.157**

Matilda is 6 weeks old. Her mother brings her to see you as she is concerned about the appearance of her nappy area. Matilda came to you a couple of weeks ago with mild eczema on her face and her mother has been applying emollients as directed. Matilda initially had mild nappy rash consisting of slight erythema confined to the nappy area when you last saw her and at that time you were not concerned, so you advised slightly more frequent nappy changes. The rash has changed over the past two days and looks redder and angrier, with small, slightly raised red spots, which spread slightly beyond the nappy area down the thighs. Her mother has read that this could be due to zinc deficiency, especially since she is vegetarian and is exclusively breastfeeding Matilda. You note there is also a family history of psoriasis.

Which is the most likely diagnosis?

1. Streptococcal superinfection of nappy rash
2. Eczema herpeticum
3. Candidal nappy rash
4. Acrodermatitis enteropathica
5. Flexural psoriasis

**Q.158 - Part 1**

Freddie is 11 months old and is an only child. His mother looks after him full-time. He was exclusively breastfed until the age of 4 months, when solids were gradually introduced alongside ongoing breastfeeding. He has just started taking some finger foods. The health visitor is concerned that his growth seems to be faltering, as he had been on the 25th centile until 6 months, and is now on the 2nd centile. His mother reports that his stool has changed and now smells offensive and is bulkier than previously. He has gone from being an easy-tempered child to being miserable for much of the day. His mother is very worried as to where she is going wrong.

Which of the following is the most likely cause of his symptoms?

1. Cystic fibrosis
2. Glucose-galactose malabsorption
3. Threadworm infection
4. Late-onset lactase deficiency
5. Coeliac disease

**Q.158 - Part 2**

Freddie has been quite a fussy eater up until now, and his mother is worried as to which of his favourite foods he will still be able to eat given his suspected diagnosis.

Which of the following need not be eliminated from his diet?

1. Fish fingers
2. Sausages
3. Porridge
4. Buckwheat pancakes
5. Chicken with gravy

**Q.159**

9-month-old Shania was taken to Accident and Emergency last week as she was febrile and had poor oral intake. She was discharged a few hours later when her parents were able to manage giving her oral rehydration solution successfully. The hospital has just notified you that her clean-catch urine sample showed a pure growth of Escherichia coli at over 105 colony-forming units per millilitre and has asked you to arrange investigations.

Which of the following investigations should be arranged as your first step?

1. Renal ultrasound
2. Abdominal radiograph
3. DMSA scan
4. Micturating cystourethrogram (MCUG) or MAG-3 scan
5. Obtain a second specimen, as investigation is required only if a second sample is positive

**Q.160**

Fawzia has just turned 8. Her mother has been concerned about her for the past four months but was embarrassed to bring Fawzia to see you. She has noticed that Fawzia has developed breast buds, and also has some sparse hair growth in the pubic region. Fawzia is the second-tallest in her class, although her mother is quite petite at 5 foot 1 inches.

Which of the following is not a potential cause of Fawzia's bodily changes?

1. Familial precocious puberty
2. Congenital hydrocephalus
3. Hyperthyroidism
4. Neurofibromatosis Type 1
5. Congenital adrenal hyperplasia

**Q.161**

15-year-old Rehana comes to see you alone for the first time. You also treat both her parents regularly for chronic medical conditions and have a good relationship with them. You know that the family's Islamic faith is very important to them and they believe that their children are also following the guidance of their faith. You are surprised when Rehana informs you that she has a boyfriend and enquires about the oral contraceptive pill.

In accordance with the Fraser guidelines for contraceptive advice in children, which of the following would be the most suitable reason for you to decline to prescribe her the oral contraceptive pill?

1. If her parents found out at a later date that you had been involved in prescribing the OCP for Rehana, this would irretrievably damage your relationship with them and thus endanger the management of their chronic medical conditions
2. Rehana understands that she could use other forms of contraception such as barriers which are available without prescription
3. Rehana is not currently sexually active with her boyfriend and she is adamant that she is not intending to commence sexual activity with him unless she is taking the OCP
4. You advise that she involves a parent in her decision if possible, but she refuses
5. You are aware that her boyfriend, also a patient of yours, has had a sexually-transmitted infection, and you feel she needs to protect herself with barrier contraception, but are unable to breach confidentiality to tell her this directly

**Q.162**

3-week-old Brandon has just been diagnosed with cystic fibrosis on the basis of the neonatal heelprick screening test. A DNA sample has been sent to the laboratory for verification. In the meantime, his parents come to see you for advice. They are shocked by the diagnosis, as they had thought up until then that Brandon was perfectly healthy. They have been reading up about all the possible complications of cystic fibrosis on the internet.

Which of the following complications can you reassure them is of no concern for Brandon?

1. Diabetes mellitus since early diagnosis allows prevention of this complication
2. Infertility, as IVF can now be used successfully
3. Pneumothorax
4. Liver failure requiring transplantation, as medical treatments are increasingly successful at preventing this
5. Meconium ileus because it is very rare in this situation

**Q.163**

9-year-old Jordan has been referred to the child psychiatry services following concerns raised at his school regarding his behaviour in class.

Which of the following would not be compatible with the diagnosis of Hyperkinetic Disorder?

1. Jordan's mother has no significant concerns about his behaviour at home, but his Cub Scout leader has reported to her in the past that he interrupts other children and is very 'forward' in his dealings with adult leaders.
2. Jordan has always been a clumsy child.
3. Jordan has a specific language impairment and has been seen by the speech and language therapists in earlier childhood.
4. Jordan's infant school, which he attended until the age of 7, felt that his behaviour was essentially within normal limits for his age. The difficulties have become evident after changing to his junior school.
5. The problems are most evident in situations where clear standards of behaviour are expected, even when these are explained to Jordan.

**Q.164**

6-month-old Marie is the daughter of a Congolese woman, who has just been granted refugee status. Marie was born in the UK, but they have had to relocate during her mother's application for political asylum. They have now settled permanently within the bounds of your practice. Her mother is aware that Marie may not be up-to-date with her vaccinations as they often had to register as temporary residents, and she asks you to check what immunisations Marie should have had by now.

Which is the correct combination of immunisations that you would expect her to have had?

1. 3 sets of HIB (Haemophilus influenzae B), diphtheria, pertussis, polio and tetanus vaccinations, 2 sets of Meningitis C vaccinations, and 2 sets of pneumococcal conjugate vaccinations
2. 3 sets of HIB (Haemophilus influenzae B), diphtheria, pertussis, polio and tetanus vaccinations, 2 sets of Meningitis C vaccinations, and 2 sets of pneumococcal conjugate vaccinations, BCG
3. 3 sets of diphtheria, pertussis, tetanus, and polio vaccinations; 1 HIB vaccination, 1 Meningitis C vaccination, 1st dose of pneumococcal conjugate vaccination due at 6 months
4. 3 sets of diphtheria, pertussis, and tetanus vaccinations; 3 Sabin (live) polio vaccinations, 2 sets of Meningitis C vaccinations, and 2 sets of pneumococcal conjugate vaccinations, BCG
5. 3 sets of HIB (Haemophilus influenzae B), diphtheria, pertussis, polio and tetanus vaccinations, 2 sets of Meningitis C vaccinations, and 2 sets of pneumococcal conjugate vaccinations, first dose of MMR with 4-month vaccinations

**Q.165**

Lennie is a 5-year-old boy. His parents bring him to your surgery with a rash. It began 2 days ago behind the ears, and now covers most of his body. On examination, you find a confluent erythematous rash with few areas of discrete macules.

Which of the following diagnoses would you suspect most strongly on the basis of the above appearances?

1. Rubella
2. Parvovirus B19
3. Scarlet fever
4. Measles
5. Coxsackie virus

**Q.166**

You are seeing 6-week-old Cameron for his routine check and you auscultate a heart murmur. His parents have not been concerned about him as he has appeared to take good volumes of milk and, although his weight has placed him now on the 25th centile rather than above the 50th where he was at birth, he seems alert and contented and is not cyanosed.

Which of the following features is most suggestive this is just an innocent murmur?

1. There is a short buzzing murmur in the 4th left intercostal space
2. There is no abnormal sound during systole, and a short, quiet murmur in diastole
3. The murmur is well-localised to the right sternal edge only and does not radiate
4. Cameron takes normal volumes of milk by bottle, completing each feed in 40 minutes
5. The murmur increases in intensity on exercise

**Q.167**

Mr Roberts comes to your surgery in a very distressed state. He tells you that his wife and 1-week-old baby Reece have been transferred by helicopter to a specialist hospital in a different city as Reece has a heart condition that was not picked up antenatally. Reece became very unwell shortly after delivery when he was born at the local midwife-led birth centre. Mr Roberts has since had to stay at home to look after the other 4 children. He has brought in a number of print-outs about different cardiac conditions from the internet as he hoped you would be able to tell him whether there was anything that could be done for Reece's condition. He has been so worked up and stressed that he has forgotten the name of the condition. What he does remember is that Reece turned blue shortly after birth and did not improve when oxygen was given.

Which of the following conditions could be Reece's diagnosis?

1. Patent ductus arteriosus
2. Pulmonary stenosis
3. Tricuspid atresia
4. Large ventricular septal defect
5. Severe coarctation of the aorta

**Q.168**

2-month-old Abdul was brought in to Accident and Emergency by ambulance. He had been waiting for some time at the GP out-of-hours service and appeared very unwell by the time the GP was able to assess him. He is now lethargic, febrile and has not fed for 8 hours. Intramuscular benzylpenicillin was administered prior to arrival.

Which of the following clinical features would least likely deter you from performing a lumbar puncture?

1. Abdul's heart rate is 80 beats per minute and regular
2. Abdul's platelet count is 49
3. Abdul is hypotensive
4. Abdul is hypertensive
5. Abdul has been rated as P on the AVPU scale

**Q.169**

An outbreak of rotavirus has forced the temporary closure of a local nursery. 6-month-old Kian seems to have been infected since, for the last 24 hours, he has been refusing most feeds, has had 5 offensive green liquid stools, and has vomited three times. His mother has brought him to Accident and Emergency and you are trying to assess how dehydrated he is to help you decide whether he may need intravenous fluid replacement or whether you should persist a little longer with oral rehydration which his mother, who is herself a nurse, has been attempting to administer to the best of her ability whilst waiting in the long queue.

Which of the following signs from the following list would suggest the most severe degree of dehydration?

1. Anterior fontanelle is sunken
2. He has not passed urine for 6 hours
3. He is lethargic
4. Skin turgor is reduced
5. Capillary refill time is 2.5 seconds

**Q.170**

Mrs Akinsola is concerned about her youngest child, Bola. Bola's older brother is 6 and attends a special needs school as he has global developmental delay of unknown cause. She wonders if her older child would have had a better outcome if she had picked up the signs of his problems at an earlier stage and had got help sooner.

In which of the following cases would you be able to reassure her that Bola's development does not appear significantly delayed?

1. Bola has smiled but not in response to his family by the age of 8 weeks
2. Bola is not reaching for objects by 5 months
3. Bola is not walking unsupported by 18 months
4. Bola is not using single words with an identifiable meaning by 18 months
5. Bola is not sitting unsupported by 8 months

**Q.171**
Yee Sook has been adopted from an orphanage and her adoptive parents have just brought her back to the UK. Her exact age is not known, as she was an abandoned baby, but her parents are keen to know what stage she is at developmentally. You observe that she is able to sit unsupported for about ten minutes before she tires. She can stand up whilst holding onto the edge of her cot, but is not yet cruising. She is able to make some consonant noises when babbling and tries to imitate sounds. She has a scissor but not yet a pincer grip of small objects. She has been finger-feeding on toast 'soldiers' since arriving in the UK and seems to enjoy this. She is also trying to hold her bottle of milk by herself and usually manages this without help.

What stage do you feel she has attained in terms of her development?

1. Roughly 6 months in all areas
2. Roughly 8 months in all areas
3. Roughly 10 months in all areas
4. Gross and fine motor around 7 months, social around 10 months
5. Roughly nine months in all areas except language, which is around 6 months

iSCMEDICAL
Interview Skills Consulting

# SECTION 8

# Pharmacology

# Therapeutics

**Q.172**

Mrs Drewberry is a 78-year-old retired housemaid. She suffers from osteoarthritis which means that she has to take a lot of opioid analgesics. She comes to you complaining of constipation. She hasn't opened her bowels for two days, and her last stool was hard and of minimal amount. She has passed flatus, which in fact is a major concern of hers. She has tried increasing the fibre in her diet but still feels bloated. She has tried senna before but found that it gave her cramping pains. On examination, her abdomen is soft and non-tender but you can palpate 'loaded bowel loops' all over.

Which of the following would be your first choice treatment for this woman?

1. Ispaghula husk
2. Movicol ®
3. Lactulose ®
4. Glycerine suppositories
5. Sodium picosulfate

**Q.173**

Mr Higgins is a 56-year-old tailor. He has hypertension and you wish to prescribe him ramipril. Having had bad experiences with medication in the past, he asks you about side effects.

Which side effect is the most likely to occur out of the following options?

1. Vertigo
2. Productive cough
3. Skin discolouration
4. Angioedema
5. Peripheral neuropathy

**Q.174**

Jenny is a 23-year-old child minder who is 4 months pregnant. She complains of urinary frequency and pain passing water. Her urine dipstick is positive for blood, leucocytes and nitrites.

Which of the following is the best option for empirical treatment?

1. Trimethoprim
2. Ciprofloxacin
3. Metronidazole
4. Doxycycline
5. Cephalexin

**Q.175**

Rachel is a 25-year-old singer. She has a 5-day history of cough and sore throat. On examination, she has acutely inflamed tonsils with obvious overlying exudate. She is 2 months post-partum and she wants to continue breast-feeding. She also has a history of penicillin allergy when she was younger, during which she experienced rash and some facial oedema.

Which of the following antibiotics is the best option for her?

1. Clarithromycin
2. Erythromycin
3. Doxycycline
4. Cephalexin
5. Ampicillin

**Q.176**

Nigel is a 49-year-old nightclub owner. He has been experiencing erectile dysfunction and demands that you write him a prescription for sildenafil (Viagra®). The prescription of sildenafil by the NHS is restricted to certain conditions.

Which of the following is NOT a specific indication to prescribe sildenafil on the NHS?

1. Varicose veins
2. Parkinson's disease
3. Prostate cancer
4. Diabetes
5. Multiple sclerosis

**Q.177**

Martha is a 69-year-old author. She has been diagnosed with osteoporosis and is about to start taking a bisphosphonate.

Which of the following is the most suitable instruction to give her regarding taking this drug?

1. Take on a full stomach with a glass of water before bed time
2. Take on a full stomach with a glass of milk, do not lie down for at least 2 hours afterwards
3. Take on an empty stomach at least 30 minutes before breakfast or any other tablets, stay upright for at least 30 minutes afterwards
4. Take on an empty stomach with calcium supplements at least 30 minutes before breakfast, stay upright for at least 30 minutes afterwards
5. Take on an empty stomach with calcium supplements before bed time, do not lie down for at least 30 minutes afterwards

**Q.178**

Katie is a 36-year-old housewife who suffers from bipolar disorder. She has recently been diagnosed with Graves' disease and has just started treatment for it. A few weeks into treatment she comes to you feeling unwell with fevers and a sore throat.

Which one of the drugs from the list below, could she be taking that would put her at risk of serious sepsis and should therefore be stopped immediately?

1. Carbimazole
2. Carbamazepine
3. Propylthiouracil
4. Propranolol
5. Paroxetine

**Q.179**

Clark is a 32-year-old sound engineer. He sustained a penetrating foot injury after stepping on broken glass. There is localised inflammation and you have started him on a combination of oral antibiotics due to the risk of a mixed bacterial infection. He wishes to know whether drinking a small amount of alcohol would do him any harm.

Which of the following antibiotics is associated with the most unpleasant reaction to drinking alcohol?

1. Erythromycin
2. Ciprofloxacin
3. Amoxycillin
4. Clindamycin
5. Metronidazole

**Q.180**

Tariq is a 32-year-old electronics engineer. He was admitted to hospital with headache and fevers, and was diagnosed with tuberculous meningitis. He has since been discharged and is continuing his therapy in the community. He comes to you complaining of dizziness and buzzing in his ears.

Which of the following antituberculous drugs is a well-recognised cause of these problems?

1. Rifampacin
2. Isoniazid
3. Pyrazinamide
4. Ethambutol
5. Streptomycin

**Q.181**

Margaret is a 37-year-old receptionist. She has been a smoker for over 20 years and has had many attempts at giving up. You are considering prescribing her bupropion (Zyban ®). All but one of the following situations fall outside the recommendations for taking bupropion.

Which one of the following situations does not fall outside of the recommendations for safe and appropriate prescribing of bupropion?

1. Patient failed bupropion therapy a year ago
2. Patient has a history of an eating disorder
3. Patient is concurrently taking ciprofloxacin
4. Patient has not set a definite smoking stop date
5. Patient is breastfeeding

**Q.182**
Angelina is a 26-year-old musician. She has poorly-controlled Type 1 diabetes. She has had a few admissions with ketoacidosis, during which she gets bad nausea and vomiting.

Which of the following anti-emetics may prove to have a particular benefit in this case?

1. Cyclizine
2. Metoclopramide
3. Domperidone
4. Ondansetron
5. Haloperidol

**Q.183**
Sally is a 32-year-old sales representative who has just been diagnosed with multiple sclerosis. She had read somewhere that steroid therapy is often indicated and that this has many side effects.

Which of the following is not a recognised side effect of steroid therapy?

1. Lowered seizure threshold
2. Hyperglycaemia
3. Postural hypotension
4. Myalgia
5. Pancreatitis

**Q.184 - Part 1**

Mr Dobson is a 66-year-old retired paramedic. He has just had a prosthetic aortic valve fitted and has commenced long term warfarin therapy.

What is the target range for INR that anticoagulation should aim for?

1. 1 - 1.5
2. 1.5 - 2.5
3. 2 - 2.5
4. 2.5 - 3.0
5. 3 - 4

**Q.184 - Part 2**

Mr Dobson once confided in you that he had managed to 'get hold of' short courses of antibiotics in the past from work colleagues. Remembering this, you wish to emphasise the risk of antibiotic drug interactions with warfarin.

Which of the following antibiotics is most recognised to enhance the anticoagulant effect of warfarin?

1. Rifampacin
2. Ciprofloxacin
3. Doxycycline
4. Trimethoprim
5. Azithromycin

**Q.185**

Mrs Bucklehurst is a 63-year-old piano teacher who is on long-term warfarin for atrial fibrillation. Her INR today is reported as 8.5. She has no signs of bleeding at present although she does report worsening indigestion and heartburn of late.

Which of the following is the most appropriate management option?

1. Omit warfarin dose and continue as normal the next day
2. Stop warfarin for now and repeat INR daily until low enough to resume therapy
3. Stop warfarin and give 5 mg of oral vitamin K
4. Stop warfarin and give 2 units of fresh frozen plasma
5. Stop warfarin, give 2 units of fresh frozen plasma and give 5mg of vitamin K intravenously

**Q.186**

Mrs Birch is a 79-year-old retired shopkeeper. She suffers from osteoarthritis of her knees, but is unsuitable for surgery. Her pain has worsened so much over the last few months that she is asking for a change in her medication to help her cope. She cannot take a non-steroidal anti-inflammatory drugs due to a history of peptic ulceration. Her current medications include bendroflumathiazide 2.5 mg OD, clopidogrel 75mg OD, atorvastatin 10mg OD and paracetamol 1g QDS.

With side-effect profiles in mind, which of the following agents would be the most appropriate choice to use alongside or instead of her current medications?

1. Co-proxamol
2. Co-codamol (8/500)
3. Co-codamol (30/500)
4. Tramadol
5. Co-dydramol

**Q.187**

Jennifer is an 9-year-old girl who has recently been diagnosed with asthma. She has had difficulty using metered-dose aerosol inhalers and so you have introduced her to using a spacer device. The following options are a list of statements regarding spacer devices.

Which of the following pieces of advice regarding spacer devices is incorrect?

1. Spacers come in different sizes and the larger ones tend to be more effective
2. After cleaning, spacer devices should be dried well with a cloth to avoid accumulation of mould
3. Despite the extra volume to pass, the same amount of puffs are required with or without a spacer device
4. Spacer devices can reduce the complication of oral candidiasis from inhaled steroids
5. Spacer devices are particularly useful in the elderly

**Q.188**

Michelle is a 19-year-old law student who has recently been diagnosed with epilepsy. She also suffers from hayfever and mild asthma. You wish to start her on carbamazepine but you have to warn her about drug interactions. Her drugs are listed in the following options.

Which one of the following drugs would be a particular cause for concern?

1. Ferrous sulphate
2. Loratadine
3. Salbutamol
4. Microgynon ®
5. Montelukast ®

**Q.189**

Harvey is a 68-year-old retired prison warden. He has recently been admitted to hospital with chest pain and palpitations. A ventricular tachyarrhythmia was discovered and he was subsequently started on amiodarone. He has since been talking to a friend of his who had been on the drug before but reacted badly to it. He has come to you today to ask you more about the drug.

Which of the following is NOT a commonly recognised side-effect of amiodarone?

1. Hyperthyroidism
2. Hypothyroidism
3. Arrhythmias
4. Yellow vision
5. Grey appearance to the skin

**Q.190**

Mervyn is a 64-year-old bank manager. He goes to Accident and Emergency because of fast palpitations and chest pain. He has a history of ischaemic heart disease, hypertension and arrhythmias. There are many reasons why he may have developed this arrhythmia today, one of which is an interaction between digoxin and one of his other medications.

Which of the following agents is least likely to potentiate the effects of digoxin?

1. Spironolactone
2. Quinine
3. Amiodarone
4. Bumetanide
5. Verapamil

**Q.191**

Charles is a 55-year-old Afro-Caribbean businessman. He has been found to have consistently elevated blood pressure. Other than chronic varicose veins with associated ankle swelling, he is otherwise well. You have already discussed lifestyle issues and are now considering drug treatment.

Which of the following would be the most appropriate first drug of choice?

1. Ramipril
2. Losartan
3. Atenolol
4. Nifedipine
5. Bumetanide

**Q.192**

Kelly is a 34-year-old poet. She has recently been diagnosed with bipolar affective disorder and is about to start lithium therapy. She wants to discuss this drug with you.

Which one of the following is not a common side-effect of lithium when given at appropriate therapeutic levels?

1. Tremor
2. Psychosis
3. Polydipsia
4. Weight gain
5. Leucocytosis

**Q.193**

Sidney is a 37-year-old train driver. He has suffered from irritable bowel syndrome (IBS) for many years, with symptoms varying between diarrhoea, constipation and abdominal pain. As a result you want to compile a mini-formulary for him, so he can select the best drugs for the symptoms affecting him at a particular time.

Which of the following drugs would you not wish to include in this formulary?

1. Mebeverine
2. Hyoscine hydrobromide
3. Ispaghula
4. Peppermint oil
5. Loperamide

**Q.194**

Mrs Keely is a 69-year-old ex-policewoman with pancreatic cancer. She requires a repeat prescription for analgesics. You have sent the prescription to the local pharmacy but it has been sent back to you because you didn't adhere to the requirements of writing a prescription for a controlled drug.

Which of the following statements is incorrect regarding prescriptions for controlled drugs?

1. The name and address of the prescriber should be stated on the prescription
2. The dose needs to be stated, but only in figures not words e.g. '100 mg' and not '100 mg (one hundred mg)'
3. The total number of dose units or total quantity (if liquid) should be written in words and figures. E.g. '10 (ten) tablets'
4. The name and address of the patient must be clearly typed or visible by printed label on the prescription
5. The form of the drug must be written out even if implied in the name e.g. MST 'tablets'

**Q.195**
Helen is 30-year-old cashier. She has bipolar affective disorder and brittle asthma. She was admitted to hospital due to a bad asthma attack that almost required ventilation in the intensive care unit. She is currently on several medications that require close monitoring.

For which of the following drugs would you not order therapeutic drug levels?

1. Aminophyline
2. Gentamicin
3. Olanzapine
4. Sodium Valproate
5. Lithium

**Q.196**
Derek is a 39-year-old man with schizophrenia, who has been brought into hospital by ambulance after his housemate finds him to be acutely confused. On examination, he is hot and sweaty with a temperature of 41 degrees Celsius. He is agitated but mute. His body is rigid with globally increased muscle tone. His blood results show mild renal impairment, a raised white cell count and raised creatine phosphokinase.

Which of the following agents is most likely to be of use?

1. Dothiepin
2. Diazepam
3. Dantrolene
4. Donepezil
5. Doxapram

**Q.197**

Rohana is an 18-year-old language student. She has recently started a course of antibiotics and she has become jaundiced. Her liver function tests are taken and the report is consistent with cholestasis.

Which of the following antibiotics is most likely to cause this picture?

1. Pyrazinamide
2. Ciprofloxacin
3. Co-amoxiclav
4. Penicillin V
5. Clarithromycin

**Q.198**

Mrs Goodwin is a 58-year-old counsellor. She is admitted as an emergency with acute abdominal pain, fevers, nausea and vomiting. She is diagnosed with acute diverticulitis and managed conservatively with antibiotics. Her blood tests show she has moderately severe acute renal impairment.

Which of the following drugs is least likely to require dose adjustment in this context?

1. Digoxin
2. Heparin
3. Morphine
4. Cephalosporins
5. Metronidazole

**Q.199 - Part 1**

Chester is a 28-year-old record producer. He was found by the police wandering in the street at midnight, mumbling to himself, and was brought into hospital. He understands that you are a doctor and is co-operative in answering questions. You note psychotic features and you suspect that the underlying diagnosis is schizophrenia.

Which of the following features is most suggestive of schizophrenia over other diagnoses?

1. Delusions that he has special powers
2. Disorientation in time and place
3. Hearing other people talking about him through the wall
4. Perseverative speech
5. Hallucinations that he can see someone else standing in the room

**Q.199 - Part 2**

Chester is later assessed by the psychiatric team and admitted under Section 2 of the Mental Health Act 1983. After a period of assessment, they believe he is likely to have a diagnosis of schizophrenia.

Which of the following factors would suggest a poor prognosis?

1. Sudden onset episode of psychosis
2. Previously stable job and social situation
3. Male sex
4. Affective disturbance congruent to the situation
5. Onset after age 25

**Q.200**

Samuel is a 32-year-old dockyard worker. He has recently been diagnosed with schizophrenia. As well as delusions and thought disorder, he also stopped turning up for work and withdrew from social interaction in the period prior to his diagnosis being made. More recently, he has become very demotivated and says very little.

Which of the following treatments is thought to be most useful for these features from the options below?

1. Olanzapine
2. Chlorpromazine
3. Flupenthixol
4. Haloperidol
5. Cognitive behavioural therapy

**Q.201**

Samantha is a 17-year-old student. She suffers from an eating disorder and has finally been encouraged by a friend to seek help.

Which of the following features is the strongest indicator that she has bulimia nervosa rather than anorexia nervosa?

1. Excessive exercise
2. Body mass index (BMI) of 18.5 $kg/m^2$
3. Induced vomiting
4. Preoccupation with her body weight and fear of being overweight
5. Amenorrhoea

**Q.202**

Harold is a 78-year-old retired caretaker. His wife died many years ago and he lives alone in a flat in a warden-controlled housing complex. His neighbour noticed that he hasn't collected the milk from his doorstep for several days and called the warden. The warden paid Harold a visit and agreed that he was behaving strangely so they called you as his registered doctor.

Which of the following clinical features would suggest a diagnosis of delirium rather than dementia?

1. Aggression
2. Hallucinations
3. Drowsiness
4. Depression
5. Personality change

**Q.203**

Martin is a 70-year-old retired shop fitter. His wife has noticed a cognitive decline for some time. You suspect a form of dementia and have referred him for a specialist assessment.

Which of the following features would suggest Alzheimer's dementia being more likely than a vascular dementia?

1. Stepwise progression
2. Personality preserved
3. Patchy cognitive impairment
4. Early loss of insight
5. Emotional symptoms at presentation

**Q.204**

Petra is a 40-year-old careers advisor. She complains of forgetfulness and impaired short-term memory. This is confirmed by her close family. This may be a case of early-onset dementia, but there are other organic causes of dementia which you would like to consider.

Which one of the following is least recognised as a cause of dementia?

1. Parkinson's disease
2. Acute intermittent porphyria
3. Wilson's disease
4. Multiple sclerosis
5. Huntington's disease

**Q.205**

Mr Warrington is a 40-year-old construction worker. He was admitted for an elective repair of bilateral inguinal hernias. Unfortunately, the procedure was complicated by bowel incarceration. Instead of a day case procedure, Mr Warrington was admitted to the ward for a few days. On the third night, the nurses calls you because he has become sweaty, agitated and confused. He is trembling under the bed sheets, petrified of scorpions which he claims are crawling all over him.

Which of the following is the best first line treatment option?

1. Lorazepam & chlorpromazine
2. Lorazepam & haloperidol
3. Chlordiazepoxide
4. Chlordiazepoxide & chlorpromazine
5. Chlordiazepoxide & haloperidol

**Q.206**

Ms Pike is a 40-year-old single mother. She was made redundant from her factory job 6 months ago and has very little in the way of a social support network. She has been a regular alcohol drinker for a while now and you suspect she needs help for this.

Which of the following is NOT a feature of the alcohol dependence syndrome?

1. Relief drinking e.g. early in the morning to avoid or escape withdrawal symptoms
2. Rapid reinstatement of drinking after a period of abstinence
3. Raised alcohol tolerance
4. Feeling guilty about their alcohol consumption
5. Presence of withdrawal symptoms

**Q.207 - Part 1**

Dennis is a 41-year-old unemployed builder. He is known to be alcoholic and has been admitted to hospital several times due to acute complications. He was brought in by ambulance after being found collapsed in the street one Saturday night. By the time he arrived at the hospital he was rousable.

Which one of the following is not a feature of Wernicke's encephalopathy?

1. Nystagmus
2. Confusion
3. Ophthalmoplegia
4. Confabulation
5. Ataxic gait

**Q.207 - Part 2**

Which other condition from those below is most commonly associated with Wernicke's encephalopathy?

1. Gastrinoma
2. Chronic pancreatitis
3. Hyperemesis gravidarum
4. Laxative abuse
5. Pernicious anaemia

**Q.208**

Frank is a 45-year-old tax collector. He has come to talk you about his wife Marlene, who has been behaving strangely of late.

Which of the following behaviours would be most significant in suggesting that she is manic rather than hypomanic?

1. She has been saying that she can win a national cake baking competition despite never having baked a cake before
2. She is really excited about the competition and can't stop thinking about it
3. She spent £50,000 to renovate the kitchen, when their existing kitchen was only 6 months old
4. She stayed up until 2am last night baking cakes
5. Her mood goes up and down depending on how successful her cakes turn out

**Q.209**
Liam is a 27-year-old set designer. He has recently been mentally ill. You have a conversation with him to explore his thoughts.

Which of the following statements outlines a delusional perception?

1. If he sees a crack in the pavement, he must avoid walking on it otherwise he will get bad luck
2. If he sees a magpie (a black and white bird) he will get bad luck
3. If he does a good deed, then a supreme being will reward him for it
4. He saw a squirrel cross the road, which means that the evil forces are going to attack him very soon
5. If he steals then he will receive punishment somehow or another

**Q.210**
Mrs Hughes is a 46-year-old woman who cleans for the Worthington family. She has been low in mood for several weeks and you suspect that her depression is worsening.

Which of the following features is most suggestive of severe depression?

1. She is convinced that she is to blame for the divorce of Mr and Mrs Worthington because their house wasn't clean enough
2. She has reduced libido
3. She wakes up at 4 am most mornings and can't get back to sleep
4. She has lost her appetite
5. She has stopped going to her bingo club because she doesn't enjoy it anymore

**Q.211**

Judith is a 76-year-old retired matron. She lives alone in a small village. She comes to you complaining of problems with her memory. You take a history and perform a number of tests which reveal that she does have some cognitive impairment.

Which of the following features is most suggestive that this is dementia rather than depression?

1. She came to you complaining of poor memory
2. She gives a detailed history
3. She is not concerned when you inform her that she has a poor result on the test
4. Lacks effort when being tested
5. Short duration of the illness

**Q.212**

Ms Peterhouse is a 42-year-old woman with severe depression. She is so unwell that electroconvulsive therapy (ECT) is to be considered.

Which of the following is NOT a recognised side-effect of ECT?

1. Headache
2. Long term memory loss
3. Joint dislocation
4. Bone fractures
5. Temporary confusion

**Q.213**

Mr Hopkinson is a 43-year-old jeweller. He complains of chronic tingling in his right arm and feels unable to use it. This has been going on for about 8 months and he has had numerous investigations and consultations with the neurologists, but they have found no organic cause. At times he has to stop working due to his symptoms. Since he is self-employed, this means a drop in his earnings because he doesn't claim disability living allowance. This also causes conflict with his wife. A year ago he witnessed a terrifying armed robbery in the bank opposite from his jeweller's shop. He wasn't hurt during the event.

Which of the following is the most likely diagnosis?

1. Somatisation disorder
2. Hypochondriasis
3. Dissociative disorder
4. Factitious disorder
5. Post-traumatic stress disorder

**Q.214**

Sandra is a 22-year-old nursing student. She is worried about her 45-year-old father who has been acting oddly of late. She thinks he might have obsessive compulsive disorder (OCD) and wants to know more about this condition.

Which of the following statements is NOT correct regarding an obsession in OCD?

1. It is a recurrent thought, image or impulse
2. It enters the patient's mind without them wishing it to
3. To others it may seem absurd, but the patient is unaware of its absurdity
4. It often leads to the compulsion to carry out an activity
5. Attempts to resist it lead to anxiety

**Q.215**
Jemima is a 22-year-old single woman who lives with her parents. She feels that she "can't cope in places where there are lots of people". It is not because she is shy, she just feels as if she is trapped and can't get out. Once before, when she tried to get a bus, she found that her breathing changed and she almost hyperventilated whilst standing at the bus shelter where a group of people were gathered. As a result, she avoids these situations and spends most of her time at home. She does her shopping through mail order catalogues and the internet.

Which of the following diagnoses best fits with this presentation?

1. Agoraphobia
2. Panic disorder
3. Social phobia
4. Generalised anxiety disorder
5. Claustrophobia

**Q.216 - Part 1**
Marcus is a 70-year-old retired greengrocer. He is admitted to hospital following a stroke which affected his vision and nothing else. The admitting doctor described his visual loss as being a left-sided homonymous hemianopia.

How would you best describe this?

1. Blindness in left eye
2. Blind in the temporal fields of both eyes
3. Blind in the nasal fields of both eyes
4. Blindness in the left half of the visual field of both eyes
5. Blindness in half the visual field of the left eye

**Q.216 - Part 2**

If this turned out to be an ischaemic stroke, which artery is most likely to be occluded?

1. Basilar artery
2. Right-sided vertebral artery
3. Right-sided posterior cerebral artery
4. Right-sided middle cerebral artery
5. Right-sided anterior cerebral artery

**Q.217**

Mary-Ann is a 31-year-old accounts clerk who is two weeks post-partum after the birth of her first child. She is a single mother, temporarily living at her mother's house. She has been acting very strangely and her mother has raised some concerns. In particular Mary-Ann thinks the baby is diseased and unclean. She has got to the point where she won't touch the baby at all because of fear of contamination of her body. As a result, her mother has to undertake all care for the baby, but she is not always around. Just today Mary-Ann mentioned she thought the baby was evil and will bring bad luck to the family.

Which of the following is the best management option?

1. Manage this case at home with antipsychotics and aid from the health visitor and mental health Home Treatment Team
2. Manage this case at home with reassurance and the aid of the midwife and health visitor, ensuring that Mary-Ann's mother takes full care of the child
3. Admit her and treat with antipsychotics and consider fostering the child
4. Admit her and treat with antipsychotics and mood-stabilising agents; try to keep the baby with her in a mother-and-baby unit
5. Admit her for observation not treatment, then watch and wait as symptoms slowly resolve with time as her hormonal balance resolves

**Q.218**

Marilyn is a 42-year-old policewoman who is right-handed. She is newly-diagnosed as having multiple sclerosis, which presented with her having difficulty with sequences of actions like getting dressed or preparing some food. She also had problems with arithmetic.

Whereabouts in the cerebral hemispheres would you expect the lesion to lie?

1. Frontal lobe
2. Right temporal
3. Left temporal
4. Right parietal
5. Left parietal

**Q.219 - Part 1**

Henry is a 68-year-old retired chef. He presents with acute leg weakness. He was able to walk normally before going to bed last night, but had an odd sense of numbness around his buttocks. He was woken early this morning from his sleep with sharp lower back pain and pain down the back of both his legs. When he tried to get up, he found that he could not move his legs and so his wife called an ambulance. He has a past history of mild asthma, hypertension and prostate carcinoma, for which he had a radical prostatectomy and adjuvant treatment 3 months ago. On examination, he has a flaccid paralysis with decreased tone and reflexes in both legs and upgoing plantars. He has decreased sensation from around the waist downwards. You discover a moderately palpable bladder in his abdomen.

Which of the following is the most likely site of pathology?

1. Frontal (motor) cortex
2. Internal capsule
3. Lower thoracic to upper lumbar spinal cord
4. Conus medullaris
5. Cauda equina

**Q.219 - Part 2**
Which of the following is the best investigation?

1. CT head
2. MRI head
3. Whole spine MRI
4. Lumbo-sacral spine MRI
5. Thoraco-lumbar x-ray

**Q.219 - Part 3**
Which of the following is the best immediate action?

1. Prioritise imaging request
2. Alert the oncologist for emergency radiotherapy
3. Give intravenous dexamethasone
4. Contact the neurosurgeons to consider emergency decompression
5. Pass a urinary catheter

**Q.220**
Mr McKinsey is 78-year-old retired baker. He has had some problems walking and, as part of your assessment of him, you examine his gait. You notice that he shifts his weight quickly from the left leg to avoid bearing weight on that side. However, there is a narrow base to his gait with no abnormal trunk stability or leg swing.

Which of the following conditions is most likely to be the underlying cause?

1. Cerebellar dysfunction
2. Cerebro-vascular disease
3. Osteoarthritis
4. Extra-pyramidal disease
5. Proximal myopathy

**Q.221**

Jonathan is a 38-year-old glazier. He has had several episodes of collapse.

The presence of which of the following is most suggestive of an epileptic seizure?

1. Tongue biting
2. Urinary incontinence
3. Loss of consciousness
4. Twitching of muscles
5. Sudden onset with no warning

**Q.222**

Kimberly is a 36-year-old photographer. Over the past few weeks, she has been suffering from severe throbbing headaches. They start fairly quickly as a sharp pain around the left eye which spreads out over the head. Her sight isn't affected but her eyes often water. She also complains of nasal stuffiness. The headache gradually worsens despite taking simple analgesia and eventually she has to lie down in a dark place to let the episode subside.

Which of the following is the most likely diagnosis?

1. Glaucoma
2. Migraine
3. Cluster headache
4. Trigeminal neuralgia
5. Tension headache

**Q.223**

Patricia is a 23-year-old sales manager. She complains of a tremor in her arms that she has increasingly noticed over the last year. It occurs any time of day or night and is more noticeable when she is holding her arms in a particular position such as holding the steering wheel of her car or if holding a drink. She has found that the symptoms lessen when drinking alcohol. She says that her late mother used to suffer from something very similar. Apart from her mild asthma, she has no other medical complaints.

Which of the following is the most likely diagnosis?

1. Friedreich's ataxia
2. Benign essential tremor
3. Hyperthyroidism
4. Anxiety
5. Salbutamol use

**Q.224**

George is a 72-year-old retired fireman. He presents with a dense left hemiparesis due to an acute ischaemic stroke. You are the admitting doctor and are about to instruct the team as to how to manage him.

Which one of the following instructions is the most incorrect?

1. Avoid pressure sores by regular turning and use of a pressure mattress
2. Avoid further platelet aggregation by giving 300mg aspirin stat
3. Avoid hypertension with use of antihypertensives
4. Avoid hypo or hyperglycaemia with insulin or dextrosas needed
5. Avoid dehydration or overhydration with careful intravenous fluid delivery

**Q.225**
Mr Jones is a 68-year-old retired banker. He had a transient ischaemic attack (TIA) 2 months ago. You are assessing his suitability for a carotid endarterectomy.

Which of the following is the strongest indication to refer for a carotid endarterectomy?

1. Bilateral carotid artery stenosis
2. At least 75% stenosis of an internal carotid artery
3. Previous TIA in a small distribution in occipital lobe
4. Age >75
5. Blood pressure >160/90 mmHg

**Q.226**
Mrs Kirkpatrick is a 36-year-old air stewardess. She presents with a sudden-onset intense headache which started 2 hours ago. You suspect that this might be a subarachnoid haemorrhage (SAH).

Which of the following statements is true regarding your management at this point?

1. A normal CT of the head can exclude a SAH
2. Stool softeners should be given to reduce excessive straining
3. The presence of neck stiffness and tachycardia is more suggestive of acute meningitis
4. A CSF samples showing fewer blood cells in successive bottles can exclude a SAH
5. Absence of xanthochromia at 6 hours after onset can exclude a SAH

**Q.227**

Mrs Emberton is a 74-year-old retired nanny. She was very well, self-caring and independent until a few weeks ago. However, over the last few weeks, she has been more sleepy than normal and, at times, seemed muddled and disorientated, with some urinary incontinence. Her difficulties have not been constant; there has been alternation between good and bad days. You arrange a number of tests, including a out-of-hours CT of her head. This shows a low-attenuation crescent-shaped mass in the fronto-temporal region.

Which of the following is the most likely diagnosis?

1. Normal pressure hydrocephalus
2. Fronto-temporal dementia
3. Subarachnoid haemorrhage
4. Extradural haematoma
5. Subdural haematoma

**Q.228**

Andy is a 23-year-old window cleaner who presents as an emergency in status epilepticus. His airway is secure and he is given 100% oxygen by mask. Intravenous access is obtained and his capillary blood glucose is found to be normal.

Which of the following is your first option to terminate the seizures?

1. Diazepam 0.5mg/kg per rectum
2. Lorazepam 4mg intravenously
3. Diazepam intravenous infusion at 3ml/kg/hr
4. Phenytoin infusion at 15mg/kg up to 50mg/hr
5. Dextrose 50ml of 50% administered intravenously

**Q.229 - Part 1**
Kyle is a 28-year-old park keeper who has just been diagnosed with epilepsy. His seizures take the form of twitches and jerks down the side of the face and down the arm on one side. After a few moments, he loses consciousness and then the jerks spread to the rest of the body with bilateral involvement.

Which definition best describes this pattern of seizure?

1. Partial
2. Partial complex
3. Partial with secondary generalization
4. Primary generalised
5. Tonic-clonic

**Q.229 - Part 2**
Which of the following is likely to be the first choice for medication to control Kyle's seizures?

1. Lamotrigine
2. Carbamazepine
3. Phenytoin
4. Sodium Valproate
5. Gabapentin

**Q.230 - Part 1**

Robert is a 58-year-old retired hospital porter. Over the last few months, he has developed parkinsonian symptoms, including slowness in initiating movements and a resting tremor. Although he has taken early retirement, his daily activities are not affected and he is currently self-caring, living with his wife. He seems to you to be relatively young to develop Parkinson's disease, and there are several conditions that can also cause Parkinsonism that you wonder whether you should exclude.

Which of the following is not a commonly recognised cause of Parkinsonism?

1. Wilson's disease
2. Arterioslerosis
3. Neuroleptic therapy
4. Post-meningitis
5. Multi-system atrophy

**Q.230 - Part 2**

Assuming this is a case of Parkinson's disease, which of the following would be the best treatment option at this stage?

1. Watch and wait until symptoms worsen then start ropinirole
2. Watch and wait until symptoms worsen then start ropinirole with an L-dopa containing agent
3. Watch and wait until symptoms worsen then start an L-dopa containing agent
4. Start ropinirole
5. Start ropinirole with an L-dopa-containing agent

**Q.231**

Fiona is a 36-year-old dentist. She presents with tingling in her thumb and first two fingers of the right hand. This is worse when her wrist is flexed during work. It also occurs at night and she has found that shaking her hand vigorously can sometimes help. Which of the following conditions is NOT typically known to be associated with this diagnosis?

1. Chronic liver disease
2. Pregnancy
3. Rheumatoid arthritis
4. Diabetes mellitus
5. Thyroid disease

**Q.232 - Part 1**

Mr Takayama is a 49-year-old property agent. He presents with disturbed sensation and weakness in his body. He has loss of sensation across his waist. His left leg is spastic with preserved pain sensation but impaired vibration and joint position sense. His right leg has normal motor function and but impaired pain sensation. Which of the following is the most likely diagnosis?

1. Syringomyelia
2. Spinal muscular atrophy
3. Brown-Sequard syndrome
4. Arnold-Chiari malformation
5. Transverse myelitis

**Q.232 - Part 2**

Mr Takayama has several investigations involving MRI of his head and spine that show several discrete lesions in the spinal cord. Which of the following is the most likely underlying cause?

1. Motor neurone disease
2. Multiple sclerosis
3. Poliomyelitis
4. Herpes virus infection (VZV or HSV)
5. HTLV-1 infection

**Q.232 - Part 3**
Which of the following factors gives the best prognosis?

1. Male sex
2. Presence of sensory symptoms
3. Late age at onset
4. Primary progressive disease
5. Secondary progressive disease

**Q.233 - Part 1**
Mrs Jefferson is a 40-year-old dog trainer. She has been told by her husband that her eyelids droop and she has come to see you about it. On further questioning, she admits to occasional episodes of double vision. On examination there is a subtle ptosis affecting the left eye. The right eye is normal. Both pupils are of normal size. The eyeball does not seem to be in an abnormal position, but there is double vision in the extreme left and right gaze when this is held for a while.

Which is of the following is the most likely diagnosis?

1. Horner's syndrome
2. Complete third nerve palsy
3. Partial third nerve palsy
4. Myasthenia gravis
5. Myotonic dystrophy

**Q.233 - Part 2**
Which of the following is the most appropriate investigation from the list below?

1. Imaging of the brainstem
2. Imaging of the neck, chest and brainstem
3. Acetylcholine receptor antibody titre
4. Nerve conduction studies
5. Genetic studies

# SECTION 9

# Reproductive

**Q.234**

Mandy is a 26-year-old estate agent. She complains of several episodes of post-coital bleeding (PCB) over the last fortnight. She has never had this before and it is not painful. She has been on depot contraception injection for 6 months. She had a bad upper respiratory tract infection a few weeks ago, for which she had a short course of antibiotics, but she is much better now. Her last smear was 2 months ago and the report read "Action required - Columnar epithelium seen only. Please repeat". A Chlamydia test taken at the same time was reported as negative.

Which of the following is the most likely cause of this problem?

1. Atrophic vaginitis
2. Breakthrough bleeding
3. Cancer of the cervix
4. Cervicitis
5. Cervical ectropion

**Q.235**

Sherrie is a 22-year-old receptionist. She complains of irregular vaginal bleeding. She describes this as a 'spotting' that she noticed yesterday and a month ago. She was treated for Chlamydia 2 months ago, which she acquired from her ex-boyfriend. She hasn't had sex since then. Her last period was 2 weeks ago and she has regular 28 day cycles.

.

Which of the following the most likely cause of this presentation?

1. Cervicitis
2. Physiological 'ovulation' bleeding
3. Endometrial neoplasia
4. Endometriosis
5. Retained foreign body

**Q.236**

Tracy is 32-year-old insurance advisor. She stopped taking the combined oral contraceptive 3 months ago after splitting up from her long-term partner. She has had no sexual intercourse since. Since then she says that she hasn't had a period. She had a laparoscopic appendicectomy 2 months ago. During this episode of abdominal pain, a gynaecologist advised a transvaginal ultrasound (TVUS) which was entirely normal. On further questioning she says that she had a little bleeding a month ago but it wasn't like the proper periods that she used to have before starting the pill. She appears well, with a little acne, and a BMI of 19 kg/$m^2$. A urine pregnancy test today is negative.

Which of the following is the most likely cause for her presentation?

1. Non-specific oligomenorrhoea
2. Turner's syndrome
3. Anorexia nervosa
4. Pregnancy
5. Polycystic ovarian syndrome (PCOS)

**Q.237**

Carmel is a 26-year-old veterinary surgeon. She complains of painful and heavy periods. You undertake several tests and conclude that this is due to dysfunctional uterine bleeding (DUB).

Which of the following is the most appropriate therapy at this stage?

1. Danazol
2. Tranexamic acid
3. Mefenamic acid
4. Endometrial ablation therapy
5. Intrauterine device (IUD)

**Q.238**
Miranda is a 24-year-old swimming instructor. She is 18 weeks into her first pregnancy when she collapses at home with abdominal pain and bleeding per vagina. She arrives at hospital, by which time the pain is controlled with analgesia. She has lost enough blood to heavily spot a sanitary towel. On passing a speculum, you notice that the os is about 1 cm open.

Which of the following best describes the situation?

1. Spontaneous abortion
2. Threatened abortion
3. Inevitable abortion
4. Incomplete abortion
5. Missed abortion

**Q.239**
Sandra is 34-year-old care worker. She has been pregnant 3 times in total, all of which have ended in a spontaneous miscarriage.

Which of the following is the most common cause for this situation?

1. Maternal endocrine disease
2. Antiphospholipid syndrome
3. Parental chromosomal abnormality
4. Cervical incompetence
5. Bacterial infections of the genital tract

**Q.240 - Part 1**
Martina is a 32-year-old beautician. She is 9 weeks into her first pregnancy. She has had severe nausea for several weeks and her blood pressure has been a bit high. She has a 4-hour history of abdominal pain and bleeding per vagina which results in admission to hospital. On examination, she has some tenderness in the abdomen and the uterus feels bulky. An ultrasound scan shows a few large cysts in the ovaries and the uterus is described as having a 'snowstorm' appearance.

Which of the following is the most likely diagnosis?

1. Multiple pregnancy
2. Ectopic pregnancy
3. Ruptured ovarian cyst
4. Hydatidiform mole
5. Choriocarcinoma

**Q.240 - Part 2**
Which of the following statements is true regarding subsequent management of her condition?

1. Human chorionic gonadotropin (HCG) levels should be monitored for up to a year
2. Pregnancy is hazardous in the short term and so a hormonal contraceptive advisable
3. Chemotherapy has a high rate of success
4. Laparoscopic exploration resulting in tubal excision is a frequent outcome
5. Elective Caesarean section is the preferred mode of delivery

**Q.241**

Linda is a 38-year-old child minder. You are performing a vaginal examination when you notice something unusual on the cervix. You see a 1mm well circumscribed, raised, pale lesion about 5mm from the os. When you prod it firmly with the swab, it doesn't break or bleed and there is no pain.

Which of the following is the most likely diagnosis?

1. Herpes simplex
2. Sebaceous cyst
3. Nabothian cyst
4. Bartholin's cyst
5. Carcinoma in situ

**Q.242**

Sandy is a 36-year-old social worker. She has a 6-month history of heavy and painful periods with abdominal fullness. An ultrasound has revealed several large uterine fibroids. She has spoken to friends who have given her lots of contradictory information about the condition.

Which of the following statements is incorrect regarding her case?

1. The combined oral contraceptive can help alleviate her symptoms and shrink the masses
2. Fibroids can cause obstruction in labour
3. Fibroids can increase in size during pregnancy and lead to miscarriage
4. Fibroids can suddenly shrink, causing severe abdominal pain
5. Fibroids are a cause of infertility

**Q.243**
Justina is a 39-year-old dinner lady. Her mother has just been diagnosed as having endometrial carcinoma and Justina wanted to know more about the risks for this condition.

Which of the following is the least likely risk factor for developing endometrial carcinoma?

1. Nulliparity
2. Late menopause
3. Obesity
4. Functioning ovarian tumours
5. Intrauterine system (Mirena ®)

**Q.244 - Part 1**
Keri is a 24-year-old telephonist. She complains of a 3-week history of a smelly vaginal discharge with some itchiness around the vulva. On examination, you note a thin off-white discharge with a strong amine odour. The vaginal pH is 4.9. Her cervix appears erythematous and swollen with tiny dimples or pits on it.

Which of the following is the most likely diagnosis/infective agent?

1. Chlamydia trachomatis
2. Neisseria gonorrhoeae
3. Bacterial vaginosis (BV)
4. Vulvo-vaginal candidiasis
5. Trichomonas vaginalis (TV)

**Q.244 - Part 2**
Which of the following is the best management strategy?

1. A course of metronidazole and advise against the use of soap products
2. A course of metronidazole and no sexual intercourse until partner is treated
3. A clotrimazole pessary and cream along with advice on prevention
4. A course of doxycycline and no sexual intercourse until partner is treated
5. A cephalosporin or quinolone according to local resistance patterns and no sexual intercourse until partner is treated

**Q.245**
Tabitha is a 22-year-old production assistant. She complains of a 2-week history of a painful ulcer on her vulva, along with a few sores in her mouth. She has also been suffering from joint pains for the last few months for which she has been taking regular diclofenac.

On examination there is a solitary, well-defined deep and tender ulcer on the left labium majorum. There are no other skin lesions anywhere else of note. Her nails are unremarkable and her lower lip shows a subtle ulceration. You take blood for serology tests and a little while later she notes a small skin swelling develop at the site.

Which of the following is the most likely diagnosis?

1. Behçet's disease
2. Psoriasis
3. Genital herpes
4. Primary syphilis
5. Fixed drug eruption

**Q.246 - Part 1**
Zoe is a 25-year-old researcher. She has been trying to get pregnant, but despite regular unprotected sexual intercourse with her partner for the last year she has not yet conceived.

Which of the following is the most common cause for subfertility?

1. Endometriosis
2. Anovulation
3. Male factors
4. Tubular blockage
5. No factor identified (unexplained subfertility)

**Q.246 - Part 2**
You take a thorough relevant history from Zoe and her partner and start arranging a number of investigations.

Which of the following is the most useful method to assess for ovulation?

1. Basal body temperature charting
2. Progesterone level one week before expected period
3. Midcycle oestrogen level
4. LH level one week before expected period
5. Late cycle drop in FSH

**Q.247**

Mischa is a 17-year-old fashion student. She comes to you one Monday morning asking for emergency contraception. Her regular form of contraception is condoms. She last had sex on Saturday night. The condom split but she realised this too late. Her last period was two weeks ago and is usually 28 days in length.

Which of the following statements is incorrect?

1. If she takes the oral emergency contraceptive she should expect disruption to the timing and consistency of her next bleed
2. Out of hours, she can get emergency contraception from a high street chemist
3. She can still take the emergency contraceptive today even if she has taken it more than once during this menstrual cycle
4. A copper intrauterine device (IUD) can be inserted within the next few days and will offer effective emergency contraception
5. Now that 24 hours have passed, the effectiveness of the emergency contraceptive pill is poor (<30%)

**Q.248**

Charlotte is an 18-year-old student. She comes to you requesting contraception advice. She has been using condoms up until now but both her and her boyfriend want to stop using them. They are about to go travelling for their gap year and won't easily be able to find condoms. She has had one pregnancy. This was an ectopic pregnancy with no serious complications a year ago. She has a history of heavy periods and migraines. The migraines are infrequent, consisting of intense headaches with no other associated features. She doesn't smoke, has a normal blood pressure and her BMI is 22 kg/m$^2$. She has no family history of vascular disease.

Which of the following is the best method of contraception for this situation?

1. Natural family planning (NFP)
2. Combined oral contraceptive pill (COCP) e.g. Microgynon ®
3. Progestogen-only pill (POP) e.g. Micronor ®
4. Intrauterine device (IUD)
5. Depot provera ®

**Q.249 - Part 1**

Janine is a 23-year-old woman 22 weeks into her first pregnancy. You find she has a raised blood pressure.

Which of the following is a recognised risk factor for pre-eclampsia?

1. Twin pregnancy
2. Smoking
3. Multigravida
4. Uterine fibroids
5. Maternal epilepsy

**Q.249 - Part 2**

Which of the following factors in isolation would be most indicative of pre-eclampsia?

1. Peripheral oedema
2. Raised serum creatinine
3. Raised liver enzymes
4. Proteinuria
5. Low platelet count

**Q.250**
Kathleen is a 32-year-old advertising executive. She is 30 weeks pregnant and has been found to have pre-eclampsia.

Which of the following statements regarding her management is true?

1. The blood pressure is a good indicator of disease severity and thus short term risk
2. The level of proteinuria is a good indicator of disease severity and thus short term risk
3. Fluid restriction plays a part in controlling high blood pressure
4. Once the baby is delivered, the risk of eclamptic seizures is removed.
5. Magnesium sulphate is indicated to reduce the risk of stillbirth and neonatal death

**Q.251**
Candice is a 27-year-old web designer. She is 33 weeks pregnant and presents as an emergency following a collapse with bleeding per vaginam. She is pale, tachycardic and hypotensive.

Which of the following features would suggest that the cause is placenta praevia rather than a placental abruption?

1. The uterus is tender and tense
2. The foetal heart rate is normal
3. There is constant intense lower abdominal pain
4. The degree of shock is inconsistent with the amount of vaginal blood loss
5. The patient is a smoker

**Q.252**
Rosie is a 26-year-old cashier. She is 24 weeks into her first pregnancy and has been reading a lot about pain relief during labour. She has come to ask you more about this.

Which of the following statements is incorrect?

1. Using transcutaneous electrical nerve stimulation (TENS) alone is effective pain relief for some women
2. Epidural anaesthesia will lead to retention of urine and so catheterisation is essential
3. Pethidine cannot be given within 2 hours of likely delivery
4. Epidural anaesthesia can only be started once there is evidence of cervical dilation
5. Entonox ® is a mixture of nitrous oxide and oxygen which is well tolerated with minimal side effects

**Q.253**
Mariella is a 26-year-old personal trainer. She is pregnant and found to have a blood group A, Rhesus D negative.

All of the following are indications to give her Anti-D immunoglobulin except one. Which one?

1. As routine at 28 and 34 weeks gestation
2. Following a threatened abortion (which fully resolves) at any stage of pregnancy
3. Following amniocentesis
4. Following placental abruption
5. Following external cephalic version of the foetus

**Q.254**

Lorna is a 32-year-old publisher who is pregnant with twins. She comes to you to ask about any particular risks to a twin pregnancy in comparison to a single pregnancy. The following is a list of complications in pregnancy. All but one are more common in multiple versus single pregnancies.

Which of the following is not more common in multiple pregnancies?

1. Hyperemesis gravidarum
2. Pre-eclampsia
3. Placental abruption
4. Oligohydramnios
5. Placenta praevia

**Q.255**

Beth is a 28-year-old occupational therapist. She is 20 weeks pregnant and an ultrasound scan has shown her baby to be in a breech presentation. She comes to you to ask for some advice about this.

Which of the following statements is NOT correct?

1. Over 90% of breech presentations at this stage will resolve to occipital presentation by term
2. Planned elective caesarean section shows better outcome than assisted 'instrumental' vaginal delivery
3. External cephalic version (ECV) should be at least attempted in the significant majority of cases
4. External cephalic version is successful in about half of cases
5. Vaginal delivery of a breech leads to an increased incidence of cord prolapse and hip dislocation

**Q.256**

Yvonne is a 27-year-old driving instructor. She has just delivered her first child, but the placenta is retained.

Which of the following options would not feature in your management plan?

1. Void the mother's bladder
2. If standard treatments fail, hysterectomy should be considered
3. Place a hand on the abdomen to steady the uterus whilst pulling the cord very tightly
4. Insert a hand into the uterus to manually separate the placenta from the endometrium
5. Put the baby to the mother's breast to feed

**Q.257**

Anne-Marie has just delivered her first child by ventouse-assisted vaginal delivery. The baby has a swelling on its head. The swelling is fluctuant and more towards one side than the other. It seems to have a margin limited to the underlying cranial bone.

Which of the following is most likely to have occurred to explain this appearance?

1. Moulding
2. Cephalhaematoma
3. Caput succedaneum
4. Chignon
5. Subaponeurotic heamatoma

**Q.258**

Carole is a 42-year-old sales representative. She has missed her periods recently and thought that it was a sign of early menopause and stress, but a pregnancy test comes back as positive. She is estimated to be about 20 weeks pregnant. She is concerned about the risk of Down's syndrome in her baby and asks your advice about this.

Which of the following statements is incorrect?

1. Chorionic villus sampling with karyotyping could provide a clear answer and would be advisable for her
2. All women should be offered the 'quadruple test' (or, if not yet locally available, the triple test) in the second trimester
3. There is a 1-2 % risk that her baby will have Down's syndrome
4. Nuchal translucency screening would not be appropriate
5. If Down's syndrome is likely, she could opt for a termination of pregnancy even after 24 weeks gestation

# SECTION 10

# Renal

# Urology

**Q.259**

Mr Nichols is a 52-year-old tiler. He complains of a few months' history of swelling of the ankles and general malaise. His urine output has decreased but his urine flow and frequency has not changed. Today he is particularly unwell and has begun vomiting. He has a history of Crohn's colitis but is currently not on any medication. On examination he is pale and hypertensive. He has palpable kidneys and ankle oedema. His urine dipstick is negative and his blood tests are shown below. You request an abdominal ultrasound, which shows bilateral slightly enlarged kidneys of normal echotexture, with hydronephrosis and medial deviation of the ureters.

| | | |
|---|---|---|
| Sodium | 131 | mmol/L |
| Potassium | 5.2 | mmol/L |
| Urea | 8.6 | mmol/L |
| Creatinine | 201 | μmol/L |
| Haemoglobin | 9.5 | g/dL |
| Mean cell volume | 89 | fL |
| Platelets | 224 | $x10^9/L$ |
| White cell count | 6.4 | $x10^9/L$ |

Which of the following is the most likely diagnosis?

1. Retroperitoneal fibrosis
2. Benign prostatic hypertrophy
3. Urethral stricture
4. Myeloma
5. Amyloidosis

**Q.260 - Part 1**

Hugh is a 72-year-old retired shop-keeper. He has been unwell recently with gastroenteritis that has been passing around the neighbourhood. He is weak and appears dehydrated but there are no other remarkable findings on examination. The laboratory call you with some blood results (see below). The phlebotomist is about to take another sample for you to confirm this result.

| | | |
|---|---|---|
| Sodium | 141 | mmol/L |
| Potassium | 7.2 | mmol/L |
| Urea | 14.6 | mmol/L |
| Creatinine | 175 | µmol/L |

Which of the following is the best next investigation?

1. Serum creatine kinase (CK)
2. Mid stream urine for microbiology (MSU)
3. Renal ultrasound
4. Urine dipstick
5. ECG

**Q.260 - Part 2**

Hugh becomes steadily more unwell over the next few hours and begins to complain of chest pain, worse on inspiration. He is not short of breath, but feels better when sat upwards. He has 98% oxygen saturation on room air. His chest is, on the whole, clear but there are minimal crackles at the bases. His pulse is raised at 98 beats per minute with 2 slightly muffled heart sounds accompanied by a squeaking sound. His chest x-ray shows clear lung fields with minor blunting of the costophrenic angles and a slightly enlarged and rounded heart border.

Which of the following would be the best therapeutic option?

1. Low molecular weight heparin
2. Haemodialysis
3. Sodium bicarbonate
4. Intravenous diuretics
5. Unfractionated heparin

**Q.261**
Logan is a 38-year-old electronics engineer who has chronic renal failure due to interstitial nephritis. He is being followed up at the local renal unit.

Which of the following measures is the best to determine the appropriate time to initiate renal replacement therapy?

1. Cockcroft-Gault calculation
2. Glomerular filtration rate
3. Serum creatinine
4. Serum : Urine creatinine ratio
5. 24-hour urine creatinine

**Q.262**
Gerald is a 52-year-old auditor. He has chronic renal failure and is on the verge of starting continuous ambulatory peritoneal dialysis (CAPD). He has done some reading and comes to you to clarify a few points before he sees the renal specialist.

Which of the following statements is NOT correct?

1. This involves connecting dialysis bags to an abdominal catheter
2. Dialysate is changed on average 2 or 3 times a day
3. Even with the best precautions, infective peritonitis may occur around once every 12-18 months for an average patient
4. CAPD is associated with abdominal hernias
5. Chronic respiratory disease is a relative contraindication to CAPD

**Q.263 - Part 1**
Andy is a 40-year-old traffic warden with end-stage renal failure (ESRF). Which of the following is the most common cause of ESRF in the UK?

1. Chronic glomerulonephritis
2. Hypertension
3. Diabetes mellitus
4. Renovascular disease
5. Undetermined cause

**Q.263 - Part 2**
Which of the following is an absolute contraindication to renal transplantation?

1. Stable angina
2. Raynaud's phenomenon
3. HIV infection
4. Chronic glomerulonephritis
5. Hepatic insufficiency

**Q.263 - Part 3**
Which of the following is the most common cause of mortality following renal transplantation?

1. Graft rejection
2. Recurrence of original pathology
3. Toxicity from immunosuppressant drugs
4. Neoplasia secondary to immunosuppression
5. Ischaemic heart disease

**Q.264**
Mr Jones is a 32-year-old stockbroker who had a renal transplant 4 months ago due to rapidly-progressive glomerulonephritis. He had done well up until a week ago, when he began to feel lethargic and unwell. He developed pain around site of the graft, fevers and a rising serum creatinine. A biopsy was taken, which showed a white cell infiltrate and tubular damage.

Which of the following is the most likely cause?

1. Hyperacute rejection
2. Acute rejection
3. Chronic rejection
4. Graft sepsis
5. Recurrence of original disease

**Q.265**

Tomasz is a 48-year-old carpenter who has immigrated to the UK from Hungary. He is found to be non-specifically unwell with malaise and lethargy. Urine microscopy shows blood and protein casts but no crystals, and a blood test shows significant renal impairment. He has a long history of arthritis affecting his knees and back, but has not been able to have surgery and has managed on pain killers alone. A urogram shows cortical scarring and clubbed calyces. Pyelography shows papillary necrosis.

Which of the following is the most likely diagnosis?

1. Reflux nephropathy
2. IgA nephropathy
3. Urate nephropathy
4. Chronic interstitial nephritis
5. Balkan nephropathy

**Q.266**

Mrs Hawthorn is a 50-year-old lecturer. She hadn't been to the doctor in a long time and had decided to book in for a routine check-up after turning 50. She was found to have consistently raised blood pressure and was started on ramipril. Shortly after starting this medication, she woke up in the middle of the night very short of breath and wheezy. She was taken to hospital by ambulance where she was found to have acute pulmonary oedema and was treated accordingly.

Which of the following is the most likely underlying explanation?

1. Anaphylactic reaction
2. Angioedema
3. Acute renal failure
4. Renal vein thrombosis
5. Renal artery stenosis

**Q.267**

Mr Ketteridge is 58-year-old locksmith who was recently diagnosed with Type II diabetes mellitus. As part of his introduction to the condition, you want to tell him about the effects on the kidney.

Which of the following statements is incorrect?

1. Urine should be dipstick-tested for protein. A negative result can usefully exclude early-onset nephropathy
2. Diabetes can lead to a form of renal tubular acidosis
3. Renovascular disease is more common in those with diabetes
4. Patients on metformin have an increased risk of radio-contrast nephropathy
5. Diabetes is associated with an increased risk of urinary tract sepsis

**Q.268**

Mr Evans is a 53-year-old inventor. He has recently been unwell with non-specific symptoms. A urine dipstick was positive for blood and protein and you sent a sample for microscopy, Gram stain and culture. The report commented on the presence of "red cell casts".

Which of the following is the most likely causative process?

1. Nephrolithiasis
2. Nephrocalcinosis
3. Nephrotic syndrome
4. Glomerulonephritis
5. Cystitis

**Q.269**

Mrs Patterson is a 54-year-old matron. She has been feeling a little unwell recently and as part of the tests you requested, she is found to have protein on her urine dipstick.

Which of the following is least likely to cause this?

1. Fever
2. Stenuous activity
3. Cystitis
4. Hypertension
5. Bence-Jones protein

**Q.270**

You are admitting Mrs Fredericks to hospital. She is a 60-year-old writer who is unwell and found to have features of nephrotic syndrome. Which of the following is the least likely complication to look out for?

1. Sepsis
2. Hyponatraemia
3. Thromboembolism
4. Hypercholesterolaemia
5. Pleural effusions

**Q.271**

Mervyn is a 42-year-old bank clerk. He complains of a urethral discharge, more so in the morning when he is on the lavatory and passing stool. At this time, there is particular discomfort around the base of his penis internally. He has also found that ejaculation is painful recently.

Which of the following is the most likely diagnosis?

1. Urinary tract calculus
2. Chlamydial urethritis
3. Gonococcal urethritis
4. Prostatitis
5. Epididymo-orchitis

**Q.272**
Carson is 22-year-old construction worker. He complains of a 10-day history of pain when passing urine.

Which of the following is the most useful test?

1. Urine dipstick
2. Mid-stream urine to microbiology
3. Gram stain of urethral smear
4. Urine cytology
5. 24-hour urine collection

**Q.273**
Roshan is a 32-year-old driver who has had some weight loss and fevers. His chest x-ray is normal but a Heaf test is strongly positive.

Which of the following options is the best investigation to demonstrate urinary tract tuberculosis?

1. Early morning urine sampling
2. Terminal stream urine sampling
3. Mid-stream urine sampling
4. Stamey procedure
5. 24-hour urine collection

**Q.274**

Mr York is a 46-year-old welder who has a family history of prostate cancer. He wishes to take a blood test for prostate specific antigen (PSA). You are aware that there are several conditions as well as prostate cancer that can raise the PSA.

Which of the following is least commonly associated with a raised PSA?

1. Benign prostatic hyperplasia
2. Vasectomy
3. Prostatitis
4. Digital rectal examination
5. Ejaculation (<24 hours from test)

**Q.275**

Leyton is a 38-year-old stockbroker. He has been unwell lately, with lethargy, malaise, weight loss and abdominal discomfort. He also complains of swelling in his scrotum. On examination, you are able to palpate a kidney on the left side. You notice that he has a left-sided varicocele in his scrotum. His basic blood tests are shown below.

| | | |
|---|---|---|
| Sodium | 134 | mmol/L |
| Potassium | 4.1 | mmol/L |
| Urea | 6.2 | mmol/L |
| Creatinine | 98 | μmol/L |
| Haemoglobin | 17.0 | g/dL |
| Mean cell volume | 89 | fL |
| Platelets | 342 | $x10^9/L$ |
| White cell count | 6 | $x10^9/L$ |

Which of the following is the most likely diagnosis?

1. Renal cell carcinoma
2. Adult polycystic kidney disease
3. Transitional cell carcinoma
4. Squamous cell carcinoma
5. Wilms' tumour

**Q.276 - Part 1**
Harvey is a 52-year-old football coach. He has a 3-month history of loin to groin pain and mild haematuria. An abdominal x-ray reveals a 5 x 4 cm staghorn calculus.

Which of the following options is the most useful non-surgical treatment you should give this patient?

1. Give analgesia and wait for stone to pass
2. Reduce calcium intake
3. Reduce chocolate and tea intake
4. Alkalinise the urine
5. Give antibiotics

**Q.276 - Part 2**
Which of the following is the most effective surgical option?

1. Retrograde ureteroscopic lithectomy
2. Extracorporeal shock wave lithotripsy (ESWL) and J-J stent insertion
3. Percutaneous nephro-lithotripsy
4. Open nephrolithectomy
5. None of the above, conservative treatment alone will suffice

**Q.277**
Mr Alexander is a 76-year-old retired electronics engineer. He is being followed up by the haematologists for chronic lymphocytic leukaemia (CLL). He has recently developed swollen ankles and increased abdominal girth. He noticed that his urine has become frothy. On examination, you detect ascites and his urine dipstick is positive for protein but nothing else.

Which of the following options is the most likely diagnosis?

1. Diffuse proliferative glomerulonephritis
2. Membranous glomerulonephritis
3. Minimal change disease
4. Cresentic glomerulonephritis
5. IgA nephropathy

iSCMEDICAL
Interview Skills Consulting

# SECTION 11

# Respiratory

**Q.278**

Keith is 32-year-old printer. He has a 10-day history of a flu-like illness and a 3-day history of increasing fevers and a productive cough. On examination, you hear coarse crepitations and bronchial breathing in his right mid-zone. A chest x-ray shows consolidation with cavity formation in the middle lobe of his right lung.

Which of the following agents is the most likely cause of this pneumonia?

1. Mycoplasma pneumoniae
2. Streptococcus pneumoniae
3. Staphylococcus aureus
4. Cytomegalovirus
5. Pneumocystis jirovecii

**Q.279 - Part 1**

Jennifer is a 48-year-old baker. She has been non-specifically unwell for a few days and has now become increasingly short of breath. Examination and x-ray is consistent with a pleural effusion, which you aim to tap for analysis.

Which of the following features or the pleural fluid would suggest it more likely to be a transudate than an exudate?

1. pH < 7.2
2. Cell count predominantly mesothelial cells
3. Glucose concentration is less than serum glucose
4. LDH > 200 IU
5. Protein <30g/L

**Q.279 - Part 2**
You confirm that the fluid is in fact an exudate.

Which of the following is the least likely underlying diagnosis?

1. Pulmonary embolism
2. Rheumatoid arthritis
3. Myxoedema
4. Systemic lupus erythematosus
5. Bacterial pneumonia

**Q.280**
Samuel is a 23-year-old medical student. As part of the preparation for his medical elective placement, he is required to have a chest x-ray. He has always been in good health, and apart from childhood illnesses, he has an unremarkable past medical history. On review of this x-ray, the lung fields are clear but there is a 1.5 cm rim of air in the pleural space on one side, i.e. a pneumothorax. Samuel feels very well with no shortness of breath or abnormal observations.

Which of the following is best management strategy?

1. Do nothing invasive and consider a repeat chest x-ray at a later date
2. Aspirate the air then repeat the x-ray
3. Place a fine bore chest drain
4. Place a fine bore chest drain and apply suction
5. Refer to a thoracic surgeon

**Q.281 - Part 1**

Jerry is a 56-year-old lorry driver. He has been complaining of tiredness for quite some time. He says that he feels sleepy during the day and can often fall asleep while watching television. He finds that some mornings he wakes up with a headache, not feeling at all refreshed from his sleep. His wife says that he doesn't sleep very well. He snores loudly, but many times in the night he seems to stop breathing for a few moments before snorting and then breathing again.

Which of the following is the most likely diagnosis?

1. Sinusitis
2. Absence seizures
3. Obstructive sleep apnoea (OSA)
4. Intracerebral space-occupying lesion
5. Narcolepsy

**Q.281 - Part 2**

Which of the following is the best initial management option?

1. Anticonvulsant therapy
2. ENT review and a course of antibiotics
3. Weight loss
4. Continuous positive airway pressure device
5. Neuroimaging and oncology referral

**Q.282**

Leon is a 47-year-old machine operator in a glass factory. He comes to see you after a long history of breathlessness over several years which he has decided to seek help for at this point because his exercise tolerance has now noticeably reduced. He is a longstanding smoker (over 30 years) and is trying to give up because he believes that it is causing his breathing problems. On examination, he has mild peripheral cyanosis and poor chest expansion. He has fine crepitations, predominantly in the upper zones. This is corroborated by a chest x-ray appearance of multiple small nodules in both upper lobes of the lung.

Which of the following is the most likely diagnosis?

1. Occupational asthma
2. Silicosis
3. Berylliosis
4. Extrinsic allergic alveolitis (EAA)
5. Asbestosis

**Q.283**

Petunia is a 28-year-old primary school teacher. Over the last 6 months, she has noticed that she has become increasingly unwell when she visits her parents, which she does most weekends. She becomes very tired, shivery and feverish with headaches and myalgia. She also gets chest tightness and shortness of breath at times. The symptoms ease if she rests in the 'guest room'. By midweek, she is completely better again. Her parents live on a farm where they keep cattle, sheep and pigs. Her parents also have a dog, two cats and 3 budgerigars, which they have acquired for company since their children have left home.

Which of the following is the most likely diagnosis?

1. Psittacosis
2. Extrinsic allergic alveolitis (EAA)
3. Acute bronchopulmonary aspergilosis (ABPA)
4. Allergen-induced asthma
5. Brucellosis

**Q.284**

Harriet is 70-year-old retired seamstress. She is admitted to hospital with increasing breathlessness, fevers and a productive cough. Examination and chest x-ray confirm that she has a lobar pneumonia.

Which of the following features is of the least prognostic value?

1. Oxygen saturation
2. Abbreviated mental test score
3. Blood pressure
4. Respiratory rate
5. Serum urea

**Q.285 - Part 1**

Lee is a 23-year-old musician who is admitted to hospital with an acute asthma attack. His asthma is particularly bad at the moment and he had a minor attack last week, following which his GP gave him some extra medications. His current medications include: Seretide ®, Phyllocontin ® and prednisolone.

Which of the following features is suggestive of a life-threatening attack?

1. Use of accessory muscles of respiration
2. Pulse rate > 110 beats / minute
3. He cannot complete sentences
4. Respiratory rate > 25 breaths / minute
5. Peak expiratory flow (PEF) < 33% of normal

**Q.285 - Part 2**

Which of the following drugs would you consider to be inappropriate in managing his asthma attack?

1. Nebulised salbutamol
2. Nebulised ipratropium bromide
3. Magnesium sulphate infusion
4. Aminophylline infusion
5. Prednisolone

**Q.286**

Mr Giles is a 57-year-old nightclub owner. He has been unwell for a few months with lethargy, weight loss and a cough. After a series of investigations he is found to have a carcinoma of the lung.

Which of the following is the most common type?

1. Adenocarcinoma
2. Bronchio-alveolar cell carcinoma
3. Large cell
4. Small cell
5. Squamous cell

**Q.287**

Paul is a 50-year-old ex-naval engineer. He has had a persistent productive cough and several respiratory tract infections over the last 6 months and you suspect that he may have chronic obstructive pulmonary disease, secondary to his long-term smoking habit. As part of his initial investigations, you organise a chest x-ray. The report mentions the presence of pleural plaques.

Which of the following statements is true regarding this finding?

1. With time, they are likely to transform into a mesothelioma
2. With time, they will progress to form diffuse pleural thickening causing a restrictive lung deficit
3. They are generally asymptomatic and rarely cause a restrictive lung deficit
4. They are a useful indicator of underlying asbestosis
5. They start to form a few years after regular asbestos exposure

**Q.288 - Part 1**

Sidney is a 48-year-old milkman. He has had a persistent cough for over a year. He produces thick purulent sputum on most days and has had several respiratory tract infections in this time. On examination, he is clubbed but not cyanotic. He has coarse crepitations in both lower lung fields. A chest x-ray is reported as showing thickened bronchi with a 'tramline' appearance.

Which of the following is the most appropriate long-term management option?

1. Steroid therapy
2. Long-acting beta-agonist therapy
3. Physiotherapy
4. Intravenous antibiotics
5. Lung transplant

**Q.288 - Part 2**

Which of the following is least likely to be an underlying cause for this condition?

1. Allergic broncho-pulmonary aspergillosis
2. Previous pneumonia
3. Immune deficiency
4. Idiopathic
5. Emphysema

**Q.289**

Roland is a 67-year-old retired journalist with longstanding COPD. His condition has progressed over the last few years and his oxygenation has fallen. You are considering prescribing long term oxygen therapy (LTOT).

Which of the following is not a criterion for prescribing this?

1. The patient must stop smoking
2. FEV1 < 1.5 litres
3. PO2 on air <7.3 kPa measured when clinically stable on two occasions 3 weeks apart
4. PO2 = 7.3 - 8.0 kPa (measured as above) if evidence of pulmonary hypotension or nocturnal hypoxia.
5. Oxygen to be administered for a maximum of 12 hours per day

**Q.290 - Part 1**

Dipak is a 23-year-old business student from India. He has recently come to stay with his cousins in the UK while he is studying at university. He has been unwell for a few months with fever, malaise, weight loss and cough. He was admitted a few weeks ago and subsequently diagnosed with pulmonary tuberculosis. He has never had clinically-obvious TB in the past; however, he thinks that an aunt did suffer from it a few years ago. An HIV test is negative. He has now been in respiratory isolation for over two weeks while taking quadruple anti-TB therapy. A sputum sample from yesterday is reported as positive for AFB (acid fast bacilli).

Which of the following is the best management strategy?

1. Discharge him on directly observed therapy (DOT)
2. Discharge him with regular follow-up in the TB chest clinic
3. Continue respiratory isolation until sputum samples become negative for AFB
4. Continue respiratory isolation and check levels of the anti-TB drugs
5. Continue isolation and add in an extra agent to cover for multi-drug-resistant TB (MDR-TB)

**Q.290 - Part 2**

Which of the following is correct regarding contact tracing?

1. All household contacts should have a Mantoux test
2. All household contacts should have a chest x-ray
3. All household contacts should have a Mantoux test and chest x-ray
4. All household contacts should have either a Mantoux test or chest x-ray
5. All household contacts should be treated for latent TB

**Q.291**

William is a 37-year-old postman. He has undertaken investigations for a respiratory illness that is associated with shortness of breath, wheeze and cough.

Which of the following features is the strongest in support of a diagnosis of asthma rather than COPD?

1. Marked diurnal variation in peak expiratory flow rate (PEFR)
2. FEV1/FVC ratio <70%
3. Improvement of lung function with steroid therapy
4. Age < 40
5. Productive cough

**Q.292**

Yusuf is 44-year-old builder. He is admitted to hospital with a short history of fevers, cough and malaise. He is hypoxic and has coarse bronchial breath sounds in the left upper zone of his chest. A chest x-ray shows airspace opacification in the left upper zone. He is also found to be hyponatraemic.

Which of the following is the most likely diagnosis?

1. Small cell carcinoma
2. Squamous cell carcinoma
3. Pneumonia
4. Pancoast's tumour
5. Empyema

**Q.293**
Linda is a 46-year-old social worker. She is admitted as an emergency with epigastric pain and subsequent collapse. After initial investigation, she is found to have acute pancreatitis due to biliary obstruction. She has mild renal impairment and deranged liver and clotting tests. She deteriorates steadily and becomes hypoxic. She is transferred to ITU where she is intubated, ventilated and fluid resuscitated. Her pulmonary artery (wedge) pressure is estimated at < 18cm $H_2O$. A chest x-ray shows bilateral infiltrates.

Which of the following is the most likely complication?

1. Interstitial pneumonitis
2. Pulmonary oedema
3. Multiple pulmonary emboli
4. Adult respiratory distress syndrome
5. Pulmonary haemorrhage

**Q.294 - Part 1**
Sheila is a 69-year-old postmistress. She presents to hospital with an episode of chest pain after exercise, which settles completely with rest. She is thought to have had an episode of stable angina. Apart from an appendicectomy and pneumonia as a child, she has an unremarkable medical history and is currently on no medication. The routine chest x-ray, however, shows an obvious cavity with a central opacification in the right upper lobe.

Which of the following is likely to confirm your presumptive diagnosis?

1. Radioallergosorbent test (RAST) to Aspergillus spp.
2. Serum precipitins
3. Skin prick tests
4. Perinuclear anti-neutrophil cytoplasmic antibody (p-ANCA)
5. Circulating anti-neutrophil cytoplasmic antibody (c-ANCA)

**Q.294 - Part 2**
Which of the following is the least likely complication of this condition?

1. Massive pulmonary haemorrhage
2. Fibrosis
3. Chronic cough
4. Invasive aspergillosis
5. Asymptomatic

**Q.295 - Part 1**
Angela is a 47-year-old charity worker who has seropositive rheumatoid arthritis.

Which of the following respiratory complications is she least likely to develop?

1. Caplan's syndrome
2. Pleural effusions
3. Bronchiolitis obliterans
4. Pulmonary nodules
5. Pulmonary fibrosis

**Q.295 - Part 2**
Angela happens to have several rheumatoid nodules in the chest which have recently enlarged with a change in her therapy.

Which of the following agents is the most likely culprit?

1. Gold
2. Methotrexate
3. Azathioprine
4. Cyclophosphamide
5. Prednisolone

**Q.296**

Mandy is 46-year-old barmaid. She attends Accident and Emergency complaining of increasing chest pain, shortness of breath, fevers and a cough productive of green sputum. On examination, she is febrile, tachycardic and hypotensive. You hear bronchial breathing, coarse crepitations and a pleural rub on the right side of her chest. Her arterial blood gases are markedly hypoxic. You find out that she had a total hysterectomy just over a week ago and you suspect a pulmonary embolus (PE) as well as a respiratory tract infection.

Which of the following tests will be best to confirm your suspicion of a PE?

1. Ventilation/perfusion scan (V/Q)
2. Serum D-Dimer
3. CT- pulmonary angiogram (CTPA)
4. Chest x-ray
5. ECG

**Q.297**

Kerry is a 32-year-old cleaner. She is brought into hospital one morning by ambulance after a friend called her but heard no reply. The police had to break in and they found her unrousable in bed. Although her pulse oximetry reads 99%, her arterial blood gas is as follows.

| | | |
|---|---|---|
| pH | 7.31 | |
| $PaO_2$ | 7.9 | kPa |
| $PaCO_2$ | 5.1 | kPa |
| Base excess | -3.8 | mmol/L |

Which of the following is the most likely cause for this discrepancy?

1. Venous blood gas sample
2. Methaemoglobinaemia
3. Poor peripheral perfusion
4. Carboxyhaemoglobinaemia
5. Nail varnish interfering with signal

**Q.298**

Mr Taylor is 58-year-old butcher. He is brought into hospital with increasing breathlessness. He suffers from a condition that has caused shortness of breath and resulted in hospital admissions previously. His arterial blood gases are shown below.

| | | |
|---|---|---|
| pH | 7.32 | |
| $PaO_2$ | 7.8 | kPa |
| $PaCO_2$ | 6.7 | kPa |
| Base excess | -5.6 | mmol/L |

Which of the following is the least likely cause of his respiratory problems?

1. Pulmonary fibrosis
2. Poliomyelitis
3. Pulmonary oedema
4. Kyphoscoliosis
5. Motorneurone disease

**Q.299**

Mrs Patterson is a 61-year-old civil engineer. She was diagnosed as having a thyroid goitre many months ago. Medical treatment has failed and she is due for a partial thyroidectomy. She is a long-term smoker and is on regular inhalers for her COPD. Over the last few months she has developed stridor and you suspect a degree of airways obstruction. You want to assess the degree of functional airways obstruction due to this mass, so that you can reassess it post operatively.

Which of the following would be the best test for this purpose?

1. CT scan of the neck and thoracic inlet
2. Peak expiratory flow rate (PEFR)
3. Spirometry
4. Flow volume loop
5. Gas transfer

**Q.300**
Mr Dawlings is a 39-year-old barrister. He has had a 2-month history of dry cough and increasing shortness of breath. Just a few days ago, he noticed painful swollen lumps on his shins. Today, he has developed increasing pain in his right eye with blurred vision. A chest x-ray reveals bilateral hilar lymphadenopathy on a background of reticulo-nodular changes.

Which of the following tests would be the most useful in supporting the likely underlying diagnosis?

1. Serum circulating anti-neutrophil cytoplasmic antibody (c-ANCA)
2. Serum calcium
3. Serum angiotensin converting enzyme (ACE)
4. Serum alpha-1 anti-trypsin levels
5. Serum anti-nuclear antibody

# SECTION 12

# Answers

## CARDIOVASCULAR

**Q.1 - Part 1 - Answer: 2**

While all the options are associated with an ejection systolic murmur, it is the additional clinical features that aid diagnosis. This is a fit 72-year-old man with no angina or dyspnoea, therefore functional valve disease or left ventricular outflow obstruction is unlikely. This rules out options 1, 3 and 5. Aortic sclerosis is a thickening of the aortic valve - very common with advancing age - and can be differentiated from stenosis by the absence of radiation to the carotid arteries. While flow murmurs are also benign and commonly detected on examination, they are a result of turbulent flow associated with a hyperdynamic state e.g. anxiety, sepsis or pregnancy. Since the pulse rate and blood pressure are not elevated, a flow murmur is unlikely.

**Q.1 - Part 2 - Answer: 5**

Aortic sclerosis is a benign condition. Since this patient exhibits no signs of functional valve disease, an echocardiogram would not be appropriate. Ambulatory blood pressure monitoring and 24-hour ECG recording are of use in those who have paroxysmal symptoms or in whom symptoms or signs are precipitated by triggers during a daily schedule outside of the consultation room. Since Mr Jaye is able to walk for an hour at a time with a young dog and he experiences no ischaemic symptoms, an exercise tolerance test would also seem to be unnecessary. It would be most appropriate just to organise a 12-lead ECG and to review him at regular intervals (every 3-6 months).

**Q.2 - Answer: 4**

The question is really asking you to identify a modifiable risk factor which requires a patient's commitment to change and hence time spent on education. Although blood pressure and cholesterol can be improved with drugs, diet is the only factor in this scenario that he can directly affect by changing his lifestyle. Furthermore, dietary changes can improve other factors such as weight, glycaemia, blood pressure and cholesterol. Smoking is a distractor here. Since he gave up over 10 years ago, it is minimally significant as a coronary risk factor. The scenario does not indicate whether or not he suffers particularly high levels of work stress, so we cannot assume that this requires modification without further information. A family history of two first-degree relatives with cardiac events before the age of 65 is a strong predictor of him having coronary heart disease, but it is not a modifiable factor.

**Q.3 - Answer: 3**

The scenario describes several distinct cardiac events: inferior myocardial ischaemia and infarction (pain radiating to neck and jaw with hyperacute T waves in II and III), rhythm abnormalities and aortic incompetence. Although these events may be individually attributed to one or more of the options offered, when grouped together they point towards aortic dissection as a unifying diagnosis. Although infective endocarditis can lead to valvular abscess and valve breakdown, one would expect a story of symptoms in the run up to this presentation. It is typically aortic dissection that would give sudden onset pain that radiates to the back, haemodynamic shock with unequal blood pressures in the arms, and disruption of the aortic root, leading to aortic valve incompetence and limited blood flow to the coronary ostia, resulting in coronary ischaemia and rhythm abnormalities.

**Q.4 - Part 1 - Answer: 1**

All of the options are useful discriminators when assessing chest pain; however it is only reproduction of pain by palpation of the chest wall that can easily point away from cardiac causes i.e. towards costochondritis. GTN can cause relief in oesophageal spasm, albeit slower than for coronary ischaemia. Pain at rest occurs in several cardiac and non-cardiac conditions. Tachycardia and shortness of breath are also non-specific features that can occur when pain is experienced at any site.

**Q.4 - Part 2 - Answer: 2**

Costochondritis is the best option since the pain is affected by touch to the anterior chest wall, as demonstrated by its worsening when Mrs Jones lies on her front. While pericarditic pain responds to posture, it is somewhat relieved when sitting forward but is not particularly relieved by lying on the back. Gastro-oesophagitis also responds to posture but again it is maximal when the patient is horizontal, whether prone or supine. Pancreatitis tends to give epigastric pain that radiates to the back rather then chest pain across the chest wall. Somatisation is a psychiatric term for the presence of a variety of symptoms with no medical explanation.

**Q.5 - Answer: 1**

Systemic hypertension is associated with increased left-sided heart strain, leading to left-sided hypertrophy and left axis deviation. All the rest are associated with right axis deviation either by increased work or conduction changes affecting the right side of the heart.

**Q.6 - Answer: 5**

Multiple lesions per vessel, multi-vessel disease, distal lesions and left main stem disease are indications for bypass grafting over PTCA and are all particularly common in patients with diabetes.

**Q.7 - Answer: 3**

Option 3 is the best since despite taking warfarin, aspirin at 300mg is still indicated and although the doses of other drugs are adequate in options 1 and 4, drugs should not be given IM if there is a potential for thrombolysis.

**Q.8 - Answer: 1**

Options 2 to 5, along with ST segment depression 80ms after the 'J' point, poor workload capacity, and failure to achieve target heart rate, are all indicators of a positive response to the exercise tolerance test. This is not a question to test your memory of these factors; it is to show an understanding of the test itself. Option 1 has to be the answer because raising the heart rate is a fundamental requirement of a valid test in the first place, i.e. to place stress on the heart.

**Q.9 - Answer: 2**

Left ventricular failure leading to acute pulmonary oedema and haemodynamic collapse can occur subsequent to myocardial failure with or without dysrhythmia (options 1,3 or 4). Anaphylaxis is well-reported with thrombolysis, particularly with streptokinase, which can also lead to generalised hypotension. Although mural thrombus is a well-recognised complication from myocardial infarction, one would not expect it to occur in this time frame, especially following thrombolysis.

**Q.10 - Answer: 3**

This is mainly a question of timing. Further myocardial infarctions can certainly occur quite rapidly following the first event, and myocardial damage can result in mural defects and rupture of papillary muscles, causing functional mitral regurgitation. However, ventricular aneurysms take time to evolve following the myocardial injury and resultant structural deterioration, and may take up to 4 weeks to develop.

**Q.11 - Answer: 2**

Thrombolysis is contraindicated up to 18 weeks post-partum. Whilst severe hypertension (>200/120mmHg) is an absolute contraindication to thrombolysis, this may often be controlled with antihypertensives, including nitrates, to allow safe thrombolysis.

**Q.12 - Answer: 5**
The presence of pericarditis, pleural effusions and fever 3 weeks after a myocardial infarction makes Dressler's syndrome - an autoimmune-mediated inflammatory condition - the most likely. One would also expect to see a mild anaemia and raised ESR. Treatment comprises non-steroidal anti-inflammatory drugs or steroids in severe cases.

**Q.13 - Answer: 5**
Ramipril is the only drug that has evidence for aiding cardiac remodelling. Carvedilol is likely to be contraindicated if this man requires salbutamol for bronchospasm. The others may benefit morbidity, but would be unlikely to add any additional benefit in terms of his long term survival.

**Q.14 - Answer: 1**
Although associated with cardiac failure, heart sounds would be anticipated in patients with cardiomyopathies. Options 2 to 5 all obstruct the transmission of heart sounds to the chest wall.

**Q.15 - Answer: 4**
This scenario describes second degree or Mobitz type I heart block, also known as the Wenckebach phenomenon. It can be quite common following inferior coronary infarction and as long as there is no haemodynamic compromise, as in this case, observation is all that is required. Mobitz type II involves missed P waves with QRS complexes occurring in a regular ratio, e.g. 2:1 or 3:1 block. This type of second degree heart block is associated with progression to complete heart block and pre-emptive pacing is often indicated. Atropine is indicated in bradycardia with haemodynamic compromise and synchronised DC shock would be used in a supraventricular tachyarrhythmia. With no evidence of evolving ischaemia, urgent angioplasty is not indicated.

**Q.16 - Part 1 - Answer: 1**
The ECG tracing shows flat T waves with occasional inversion, prolonged PR interval, some ST segment depression and an extra U wave following the T. This is typical of hypokalaemia.

**Q.16 - Part 2 - Answer: 3**
TPN is associated with magnesium deficiency. Hypothyroidism can lead to hypothermia. Furosemide is a common cause of potassium loss. Spironolactone is a potassium-sparing diuretic which can precipitate

hyperkalaemia. Small cell lung carcinomas can secrete parathyroid like hormone substances which lead to hypercalcaemia.

**Q.17 - Answer: 5**

This man has a narrow complex or supraventricular tachycardia (SVT). Although vagal manoeuvres are often the first option, followed by adenosine, he is decompensating and fast becoming unconscious. Furthermore adenosine can precipitate bronchoconstriction and would be contraindicated in an asthmatic. Electrolyte disturbance can cause SVTs, and it is important to investigate this at the earliest suitable opportunity, but the immediate priority is to stabilise the patient. The best and quickest option for this man is therefore DC cardioversion.

**Q.18 - Answer: 4**

Most pacemakers either sense and pace in the ventricles or sense and pace in both chambers to allow synchrony of cardiac contraction. The demand is level-sensed, below which the pacemaker will cut in. The pacing spike is only seen when the pacemaker cuts in, however this is not determined by haemodynamic state; it is determined by the 'demand' which, if at a 'normal heart rate', would definitely be above the current 46 beats per minute that John is experiencing. Driving restriction is indeed for 1 week after pacemaker insertion; however, John has also has a myocardial infarction so he must refrain from driving for at least 4 weeks.

**Q.19 - Answer: 1**

This seems like a complicated question, but once you make a few diagnostic conclusions from the text, then logic will see you through. Firstly this is a case of atrial fibrillation (AF), but what type? Well, there is an acute febrile illness which may be transient, but this woman also has signs of mitral regurgitation and in particular with likely left atrial enlargement. In other words, despite her being unaware of palpitations, which would help to time the onset of the AF, she has a structurally abnormal heart which suggests it is safer to anticoagulate but also implies that cardioversion is unlikely to be successful. For that reason, options 3, 4 and 5 are discounted. Furthermore, she has a controlled heart rate probably due to her atenolol and is she is haemodynamically stable so emergency action or rate control is unnecessary. This leaves option 1 the best from those available.

**Q.20 - Answer: 2**

Renin is released by the kidneys in response to reduced renal perfusion and in turn leads to angiotensin I conversion to angiotensin II by ACE. This can occur in heart failure when poor cardiac output leads to poor renal perfusion, in turn maintaining a vicious cycle of further salt and fluid retention and further heart failure, but drug therapy and hypovolaemic states will also cause these hormones to rise. The BNP, as the name suggests, is a peptide that can lead to salt loss and is secreted by the heart in response to stress of heart failure. Ground glass shadowing on high resolution is caused by several conditions besides pulmonary oedema, which is not in itself a specific indicator of heart failure in any case. The third heart sound or 'S3' occurs due to passive filling of the ventricles following atrio-ventricular valve opening. This occurs in cases of heart failure when the atria are overloaded and readily refill the ventricles; however this is also a normal physiological finding in the young and athletic.

**Q.21 - Answer: 4**

This is a case of severe hypertension with the resulting features of headache and retinal damage. Although this gentleman has a 'tanned' appearance, it is a red herring since it may well just be due to ethnicity and outdoor work. Although linked to changes in skin pigmentation, options 2 and 3 are not associated with malignant hypertension. Glomerulonephritis does cause hypertension, though one would expect a much higher creatinine and blood on dipstick. Cushing's patients would exhibit a rotund habitus and glycosuria would be expected from impaired glucose tolerance. With the slightly raised Na and lowered K, Conn's is the most likely diagnosis here.

**Q.22 - Answer: 3**

The story is of likely unsanitary surgical procedures leading to bacteraemia. Splenomegaly, a new murmur and dipstick haematuria fit with endocarditis. A prolonged P-R interval on ECG does occur in rheumatic fever and Lyme disease due to conduction defects but in endocarditis signifies aortic root abscess. Schistosomiasis can cause haematuria; yet, as for Lyme disease, Myriam did not travel to endemic areas. Finally typhoid, although present in Asia, is more often associated with fever, bowel disturbance and bradycardia.

**Q.23 - Answer: 2**

These episodes are likely to be due to an arrhythmia because she experiences palpitations and since they are paroxysmal, a 24-hour tape or ambulatory ECG would be best. She has osteoarthritis so, although an exercise test may bring these episodes on, she is unlikely to be able to take the test. An arrhythmia may or may not be secondary to a structural heart defect so an echo may later prove appropriate but is not the next best step.

A tilt test is best to investigate postural effects on blood pressure and dizziness; Annie's symptoms occur at any time of day or night, therefore are independent of posture. EPS are useful for finding aberrant conduction pathways. Such problematic conduction pathways are congenital and would be expected to have shown themselves before Annie reached 70 and may have left signs on a 12-lead ECG. EPS involves invasive techniques and option 2 is still the best for this case.

**Q.24 - Answer: 1**

Prophylactic antibiotics are also not usually required for low-risk cardiac catheterisation, fibre-optic bronchoscopy and Caesarean or normal deliveries.

**Q.25 - Answer: 2**

Patients should not drive for 4 weeks after a myocardial infarction or for one week after an angioplasty, but they do not need to inform the DVLA unless there is ongoing disability thereafter. The regulations are of course much stricter for those with commercial vehicle licenses and these patients should ensure that their condition is discussed with the DVLA.

**Q.26 - Answer: 3**

Although it is conceivable that this woman has missed or taken an inadequate dose of her insulin in the context of a concurrent gastric illness, the sharp chest pain with sloping ST segment elevation fits with pericarditis; uraemia due to renal failure is a recognised cause. Myocardial infarction in diabetic patients does not always give chest pain and certainly not sharp in nature. The timescale and severity do not point to an established salmonella bacteraemia and although she has an indwelling catheter, there are no other features suggestive of endocarditis.

**Q.27 - Answer: 1**

This is a question about managing stable angina in a patient experiencing more pain on exertion. Such patients often have combinations of nitrates, calcium channel blockers and/or nicorandil titrated to symptoms and tolerance before angiography is opted for. Regarding options 2 to 4, Mr Frederick gets dizzy when taking extra GTN and his blood pressure is borderline, so further hypotensives may not be sensible. In particular, diltiazem (unlike verapamil, which is completely contraindicated) should be used with caution in those already on a beta blockers. This patient also has evidence of peripheral venous stasis and oedema which can be worsened by calcium channel blockers. This pushes the choice to option 1; however the main reason that this is the best step is because this is a story of nitrate tolerance. Imdur ® is a slow release nitrate meant to be taken once a day. On a BD basis, Imdur ® doesn't allow for a nitrate free period and tolerance with efficacy will diminish as it has done in this patient. Changing to 60mg OD may be the best first step.

## DERMATOLOGY / ENT / EYES

**Q.28 - Answer: 2**

Annular lesions are ring like. Macules are flat and papules are raised. Purpuric regions or purpura are purple like bruises; pruritic lesions are itchy. Induration is thickened dermis and subcutaneous tissue whereas lichenification is increased skin markings and thickening due to repeated rubbing (like the heel of the foot). Excoriation occurs when the skin breaks due to scratching.

**Q.29 - Answer: 4**

Pityriasis versicolor is caused by pityrosporum yeasts, hence the subtle itch and scale. The lesions may appear darker than surrounding skin in caucasians but lighter than surrounding skin after tanning or in darker-skinned people. Discoid eczema is just a term for a disc shaped area of eczema. Vitiligo is hypopigmentation and is associated with autoimmune diseases (including thyroid disorders and Type 1 diabetes); however the loss of pigment is usually well-defined rather than subtle; it is non-pruritic and has no scale. A more widespread distribution over traumatised surfaces would be expected. Chloasma refers to facial hyperpigmentation associated with pregnancy or hormonal contraception. Pityriasis alba is a type of postinflammatory hypopigmentation following an eczematous lesion.

**Q.30 - Answer: 3**

The pustulo-nodular lesions in the context of inflammatory bowel disease point toward pyoderma gangrenosum. Dermatitis herpetiformis is an intensely itchy vesicular eruption classically seen on the elbows of those with coeliac disease. Erythema multiforme comprises macular 'target' lesions that can be widely distributed. It is associated with viral infections and drug reactions. Erythema nodosum does cause nodular tender lesions on the shins in those with inflammatory bowel and other granulomatous diseases; however it doesn't break down into pustules as described here. Necrobiosis lipoidica is a flat, waxy and shiny lesion with telangectasia that is found on the limbs of those with overt diabetes mellitus.

**Q.31 - Answer: 2**

The description indicates a slow-growing ulcer with a rolled pearly edge and telangectasia, i.e.a basal cell carcinoma, also known as a rodent ulcer. Actinic keratoses do occur on sun-exposed skin and can lead to squamous cell carcinomas, but both of these are scaly and crusty. Bowen's disease is a red scaly plaque that can also progress to a squamous cell carcinoma. A seborrhoeic keratosis or seborrhoeic wart is a common and benign waxy lesion that is often pedunculated and friable.

According the Glasgow criteria for dysplastic naevi, major features are: change in colour, change in size, change in shape. Minor features are: inflammation, oozing or bleeding, itch or altered sensation and a diameter >7mm

**Q.33 - Answer: 5**

When eczema cause blistering on the soles or palms it is referred to as pompholyx. The Koebner phenomenon is when a dermatological process can be induced at the site of skin trauma. Dermatographism literally means writing on skin but refers to the weal and flare caused by local histamine release after scratching the skin. The Auspitz sign refers to pinpoint bleeding that occurs when a psoriatic scale is scraped away.

**Q.34 - Answer: 4**

Although groin lesions can occur in flexural psoriasis, they are 'wet-looking' rather than scaly. Psoriatic arthropathy can be asymmetric oligoarthritis, rheumatoid-like, symmetrical distal polyarthritis, spondyloarthropathy or destructive arthritis mutilans.

**Q.35 - Answer: 4**

Lichen simplex, also known as lichen simplex chronicus or neurodermatitis, refers to a condition where one repeatedly scratches a particular area of the skin and over time it thickens and can even hyperpigment. It is more of a sign of a habit of scratching rather than a disease in itself. Although it is a skin change in an area of trauma i.e. excoriation, it is not strictly speaking a true Koebner phenomenon, which is when a single act of trauma may cause a disease process to occur at that site. All the other options exhibit 'Koebnerisation'.

**Q.36 - Answer: 2**

This is a description of a mundane yet troublesome problem of dry skin. Zack is likely to be outside in harsh weather conditions and dry skin is a predictable consequence. One may be tricked into thinking there is a form of inflammatory process or eczema which may require a steroid preparation; however the absence of significant changes in appearance and only a mild itch which occurs in any dry skin counts against this. For that reason, and since topical steroids should be used with caution on the face especially near the eyes, options 1 and 4 should be disregarded. Benzoyl peroxide is an anticomedonal agent used for acne which may further dry the skin. This leaves aqueous cream and emulsifying ointment which are emollient and therefore able to provide symptomatic relief. The main reason to choose aqueous cream in the first instance is because it is the least greasy and best tolerated of the two options.

**Q.37 - Part 1 - Answer: 5**

This is a picture of herpes zoster ophthalmica with secondary bacterial infection. Complications can be serious and treatment would therefore involve intravenous antibiotics with antivirals and well as review in an acute setting. Yellow crusting on an erythematous base on the face is also seen in impetigo, a staphylococcal infection seen in children and requiring topical fusidic acid or systemic therapy.

**Q.37 - Part 2 - Answer: 4**

Periorbital cellulitis can lead to abscess formation.In that case, imaging with a CT of the head as well as ophthalmology review may be required.

**Q.38 - Answer: 2**

Itching is worse when the skin is dry; for that reason reducing the central heating will reduce skin drying at home. Towel drying has the potential to aggravate eczema especially if the skin is rubbed rather then wrapped to dry. Cotton clothing, like most natural fabrics, may be better than synthetics. They are less occlusive and are unlikely to react with the skin. Options 3 and 4 are of unproven benefit unless specifically indicated.

**Q.39 - Answer: 4**

The presence of flat pink macules with scale occuring after a single 'herald' lesion makes pityriasis rosea the best option. Guttate psoriasis does form multiple lesions but one would expect to see raised plaques with more obvious scaling and a herald lesion is not commonly noted. Porphyria cutanea tarda involves blistering lesions with hyperpigmentation and increased hair growth (hypertrichosis). Seborrhoeic dermatitis is linked to pityrosporum yeasts and in the adult commonly causes an itchy, flaky scalp. Rosacea is a chronic facial skin disorder involving pustule, papule and telangectasia formation. It is often triggered by alcohol and sun exposure.

**Q.40** - **Answer: 3**

Lichen planus is an inflammatory condition of unknown origin. It classically gives irregularly shaped (polygonal) flat-topped 'violaceous' plaques on flexor surfaces. Wickham's striae are characteristic white lacy streaks seen overlying such plaques and oral lesions are also noted. Lichen simplex refers to an area that has been thickened or lichenified with time due to repeated abrasion. Lichen sclerosus (et atrophicus) is an itchy, autoimmune, destructive process that can affect the vulva leading to whitening of the skin, sclerosis and loss of architecture around the labia and clitoral hood. It is also known to be premalignant. Leukoplakia means white plaques. Oral hairy leukoplakia manifests as rough white plaques or streaks in the oral cavity due to EBV activity in those who are immunosuppressed e.g. due to HIV.

**Q.41 - Part 1** - **Answer: 3**

Pure tone audiometry is the most exact method of determining conductive, sensorineural or mixed hearing loss. Skull imaging may outline space-occupying cerebral lesions and opacities in the middle ear, but it is unlikely to be able to define the type of hearing loss. Although otoscopy can reveal material in the external auditary canal and allow one to visualise the ear drum thereby indicating middle ear disease, findings may be negative even in cases of middle ear disease i.e. conductive hearing loss. Weber's test involves placing a vibrating tuning fork on the glabella and asking the patient to indicate which side it is heard the loudest. This can suggests bone conduction superior to air on one side; however if there is unequal deafness in both ears, interpretation of the test is complicated. The Valsalva manoeuvre, along with holding one's nose, can put pressure on the Eustachian tubes and can be useful to help equalise pressure in Eustachian tube dysfunction, for example when descending in an aeroplane; however it is unlikely to be the most useful action here.

**Q.41 - Part 2** - **Answer: 2**

This is a case of bilateral otitis media or 'glue ear'. In the young, glue ear is very common and spontaneous resolution often occurs, therefore prompting a watch and wait strategy. If after a few months things are no better then grommet insertion is an option. Pharmacological therapy has very little proven benefit. Despite a significant number of patients having fluid aspirates that grow bacteria, the role of antibiotics is still uncertain. Bilateral otitis media in an adult may suggest a sinister underlying cause therefore grommet insertion accompanied by biopsy of post nasal space in suspicion of a tumour is prudent.

**Q.42 - Answer: 5**

Exostoses are swelling of the bony portions of the external auditory canal secondary to cold exposure, and are often found in regular swimmers and divers. A basal cell carcinoma could present on the pinna but would have irregular skin markings and possible ulceration rather than subcutaneous swelling. A cauliflower ear results from failure of surgical intervention following a pinna haematoma (likely due to trauma). Cerumen is another name for ear wax. Chondrodermatitis nodularis chronica helicis is the diagnosis here and is thought to be caused by localised vasoconstriction secondary to exposure to the elements, which then precipitates avascular chondritis.

**Q.43 - Answer: 3**

A cholesteatoma is a serious complication of acute otitis media whereby an ingrowth of squamous epithelium leads to localised destruction and the potential for meningitis and formation of a brain abscess. Its characteristics are described in the case summary given. Chronic suppurative otitis media is typically a continued painless inflammation with discharge (glue ear). Problems were noted with the middle ear but not the external canal, therefore ruling out otitis externa. Labyrinthitis would be a deeper, inner ear infection, causing vertigo as a predominant symptom.

**Q.44 - Part 1 - Answer: 1**

Presbyacusis or old age hearing loss is the most likely since deafness per se would be the most likely cause of tinnitus in this case: as external noise perception dimishes, internal ringing becomes more apparent. Acoustic neuromas do cause tinnitus but one would expect more profound deafness and bilateral neuromas are fairly rare. Drugs, including loop diuretics and aminoglycosides can lead to hearing loss or tinnitus. Some atypical antituberculous medications, including macrolides, have also been associated with ototoxicity. However, it is unlikely these would have been available to Mr Dobson when he was young. With Meniere's disease one would expect vertigo. Tinnitus and sleep disturbance can be a feature of depression; however there are better causes for the tinnitus in the list and his lifestyle doesn't suggest depression.

**Q.44 - Part 2 - Answer: 1**

With presbyacusis as the diagnosis, a hearing aid is the best option. In effect it allows amplification of background noise which can drown out the tinnitus. Option 2 would be a reasonable option for suspicion of an acoustic neuroma and option 5 for depression but 3 and 4 are of unproven benefit.

**Q.45 - Answer: 2**

This lady has a story suggestive of benign positional vertigo, due to the chronicity of the symptoms without other ENT features and her experience of vertigo prompted by sudden movement. For that reason the Hallpike test, which involves brisk head movement to trigger the vertigo, is the test best suited to clarify the diagnosis. The tilt test does use positional changes to prompt a pathological response, however it is best suited to postural hypotension. An electroencephalogram can suggest abnormal brainwave activity if we were thinking about seizures. Calorimetry can test activity of semicircular canals but usually opted for after the Hallpike test. Romberg's test can suggest cerebellar dysfunction, however the story is not in keeping with cerebellar disease.

**Q.46 - Answer: 3**

This is a case of nasal polyps, i.e. insensitive mucosal protrusions presenting with rhinorrhoea, post nasal drip (nocturnal cough) and anosmia. Although associated with cystic fibrosis, Mr Plotski has managed to reach the age of 42 as a tennis coach, which makes allergic rhinitis a more likely underlying cause. A tumour would not give such a long history of these rhinitic symptoms; neither would a foreign body which is not only unlikely in an adult but would give a shorter history of purulent nasal discharge. Although a hypertrophied turbinate can give nasal obstruction and rhinorrhoea, the key is in the palpation since turbinates have preserved sensation to touch.

**Q.47 - Part 1 - Answer: 1**

At this stage, the patient is not haemodynamically compromised so she is able to sit up and option 5 is quite over the top. If bleeding worsened with ensuing hypovolaemic shock and an accessible bleeding point could not be found then ENT help would certainly be required. The bridge of the nose is bony and applying pressure to this is unlikely to stem a bleed, especially since the majority of bleeding vessels are in the anterior part of the nose.

**Q.47 - Part 2 - Answer: 5**

For the vast majority of nose bleeds, the cause is unknown. Hypertension is not proven to be a cause of epistaxis and bleeding due to nose picking or trauma is postulated in cases; but, unless the patient is neurotic, this is anecdotal. From the history, the patient is likely to be on warfarin which will inhibit clotting mechanisms, making resolution of a spontaneous nose bleed unlikely to occur naturally. Cocaine abuse can cause destruction of nasal tissues and microvascular tears, but this would be not be the most likely cause here. The factor V leiden deficiency is a thrombophilia which would have made her deep vein thrombosis more likely i.e. the opposite to a bleeding tendency.

**Q.48 - Answer: 2**

This patient does have features of sinus inflammation; however at this early stage most cases are self-limiting and the evidence for antibiotic use is limited; neither would an inhaled steroid be advised. Decongestants are useful in the short term, but work by causing vasoconstriction which in the longer term can cause ischaemic damage in the mucosa, leading to rebound oedema and swelling. For that reason, such agents should not be used for more than a week at a time. Chronic cases of longer duration may benefit from a trial of antibiotics or surgical intervention such as sinus washout.

**Q.49 - Answer: 3**

Like most conditions, referral for specialist treatment with tonsillitis is individualised with local guidelines but there are some general rules. Commonly accepted indications for referral include: recurrent episodes greater than 5 or 6 days' duration on at least 5 or 6 occasions over the preceding 2 years; obstruction to the airway (manifesting as sleep apnoea); chronic inflammation (>3 months); suspicion of malignancy; or likely peritonsillar abscess (also called a quinsy). The accumulation of saliva dues to swallowing difficulties suggests considerable obstruction and a likely quinsy in this case.

**Q.50 - Part 1 - Answer: 4**

Classification of diabetic retinopathy can be confusing especially since different sources may disagree as grading systems become outdated.
A rough guide is:

- BDR - Microaneurysms, dot and blot haemorrhages and hard exudates
- PPDR - as with BDR, plus cotton wool spots, larger blotch haemorrhages and beading of retinal veins

- PDR - neovascularisation
- Maculopathy - any of the retinal changes within one disc space of the macula. Circinate groups of hard exudates (in rings) often feature.
- Retinal haemorrhage - tends to refer to larger vitreous bleeding from neovascularisation.
- BDR and PPDR can also be grouped as non-proliferative diabetic retinopathy.

The changes noted here are indeed those of BDR; however because they are found at the fovea (within one disc space of the macula), maculopathy is a better term. Furthermore the presence of these hard circinate exudates are characteristic of maculopathy.

**Q.50 - Part 2 - Answer: 3**
This is a complicated question since different trusts will have different guidelines and referral pathways. The essence however is that with diabetic maculopathy, referral for laser therapy is required but this is not as urgent as with established proliferative retinopathy. Same day referral would be more appropriate for evolving vitreous haemorrhage or retinal detachment.

**Q.51 - Answer: 4**
Options 1, 3 and 4 occur in both diabetic and hypertensive retinopathy, however 'flame haemorrhages' are more suggestive of hypertension. Microaneurysms are noted in diabetic retinopathy. Changes in hypertensive retinopathy in order of progression are: arteriovenous 'nipping', shiny arterioles ('silver wiring'), narrowed arterioles that lead to cotton wool spots (infarctions), flame haemorrhages, hard exudates (leaking vessels) and finally papilloedema in severe cases.

**Q.52 - Answer: 2**
This is a picture of transient visual disturbance with localised pain and signs of later optic atrophy. Options 1 and 4 do cause optic atrophy but one would expect them to give bilateral problems without pain. Artery occlusion could also cause these problems but like toxic and vitamin deficiency, it is fairly rare and would tend to give a persistent deficit. Migraine can cause transient painful unilateral visual disturbance and, with a vascular association, may result in a degree of atrophy; however Charlotte has never experienced this before. Overall, multiple sclerosis is the most common cause of optic atrophy in this age group and the presentation of painful unilateral visual

disturbance during strenuous activity fits best with a retro-orbital neuritis or papillitis in this case.

**Q.53 - Answer: 3**

The story of acute onset intense, nauseatingly painful red eye provoked by iris dilatation and accompanied by visual 'haloes' is typical of acute closed angle glaucoma. Scleritis tends not to be so acutely or severely painful and both scleritis and episcleritis are associated with connective tissue diseases, neither of which are present here. Although retrobulbar neuritis can give acute pain and visual disturbance, the other features, along with a misty or cloudy cornea, are more suggestive of acute glaucoma. The raised pulse and respiratory rate with tremors is a result of the severe pain rather than being indicative of a panic attack.

## ENDOCRINOLOGY / METABOLIC

**Q.54 - Answer: 1**

Hyperventilation is often accompanied by paraesthesia. This is caused by respiratory alkalosis which interferes with calcium binding in the blood, leading to membrane destabilisation of peripheral nerves. Although capillary blood tests are not always reliable, the normal blood glucose reading does make options 3 and 4 less likely. Amphetamine abuse is also less likely since her neurological and haemodynamic markers count against it. Finally, Addison's disease, although associated with other autoimmune disorders like diabetes mellitus, is relatively rare in comparison to hyperventilation and one would expect to see postural hypotension.

**Q.55 - Answer: 1**

It is now recognised that HbA1c can be very difficult to reduce in type 2 diabetes, even with adherent patients. The successful weight loss and meticulous records at the slimming club and the glucose measurements should support your trust in this patient. Haemoglobinopathies such as sickle cell can alter HbA1c but would reduce it, not increase it. Thalassaemia can increase the HbA1c but is unlikely in this lady. Fructosamine is used to monitor shorter term changes in glycaemia such as in pregnancy. Orlistat is drug used to promote weight loss but is generally indicated when over 2.5 kg of weight has already been lost, but in someone of BMI> 28 kg/m$^2$.

**Q.56 - Answer: 2**

This is a very complicated history with a a few red herrings but if you outline the clear facts then you can work it through. Allyson is definitely hypoglycaemic, but has no other electrolyte imbalance, neurological or haemodynamic disturbance. This should rule out option 1, 4 and 5. She also has a high insulin level which also channels you to option 2 or 3. Finally, you are fortunate to get a quick C-peptide level. This substance is made by the pancreas during endogenous insulin production. Exogenous administration of insulin inhibits natural insulin and C-peptide production; however in the presence of insulinoma this is not the case and both remain high. Allyson 's sister is diabetic so she would have ready access to insulin.

**Q.57 - Part 1 - Answer: 3**

Options 1, 2 and 3 often occur, co-exist and even synergise in diabetic patients, but the question specifically asks what is the cause of his symptoms rather than signs. For that reason, the burning neuralgic pain at rest at night is characteristic of a painful diabetic polyneuropathy. The convoluted description of his feet is an example of what another healthcare professional may describe. We all should realise this is just a hallux valgus or bunions which are common with advancing age but are prone to trauma, which is a danger in a diabetic. A Charcot's joint is a severely deformed joint one which would expect in a diabetic patient with a much more clinically evident degree of neuropathy. The broken skin is a result of poor footwear with this deformity. The reduced sensation over the thickened skin is common in anyone. Although we can't find the pulses, this doesn't mean there is limiting ischaemia. You can feel his warm toes which is a good sign and, in patients with atherosclerosis, the thickened walls may reduce the ability to detect a pulse but still allow a patent lumen. Finally, despite proprioception and vibration sense both being carried by fibres of the dorsal column in the spinal cord, vibration sensation may be the first modality to be lost, hence the most discriminatory test of early neuropathy. Lesson - buy a 128Hz tuning fork.

**Q.57 - Part 2 - Answer: 3**

As already discussed, this is likely to be due to painful sensory polyneuropathy and although simple analgesia would be tried first, the best step from the list is a tricyclic antidepressant which, as well as being useful in this type of chronic pain, also has a useful hypnotic effect. Other agents including carbamazepine or gabapentin can be tried before the chili pepper extract capsaicin is used. Option 2 is definitely indicated here but will not directly help with his nightly pain. Since we do not think there is significant ischaemia, option 5 is a bit hasty.

**Q.58 - Answer: 4**

This is a situation of impaired fasting glycaemia (fasting glucose between 6.1 and 7 mmol/L). It is suggestive of diabetes but not diagnostic and the British Diabetes Association recommend that such patients should have an OGTT to clarify the diagnosis. It must be noted that random urinalysis is poorly sensitive for glycosuria.

**Q.59 - Answer: 1**

Metformin is the best first-line drug in this case since the patient is overweight and has no obvious contraindications - e.g. creatinine >150 µmol/L - or evidence of tissue hypoxia. Gliclazide is used as an adjunct to metformin if this fails to control glycaemia alone, or in place of metformin if this is poorly tolerated or contraindicated. Rosiglitazone is not a first-line drug and is used in combination with either metformin or a sulphonylurea. Acarbose is an adjunct that can reduce starch conversion to sugar in the gut but is not the drug of first choice. Enalapril is indicated in diabetic patients who have evidence of nephropathy indicated either by raised serum creatinine or by microscopic proteinuria (as detected by increased protein levels on a 24hr urine collection).

**Q.60 - Answer: 4**

Tight blood pressure control has been shown to have the most important impact on macrovascular complications such as ischaemic heart disease in this setting.

**Q.61 - Part 1 - Answer: 1**

Although infertility is associated with all these causes, the features of hirsutism and obesity point to polycystic ovarian syndrome (PCOS) as the most common cause. Cushing's disease refers to Cushing's syndrome due to a pituitary adenoma causing a raised ACTH which in turn causes raised cortisol. Questions describing pituitary adenomas including a prolactinoma would tend to mention the effects of a space occupying lesion in the pituitary fossa. Hypothyroidism can cause weight gain and menstrual irregularities, however more often increasing rather than decreasing menstruation. The hirsutism and acne is more likely to be due to PCOS. Kallman's syndrome is a rare form of hypogonadotrophic hypogonadism. It is caused by the failure of GnRH secreting neurones to migrate to the hypothalamus. The syndrome includes hypogonadism, colour blindness and anosmia but not obesity and virilisation as seen here.

**Q.61 - Part 2 - Answer: 3**

As described previously, this is polycystic ovarian syndrome and insulin resistance with infertility, and can be treated successfully with metformin. 24-hour urinary free cortisol can aid diagnosis of Cushing's syndrome. The transsphenoidal approach is used to resect pituitary tumours. Bromocriptine is a dopamine agonist that can inhibit prolactin secretion from the anterior pituitary.

**Q.62 - Answer: 2**

Cannabis is known to cause gynaecomastia, as can alcohol in great excess, though in this case is more often related to chronic liver disease and cirrhosis, of which he has no signs. Gynaecomastia is related to an increased oestrogen to androgen ratio, so any disruption in this balance, including oestrogen-secreting tumours, are implicated. Drugs like spironolactone, digoxin or cimetidine are also noted to cause this condition. A prolactinoma can lead to galactorrhoea rather than gynaecomastia, and moreover the headaches in this story sound more likely due to a hangover than a space-occupying cerebral lesion.

**Q.63 - Answer: 4**

Mr Brooks is overweight, hypertensive and glycosuric (possibly diabetic) these are feature of Cushing's syndrome, however with the addition of soft tissue swelling (hands and neck), obstructive sleep apnoea and increased sweating this more likely to be a description of acromegaly. Options 2 and 3 are excluded since they test for Cushing's syndrome. An OGTT will assess impaired glucose tolerance but can only help assess acromegaly if followed by serial growth hormone measurement. Growth hormone is usually secreted in a pulsatile manner, so random levels can be uninformative. The best test here to assess for growth hormone excess is to measure IGF-1, which is released from the liver in response to growth hormone.

**Q.64 - Answer: 3**

Lucy is likely to be in diabetic ketoacidosis precipitated by urinary tract sepsis and possible developing pyelonephritis. All options will give her some benefit, however with vomiting, fevers and likely dehydration along with a 'Hi' (high) glucose, fluid resuscitation is the immediate first step, then insulin (usually intravenously stat before a sliding scale) would follow. A broad spectrum antibiotic would be valuable here but not as the most important next step. An antiemetic, especially a prokinetic such as metoclopramide, along with a nasoogastric tube is useful in these cases with vomiting, especially where gastroparesis is possible.

**Q.65 - Answer: 4**

This is a question about recognising actions of insulins as well as evaluating insulin choices for an individual. From the story we can make out, Nadia is a highly motivated and likely intelligent individual who would be happy with a degree of complication in her treatment to keep her lifestyle, i.e. she would cope with several times a day rather than once a day if that allowed her to get on with life. Also the inconsistency of eating times and amounts from day to day would make a standard daily dose of insulin unsuitable, because she would have little freedom to eat at times determined by other people. Nowadays there is an emphasis on giving patients the lifestyle control and fitting the insulin around it rather than vice-versa, e.g. the dose adjustment for normal eating (DAFNE) programme. Since her eating plans can be delayed or changed at short notice, an ultrafast-acting insulin that can be taken inconspicuously just before or after eating such as option 4 would be ideal. Glargine is a once-a-day insulin. Insulatard ® is intermediate, Actrapid® or Humulin ® are fast acting and Mixtard ® is a mixture of types.

**Q.66 - Answer: 1**

Here we see a low TSH and low T4. This should straight away rule out hyperthyroidism in which the T4 would be high or normal if subclinical. It would also rule out hypothyroidism in which the TSH would be high. Hashimoto's thyroiditis is also a primary hypothyroidism and would likewise tend to give a high TSH. This leaves option 1 and 4 both of which give a low TSH leading to a low T4 i.e. 'top down dysfunction'. Despite the headaches, secondary hypothyroidism (due to a pituitary adenoma) is still less common than sick euthyroid syndrome which is much more common in times of intercurrent illness, such as in this case.

**Q.67 - Answer: 4**

Despite all the text in the case and confusion between weight loss and anxiety due to carcinoma versus weight loss and agitation due to thyrotoxicosis, the most useful piece of information is detection of a 'hot nodule'. This makes a carcinoma very unlikely, and since Graves' disease would give diffusely high uptake of radioactive iodine, a functional adenoma is most likely. Incidentally, a papillary carcinoma is more common than anaplastic or medullary, and a medullary tumour does not secrete T4 or T3; it secretes calcitonin instead.

**Q.68 - Answer: 5**

This case describes Sheehan's syndrome - pituitary failure following an acute hypovolaemic episode. Kallman's syndrome is congenital hypogonadotrophic hypogonadnism. Waterhouse-Friederichsen's syndrome denotes adrenal failure as a result of adrenal haemorrhage, these days usually secondary to severe meningococcal sepsis. Sipple's syndrome is also known as multiple endocrine neoplasia (MEN) type II or IIa, which is an inherited combination of phaeochromocytoma, parathyroid and medullary thyroid carcinomas.

**Q.69 - Part 1 - Answer: 1**

The startled expression, with visible cornea, dry eyes and ophthalmoplegia, suggests proptosis and lid retraction. Although eye signs are a feature of myaesthenia gravis and myotonic dystrophy, one would expect ptosis instead of lid retraction as well as weak facial muscles, so she would be unlikely to smile well. Sjögren's syndrome involves dry eyes but none of the other neuromuscular problems. Eyelid retraction is associated with all forms of hyperthyroidism, but opthalmoplegia and proptosis are specific to Graves' disease. It is also important to remember that eye signs in Graves' disease can predate other features of hyperthyroidism.

**Q.69 - Part 2 - Answer: 2**

As established, this is Graves' eye disease and so option 5 can be eliminated. Such eye disease doesn't always respond to treatment of hyperthyroidism and since there are no other apparent features at this stage for Mrs Garcia, options 3 and 4 can be excluded. This leaves options 1 and 2. Artificial tears are used for such patients where dryness is a problem, however since there is evidence of overt orbital infiltration and ophalmoplegia, this would be inadequate as a sole treatment, and radiotherapy is best from the list. While radiotherapy may not be the next appropriate step since other therapies such as high dose steroids may be used at this stage, the question does not ask for the next step, only the most effective from the list given.

**Q.70 - Answer: 4**

Doris is hypothyroid and, as an elderly woman, care must be taken when starting thyroxine as to avoid cardiac overdrive, thereby precipitating angina. Although other complications from thyroid replacement have been noted, this is the best answer.

**Q.71 - Answer: 4**

Below is a table showing the biochemical changes expected with these conditions, but before you just memorise it, take a moment to think about the principles behind bone metabolism that can help you to work through the answer.

Step 1 - What is happening to the calcium? Remember which conditions are related to high calcium : primary and tertiary hyperparathyroid (PTH), myeloma and sarcoidosis. Low calcium is found with hypoPTH and vitamin D deficiency (osteomalacia). In osteoporosis, minerals may be normal because the problem is overall bone formation, not lack of substrate. This should straight away eliminate options 3, 5 and 1.

Step 2 - What does alkaline phosphatase (ALP) do? ALP is raised when there is osteoblastic activity, so will be raised in osteomalacia and in primary hyperPTH where there is increased bone turnover. This should discount option 2.

Step 3 - What does PTH do (even if you have no result for it)? - PTH leads to calcium resorption and phosphate elimation. Therefore any condition which involves a disturbance of PTH (including paraneoplastic syndromes) would be expected to show these to ions moving in opposite directions. This should all point to option 4, hypoparathyroidism, which in this case may be just coincidental with the wrist fracture. Alternatively, you can just memorise the table!

| | Calcium | Phosphate | ALP |
|---|---|---|---|
| Primary hyperparathyroidism | ↑ | ↓ | normal or ↑ |
| Hypothyroidism | ↓ | ↑ | normal |
| Osteomalacia | ↓ | ↓ | ↑ |
| Osteoporosis | normal | normal | normal |
| Multiple myeloma | ↑ | ↑or normal | normal |
| Paget's disease | normal | normal | ↑↑ |

**Q.72 - Answer: 3**

Hypocalcaemia is a common complication of chronic renal failure. It is linked to reduced 25-hydroxy vitamin D transformation into the active 1,25-dihydroxy vitamin D or calcitriol. Calcium absorption from the gut is dependent on calcitriol, so simply increasing calcium intake would not overcome hypocalcaemia. Increasing dairy consumption is furthermore a bad idea since they contain high levels of phosphate which should be limited in renal patients. Calciferol is another name for vitamin D3 similar to that in the diet, i.e. non activated, so unhelpful here. Alfacalcidol is an activated form of vitamin D and so is the best option.

**Q.73 - Answer: 2**

Phaeochromocytoma is due to a catecholamine-producing tumour which typically gives episodic syptoms related to adrenergic overdrive e.g. chest pain, bronchoconstriction, hypertension, sweats, facial flushing, tremor, nausea and vomiting, as well as peripheral and central nervous system effects of vasospasm. During an episode, thyroid enlargement has been noted. The key here is the constellation of symptoms but also their episodic nature. Conn's syndrome is primary hyperaldosteronism that would give constant hypertension. Again Cushing's syndrome could give similar symptoms including glycosuria, but one would not expect attacks as described here. Thyroid storm may well give a severe attack with adrenergic overdrive, however simple resolution would not be expected. Carcinoid syndrome results from a serotonin (5-HT) secreting tumour that presents with diarrhoea, wheeze and flushing.

**Q.74 - Answer: 3**

A 24-hour urinary free cortisol or even better an overnight (low dose) dexamethasone suppression test is the best way to screen for Cushing's syndrome. From that point on, as long as you exclude exogenous hormonal treatment, you want to distinguish between the three likely causes: 1) Cortisol-secreting adrenal adenoma, 2) ACTH-secreting pituitary adenoma (Cushing's disease) and 3) Ectopic ACTH production from another tumour. Only ACTH can distinguish between an adrenal adenoma (when ACTH is low) and the other two causes. All other tests suggest whether the ACTH is pituitary or ectopic.

**Q.75 - Answer: 3**

Gastric lavage is only of use if started within an hour of likely poisoning; there is no such limit for the activated charcoal. If a large overdose i.e. >150 mg/kg or >12g is suspected, the risk of treatment with N-acetyl cystine immediately is outweighed by its benefits. Since 1 tablet = 500g, it is certainly worth the risk in this case.

**Q.76 - Answer: 1**

This is a picture of normal anion gap metabolic acidosis of which there are only a few causes including: renal tubular acidosis, hypoaldosteronism, treated ketoacidosis and diarrhoea. This girl is thin and likely to have bulimia nervosa with finger callouses from induced vomiting (Russell's sign). Although carcinoid syndrome does give diarrhoea, Tarina doesn't show any of the other features which makes laxative abuse the most likely. Note that aspirin and lactic acidosis give increased anion gaps.

**Q.77 - Answer: 5**

ADH is secreted from the posterior pituitary and is responsible for managing water conservation in the kidneys. Diabetes Insipidus (DI) results either from a lack of pituitary ADH (cranial DI) or lack of responsiveness to ADH (nephrogenic DI) thereby leading to water loss and increasing plasma osmolality. This may present with polyuria and polydipsia. A water deprivation test can help distinguish between CDI and NDI and between primary polydipsia which is a purely psychogenically-driven increased fluid intake. In this case the initial low plasma osmolality indicates there is no failure of the ADH axis and so a water deprivation test or specialist referral are all unnecessary. Exposure to toxins in the workplace is are unlikely to cause DI even if she did have this condition, so option 4 is eliminated also.

**Q.78 - Answer: 2**

This is an example of tumour lysis syndrome in which potassium, phosphate and urate rise due to rapid tumour destruction. Urate can lead to renal failure and gout. This can be pre-empted with prophylactic allopurinol.

## GASTROENTEROLOGY / NUTRITION

**Q.79 - Part 1 - Answer: 3**

Aphthous ulceration, as the name suggests, refers to ulcers, which are not present here. They can be spontaneous or related to inflammatory bowel disease or secondary to other dermatological conditions including pemphigoid and erythema multiforme. Cheilitis is also called angular stomatitis i.e. inflammation of the corners of the mouth. This is often secondary to oral candidiasis or poorly fitting dentures. Oral candida can give a sore mouth and tongue with a base of erythema; however one might expect to see a covering of white/creamy material that can be easily lifted away. Gingivitis is inflammation of the gums usually associated with poor dental hygiene. One would expect to see erosions and some discharge as well as noting halitosis. Glossitis is inflammation of the tongue which presents as being smooth, red and sore.

**Q.79 - Part 2 - Answer: 3**
Amyloid can deposit in the tongue and gives a characteristically large tongue. Vitamin C deficiency would lead to healing problems and is associated with gingivitis. Candida albicans is the most common organism causing thrush. Anti-smooth muscle antibodies are raised in autoimmune hepatitis. Iron, B12 and folate deficiencies are all linked to glossitis.

**Q.80 - Part 1 - Answer: 5**
Both malignant lesions and motility disorders are able to cause all of the first four options. A motility or neurological lesion is able to cause complete obstruction to liquids and solids from the start whereas a tumour that occludes the lumen would be expected to cause gradually worsening obstruction from solids to liquids.

**Q.80 - Part 2 - Answer: 2**
A corkscrew appearance on barium swallow is characteristic of the abnormal contractions caused by oesophageal spasm. Achalasia is characterised by abnormally high tone in the lower oesophageal sphincter causing failure of relaxation leading to a tight blockage of food entry into the stomach. This is fundamentally neurological, due to degeration of the myenteric nerve plexus. Barium swallows typically show a wide dilated lumen down to a sharp stricture and tapering 'rat's tail' appearance. Bulbar and pseudobulbar palsies are lower motor and upper motor neurones respectively. They affect the lower cranial nerves that are involved in tongue and palatal movement and hence palsies lead to swallowing difficulties due to problems with the action of swallowing rather than abnormal peristalsis down the oesophagus.

**Q.81 - Answer: a3 b2**
Andrew is a man with a history of dyspepsia, with no symptoms of reflux disease or any alarm features (see below). In this instance, simple lifestyle measures and antacids are the first option. The next steps in order would be a H.pylori test with triple therapy if positive or a trial of a proton pump or H2 blocker if negative. If these strategies fail then an endoscopy is indicated. A referral to endoscopy is the first option in those with alarm features: non-steroidal anti-inflammatory drugs, unintentional weight loss >3kg, dysphagia,

odynophagia, frequent vomiting, bleeding, anaemia, epigastric mass or age over 55.

**Q.82 - Answer: 4**

Unlike the previous question, this is more a case of reflux disease than pure dispepsia. The long hours suggests he eats late at night and close to bed times. This, coupled with pain when lying down and after a large meal, agrees with the picture of reflux. He has tried lifestyle changes and simple medications, but unlike dyspepsia, an endoscopy is the next preferred step to other medications.

**Q.83 - Answer: 5**

H.pylori is more often associated with peptic ulcer disease rather than GORD so options 1 and 2 are wrong. A barium swallow can show some motility and structural lesions and endoscopy can visualise the mucosa, however both of these can be normal in reflux disease and for those cases option 5 may be the only way to make a diagnosis.

**Q.84 - Answer: 1**

H. pylori is the most common cause (approx. 80% of gastric ulcers). Corticosteroids are associated with peptic ulcer, but more often duodenal ulcers and usually following higher doses or prolonged therapy. A Cushing's ulcer follows the stress of neurosurgery and a Curling's ulcer follows the stress from burns. Zollinger-Ellison syndrome involves a functional gastrinoma which causes multiple severe peptic ulcers and it is relatively rare.

**Q.85 - Answer: 4**

Jake could well have a bout of infective gastroenteritis, but although he is mildly dehydrated he is not systemically unwell. Moderate to severe dehydration, fevers over 39 degrees Celsius or bloody diarrhoea over 2 weeks in duration would prompt a hospital admission. Some authorities do not like to give loperamide if possible, but just like mild travellers diarrhoea, it might be for the best if symptoms are unmanageable or risking further dehydration. At this stage stool culture is unnecessary and besides, a viral agent may be the cause. There is little evidence to suggest a major outbreak of food poisoning and neither him or his girlfriend are food handlers so there is no need to notify this as a possible outbreak. The blood on paper and painful defecation is likely to be due to an anal fissure.

**Q.86 - Answer: 3**

Pain waking from sleep, symptoms less that 6 months' duration, loss of weight, blood in stools and age over 40 are some of the indicators of a disease other than IBS, warranting further investigation. All the other options are recognised features in IBS. That is not to say they are required for the diagnosis, or do not suggest other conditions e.g. cyclical pain and endometriosis; however their presence does not discount IBS as the diagnosis.

**Q.87 - Answer: 1**

This lady is likely to have had an upper gastrointestinal bleed secondary to non-steroidal anti-inflammatory agents. From her drug history we can accept that she has stable angina and heart failure. The urea is raised, which is likely due to blood absorption from the gut rather than acute renal failure considering the normal creatinine. Similarly the elevated potassium may in part be due to the bleed and her spironolactone. Her blood pressure is low normal but she is not compromised by this so, all in all, considering her heart disease, liberal fluid replacement is a bad idea. This eliminates options 2 and would suggest caution is required with 3, 4 and 5. Option 5 is certainly not necessary as there is no indication for fresh frozen plasma since her platelet count is in fact high as a reaction to bleeding and she does not have a high INR. Although we would not normally consider tranfusion for those with a haemoglobin over 8g/L, we would transfuse her in order to prevent triggering her angina. Compared to the other choices, Option 1 is the best option overall.

**Q.88 - Answer: 1**

Gilbert's syndrome is a benign defect of bilirubin conjugation leading to an unconjugated hyperbilirubinaemia, which is more clinically evident at times of intercurrent illness and starvation. Hepatitis A causes a hepatocellular defect leading to a mixed picture of conjugation. Gallstones cause obstructive jaundice and one would expect a mainly conjugated hyperbilirubinaemia. Haemolysis, elevated liver enzymes and low platelet count or the HELLP syndrome is related to pre-eclamptic toxaemia of pregnancy and is therefore not a contender for this patient. Although it is conceivable that a man in his early twenties may have a cardiomyopathy or another condition predisposing to right sided heart failure, this would be quite rare and one might expect more clinical details.

**Q.89 - Answer: 2**

The question asks which option will eradicate the varices. Only options 1 and 2 can do this and ligation has now found to be more effective therefore is the best option. Options 3 and 4 are primary bleeding prevention and used alone in small varices, however larger ones must be approached with eradication in mind. Similarly TIPSS aims to reduce the pressure in the varicose system thereby reducing the bleeding risk, but not eradicating the varices.

**Q.90 - Answer: 4**

The story of streaks of fresh blood at the end of a heavy bout of vomiting in an otherwise healthy person characterises a Mallory-Weiss tear. If Michael is stable and there are no other abnormalities one would discharge him. There is no doubt that his alcohol consumption is excessive and the opportunity should be taken to address this with him. Option 5 refers to a treatment for a hiatus hernia, for which we have no evidence here and it certainly doesn't constitute an emergency. Options 1 to 3 are strategies for oesophageal varices. Option one is an option for primary prevention of rupture. Options 2 and 3 are equivalent, although terlipressin (similar to glypressin) is often preferred. Although Michael does abuse alcohol, there is no evidence of chronic liver disease from this story nor any indication of large volume or warning bleeds from varices, with hypotension or shock.

**Q.91 - Answer: 3**

This is a picture of hepatic encephalopathy. Triggers include: alcohol, drugs including sedatives and opiates, gastrointestinal haemorrhage, infections and constipation which allows increased absorption of toxic amines that can bypass the porto-systemic circulation and affect the brain. Potassium is a problem in renal failure. Hypoglycaemia may be present as a result of liver failure but is not a precipitant per se of encephalopathy.

**Q.92 - Answer: 5**

The two questions here are: does she have spontaneous bacterial peritonitis? And if not, which is the best way to treat the ascites? It may be too much to be expected to know the cut-off white cell count to diagnose peritonitis (which is >250 /mm$^3$) However, logic tells us that 10 cells/ mm$^3$ is actually a small number. More to the point though, clinical sense tells us that the patient is otherwise systemically well and the fluid is clear. To treat simple ascites in this case, spironolactone is the first choice; furosemide can be added if this fails. Paracentesis with albumin replacement should be a last resort from the list.

**Q.93 - Part 1 - Answer: 1**

HH is an inherited condition leading to excessive iron accumulation. Iron deposits lead to widespread organ damage: Liver - cirrhosis: Heart - cardiomyopathy and arrhythmias; joints - chondrocalcinosis and pseudogout; pancreas - diabetes mellitus and rarely exocrine failure; pituitary - hypogonadism; skin - bronze pigmentation. The other distractors relate to alpha-1 anti-trypsin deficiency (emphysema) and Wilson's disease (neuropsychiatric problems) both of which also cause cirrhosis.

**Q.93 - Part 2 - Answer: 2**

Ideally, a raised serum ferritin is used as a screening test; however this is also an acute phase protein which would be raised in acute infection such as his urinary tract infection. A full blood count would not prove sufficiently informative even if the haemoglobin was raised; polycythemia could be related to haematological neoplasia or raised erythropoietin, or due to lung disease, rather than increased body iron. Both options 4 and 5 are appropriate to confirm HH but not as a first step as in this case.

**Q.94 - Answer: 1**

Weight loss, steatorrhoea and other non-specific symptoms are suggestive of coeliac disease, which can be detected at any age. Although anti-gliadin antibodies may be raised, the anti-endomysial antibody has the greatest specificity for coeliac disease. Option 3 refers to a test for pernicous anaemia. Villous atrophy is a feature of coeliac disease, but it also occurs in: lymphoma, tropical sprue, Whipple's disease and other conditions; therefore it is not specific to coeliac disease. A small bowel enema is of limited use here, unless imaging of ulceration or tumours is required.

**Q.95 - Answer: 3**

Options 1, 2 and 5 are associated with primary biliary cirrhosis. Pernicious anaemia is associated with autoimmune hepatitis.

**Q.96 - Part 1 - Answer: 3**

Mrs Millen has no constitutional symptoms (fever, sweats, weight loss, rash or arthritis), which one would expect from options 1, 2 and 4. Furthermore, her liver dysfunction is present yet mild making options 3 and 5 less likely. Overall, the pruritis can be the most significant problem in primary biliary cirrhosis long before other problems become apparent.

**Q.96 - Part 2 - Answer: 1**
Osteomalacia is also common, being related to malabsorption of vitamin D, a fat soluble vitamin.

**Q.97 - Answer: 4**
This question really comes down to logic and epidemiology. Option 4 is the most common cause in the UK out of the other options. Don't get confused with the likelihood of developing an HCC, which is higher with hepatitis C than B; however there are vastly more cases of hepatitis B than C in the UK, which makes up for this difference. Primary biliary cirrhosis and autoimmune hepatitis are relatively rare and would tend to cause death by liver failure, though essentially any condition that can cause cirrhosis can progress to cause HCC.

**Q.98 - Answer: 3**
Pancreatic cancer is by far rarer than the others, and would be far more likely cause jaundice by biliary obstruction directly, rather than by metastatic lesions causing obstruction.

**Q.99 - Answer: 4**
Suzie is obviously unwell and appears peritonitic. The main concern is of toxic megacolon with or without perforation. One may argue that a chest x-ray is better to diagnose air under the diaphragm, however it may be particularly difficult to sit her up for long enough and one could miss the megacolon. Besides, it is still possible to make out a perforation on an abdominal x-ray, due to air being on both sides of the lumen, giving it a 3-D appearance. A barium enema would be strictly contraindicated in this acute setting for fear of perforation and peritoneal contamination with barium.

**Q.100 - Answer: 4**
In fact, all these features have been noted in both ulcerative colitis and Crohn's disease. Furthermore, the systemic manifestations of inflammatory bowel disease are much more common in Crohn's than ulcerative colitis. However, remember the anatomical distinction. Ulcerative colitis shouldn't affect the small bowel and should therefore have little effect on the absorption of nutrients, including the fat soluble vitamin D which, when deficient, leads to osteomalacia.

**Q.101 - Answer: 3**

Follicular bleeding, gingivitis and purpura are features of vitamin C deficiency. Also noted are short question mark or corkscrew hairs. The other options don't adequately explain all the signs including gingivitis. Scabies would typically cause intense pruritis in skin creases, particularly at night.

**Q.102 - Answer: 1**

All of the above are water-soluble B vitamins that can be deficient in such patients, although some are more common than others. Niacin deficiency, also known as pellagra, has the classical features of dermatitis, diarrhoea and dementia (death is also added). Neuropathy, behavioural and mood disturbance and ataxia are also recognised. Riboflavin or vitamin B2 deficiency leads to angular stomatitis and glossitis. Thiamine or B1 deficiency should be well recognised in alcoholics, leading to the Wernicke-Korsakoff syndrome, or in chronic deprivation it leads to wet beri-beri, which involves fluid retention leading to high output heart failure. Cyano-cobalamin or B12 can be deficient from diets lacking any animal products and in pernicious anemia, and of course does give neurological complications including subacute combined degeneration of the spinal cord, as well as optic atrophy. Pyridoxine or B6 deficiency also gives peripheral neuropathy, dermatitis and glossitis and is more often associated with drugs such as isoniazide in the treatment of tuberculosis.

**Q.103 - Part 1 - Answer: 2**

Andrzej has no clinical jaundice and his urine is pale, so obstructive jaundice is unlikely, thereby ruling out options 3, 5 and rendering 4 less likely. He is afebrile with no right upper quadrant signs also counting against option 4. A cancer confined to the tail of the pancreas may occur with no jaundice in a chronic pancreatitic; however we would expect some cachexia at this stage. Ultimately, epigastric pain that goes through to back is more likely pancreatitis than biliary colic and, although peptic ulcers may be similar in presentation, the chronic history of abdominal pain in a former alcoholic along with steatorrhoea is more suggestive of chronic pancreatitis.

**Q.103 - Part 2 - Answer: 5**

Serum amylase is unhelpful since it can be normal in those with chronic pancreatitis. An abdominal ultrasound will detect gallstones and show pancreatic and biliary tract dilatation, as well as gall bladder dimensions. In this case, stones are unlikely to be present, so ducts may be of normal calibre. An ultrasound may also show a shrunken pancreas with abnormal reflectivity; however, signs may be subtle, the pancreas often being obscured by overlying bowel, and this doesn't confirm chronic pancreatic insufficiency. Both options 1 and 2 involve radiological techniques that can demonstrate dilated pancreatic and biliary ducts suggestive of gallstone disease. They can also show pancreatic calcification, a feature of chronic pancreatitis. Unfortunately pancreatic calcification may only be detected in up to 60% of those with chronic pancreatitis and so faecal fat analysis is the best option. Nowadays, the pancreolauryl or 'PABA' (P-aminobenzoic acid)' tests tend to be favoured over the less pleasant faecal fat analysis. Such tests involve administration of an oral substrate, of which the cleavage is dependent upon pancreatic enzymes. The products of this metabolism can be measured in the urine.

## INFECTIOUS DISEASES / IMMUNOLOGY / ALLERGIES / GENETICS

**Q.104 - Answer: 5**

In some parts of the UK, antenatal diagnosis of HIV is increasing rapidly and the simple principles must be understood by all members of the multi-disciplinary antenatal team. Unlike syphilis tests, a positive HIV antibody test in pregnancy is highly likely to be positive. A confirmation is always taken for anyone pregnant or not. With a multidisciplinary approach to antenatal HIV, including single or combination antiretrovirals, Caesarean section and bottle feeding, vertical transmission of HIV can be reduced to under 1%. Premature delivery may be increased, but actual numbers of stillbirths and miscarriages are not significantly raised. Termination of pregnancy is an option which may be appropriate to discuss with the mother, but the risks to the fetus can be rendered so low with current treatments that such an option is not often chosen by mothers in this situation.

**Q.105 - Answer: 3**

PEP involves a combination of antiretrovirals to be taken daily for 4 weeks. It is not a cure; it is just a strategy proven to lower the risk of HIV transmission from needlestick injuries. Guidelines indicate that it is to be given as soon as possible after the incident and ideally within an hour of exposure. Hepatitis C vaccine doesn't currently exist and John is unlikely to be in NHS employment if his Hepatitis B immunity is not up to date, though of course this must be verified and immediately addressed if not the case, as there are non-responders to the vaccine. Options 4 and 5 are correct but not the most important at this stage. It is also important that his baseline HIV and Hepatitis status should be confirmed, but again this is not the immediate priority.

**Q.106 - Answer: 2**

Boiling is the only way to inactivate amoebic cysts that may otherwise persist with other purifying methods. Bottled water is relatively safe as long as it was pure and treated and securely bottled; however, a large amount of bottled water has been refilled by the road side, improperly sealed, or sitting in a bucket of ice which can contaminate the rim. Copying the locals is never a good guide, since they will have a different immunity, but also at times suffer from water-borne infections themselves. The level of chemical pollution in water can be high in many developing countries and this risk cannot be eliminated by boiling.

**Q.107 - Answer: 2**

This question comes down to incubation periods. Options 1, 3 and 4 all take at least 48 hours before symptoms appear, whereas salmonella can cause symptoms after just 12 hours. Cryptosporidium takes at least 4 days to cause symptoms and, besides, its ability to cause significant illness is limited to the immunosuppressed e.g. HIV seropositives.

**Q.108 - Part 1 - Answer: 4**

Patients with falciparum malaria can appear reasonably well despite high parasitaemias up until a point when they decompensate with massive haemolysis. A parasitaemia of over 5% suggests a more severe infection than lower values but the proportion of parasites at the trophozoite or schizonts stage is significant, i.e.>20%, suggesting a particularly poor prognosis. For those with high parasitaemias (>10%) or features suggestive of impending decompensation, one should consider transfer to ITU and exchange tranfusion therapy. Likewise, cerebral malaria heralded by fits, change in conscious state and coma would prompt intensive care assistance. Local guidelines may however vary as to the point at which these extra interventions are carried out and, like most clinical scenarios, an individual case-by-case assessment would be appropriate. If in doubt, you should contact your local infectious diseases specialist or, if unavailable, your local hospital for tropical medicine. General principles, however, are as follows: as long as a patient can swallow, oral quinine (not chloroquine) is the first choice due to extra complications arising from iv therapy. Maintain carefully-balanced fluid management because of the risk of ARDS in severe malaria. Acute tubular necrosis with haemoglobinuria, also known as 'blackwater fever', is an infrequent but severe complication that would also require intensive input. The normal creatinine and only a trace of blood on dipstick make this unlikely at this stage.

**Q.108 - Part 2 - Answer: 5**

ECG monitoring is important, particularly when giving intravenous quinine, since arrhythmias can arise. An arterial blood gas can point towards metabolic (lactic) acidosis, and a urine sample and dipstick can suggest haemoglobinuria. Both of these can be signs of deterioration in this case. Cross-match of blood would be of use when preparing for a transfusion if haemolysis, which is also a possible complication, has occurred . However, out of all these options, hypoglycaemia is one of the most likely events due to the story given and as the question asks, it would be one of the quickest and easiest complications to detect and remedy.

**Q.109 - Answer: 3**

Live attenuated vaccines have a rare risk of reactivation in immunocompromised hosts. Attenuated vaccines also include: mumps, measles, BCG and Polio (Sabin), though killed Polio vaccine (Salk) is now the recommended option for UK vaccinations. Preformed antibodies i.e. 'IgG' for immediate and short-lived immunity in infants include: varicella (VZIG), hepatitis, botulism, rabies, tetanus, diphtheria. Killed organism vaccines include: typhoid, cholera, pertussis, rabies and polio (Salk). Particles of organisms or subunit vaccines include: hepatitis B, Haemophilus influenzae, Neisseria meningitidis. Pertussis used to be given as a whole-cell vaccine but in recent years a subunit vaccine has superseded this.

**Q.110 - Answer: 2**

This is a story of tuberculous meningitis, for which the four agents listed plus steroids should be initiated. The classical CSF findings are of a mononuclear leucocytosis, elevated protein and low glucose when compared to plasma. Options 3 to 5 are for bacterial meningitis, with option 4 particularly covering listeria, which, although very rare overall, is seen in neonates, the immunocompromised and the elderly. Option 1 refers to the management of a subarachnoid haemorrhage.

**Q.111 - Answer: 1**

Blood for malarial films should always be included in such a management plan, however both Anita and Ben have features of an atypical pneumonia and have undertaken good malaria prophylaxis. Furthermore, staying in a hotel with a closed circuit ventilation makes Legionella infection a clear possibility. A rapid urinary antigen test can confirm the diagnosis and is better than option 4, since comparison of acute and convalescent respiratory serology is undertaken retrospectively and would not help to direct your management this stage.

**Q.112 - Answer: 3**

Non-specific fever and myalgia with a rash that mimics flushing or sun tan is characteristic of dengue fever. This is one of the viral haemorrhagic fevers (VHF) and in endemic to South-East Asia. Yellow fever is also a VHF; however, it is more often found in South America and Africa. If Brandon did get travel advice, they would have offered him a yellow fever and typhoid vaccine as appropriate. Typhoid tends to present with enteric rather than dermatological manifestations. Photosensitivity would be conceivable if Brandon had been taking doxycycline as malaria prophylaxis; however, this would not explain the other features that he presented with. It would usually be appropriate to ensure a sexual history is taken. Body rashes occur in secondary syphilis and can take on many guises. The classical picture is a macular-papular eruption involving the palms and soles. Given the timescale here, secondary syphilis is unlikely. One might consider a rapid HIV (including p24 antigen) test since this could be acute HIV seroconversion.

**Q.113 - Answer: 2**

Influenza is a self-limiting viral infection in most people; however, vaccination is recommended for at-risk individuals, namely those with chronic respiratory disease, chronic renal impairment, significant cardiovascular disease, diabetes mellitus, those over 65 years, or those who are otherwise immunocompromised. For those unvaccinated individuals in the at-risk list above, who been exposed to someone with an 'influenza-like illness' within 48 hours, a treatment course of oseltamivir (Tamiflu) is recommended by NICE guidelines. This only applies at times when there are known to be cases of Influenza A or B in the community. At this stage, it seems very likely to be a viral infection so an antibiotic is not indicated. The vaccine itself is not useful as a post-exposure prophylaxis and amantadine is no longer recommended as a treatment.

**Q.114 - Answer: 3**

A morbilliform (measles-like) rash following penicillin (amoxycillin or ampicillin) for a sore throat along with lymphadenopathy and splenomegaly is classical for infectious mononucleosis or 'glandular fever'. It is caused by EBV infection and diagnosis suggested by the presence of large mononuclear lymphocytes on peripheral blood film, as well as a positive heterophil antibody (Monospot® or Paul-Bunnell) test. There are occasions when these tests can be falsely positive, including in lymphoproliferative disease. Therefore, serological tests showing positive EBV - IgM can help to confirm the diagnosis. In this case only IgG was ordered (which, if positive, would confirm previous infection) and so is misleading and doesn't rule out acute EBV infection. Don't forget the other rare associated features: myopathy, encephalitis, pericarditis or peripheral neuropathy. Q fever is a rare bacterial infection caused by Coxiella burnetii that leads to pneumonia, amongst other complications.

**Q.115 - Answer: 2**

It is important to recognise the features of severe HIV infection as described above, that would suggest a very low CD4 count and a vulnerability to opportunistic infections. All the options can affect the neurological system and Omara is likely to have a CD4 count below 50 cells/mm$^3$, making any of them a possible co-infection. However, given the absence of other neurological signs or meningism, and the fundoscopy appearances, cytomegalovirus (CMV) is the most likely diagnosis.

**Q.116 - Answer: 3**

Mycoplasma pneumoniae causes atypical pneumonia in epidemics which follow 4-year cycles. Constitutional symptoms may predominate before the development of a dry cough. It has a known association with erythema multiforme which is described here with the characteristic target lesions. Mycoplasma pneumoniae is also known to generate cold agglutinins, which are IgM immunoglobulins that precipitate at temperatures below 4 degrees Celsius. This is responsible for the pains that she was experiencing in the extremities as well as the abnormal precipitate noted in the blood test bottles.

**Q.117 - Answer: 2**

Hepatitis B serology concerns three separate antigens:

1) Surface antigen (Hep B sAg). If present, it signifies active infection, and if present for >6 months, it signifies chronic infection. Antibodies to surface antigen (Hep B sAb or AntiHBs) signify immunity following vaccination or infection.

2) Core antigen (Hep B cAg). It is not detected in the serum so is not reported in blood results. Antibodies to core antigen (Hep B cAb or AntiHBc) signify immunity following infection alone since the vaccine comprises subunits of the surface epitopes only.

3) 'e' antigen (Hep B eAg). If present, it reflects high level of infectivity in acute or chronic infection. Antibodies to the 'e' antigen (Hep B eAb or AntiHBe) signify declining level of infectivity in acute or chronic infection. If

cAb is positive, immunity is lifelong, unlike post vaccination sAb, which has to be boosted.

Household contacts of those infected with hepatitis B should be offered testing and vaccination. Acute Hepatitis B infection is a notifiable disease; chronic infection is not.

**Q.118 - Answer: 3**

The most likely diagnosis here is typhoid or enteric fever as characterised by the diarrhoeal symptoms after a period of constipation and the relative bradycardia despite dehydration and pyrexia. Although stool cultures may become positive later on in this condition, at this stage blood culture showing salmonella typhi would be the most likely confirmatory test. Options 1 and 2 are tests for malaria. Option 2 is more commonly available and useful to confirm P. falciparum where access to an experienced labaratory is limited. It is not, however, a 100% sensitive test, so a negative result must be accepted with caution. Stool microscopy should be sent in diarrhoeal illnesses and is useful for identifying ova, cysts and parasites, including giardia.

**Q.119 - Answer: 1**

Streptococcus remains overall the most common cause of pneumonia in HIV seropositive patients. The presentation here is characteristic, with a short onset of a productive cough and localised lobar signs confirmed on radiography. In addition, Matt is not significantly immunosuppressed, which makes option 2, the cause of 'PCP' pneumonia, unlikely. A final note to make is that desaturation on exercise is a non-specific test of respiratory function and will occur in any individual with an abnormal x-ray. It is of particular use to highlight disease in those where respiratory pathology is suspected but the chest x-ray is normal (as in around 25% of cases of PCP).

**Q.120 - Answer: 4**

Anticipation is a feature of conditions involving trinucleotide repeats, such as myotonic dystrophy, Huntington's chorea and Friedreich's ataxia. It is an important concept to explain to patients since it can explain why their parents may never have had any features of the condition, as well as preparing them for what they may expect in their children.

**Q.121 - Answer: 3**
Haemophilia is an X-linked recessive condition. If X* or Y* denotes affected chromosomes and X or Y denotes unaffected chromosomes, the genotypes are as follows:
Timothy: X* Y
Julie: X* X

This would give 4 equally likely options for their offspring:
1) X* X *= girl with haemophilia
2) X* X = girl who is a carrier
3) Y X* = boy with haemophilia
4) Y X = an unaffected boy

**Q.122 - Part 1 - Answer: 5**
This is acute anaphylaxis and patients can present anywhere on a scale from rash or wheeze, to laryngeal oedema and shock. Since Roshan has signs of haemodynamic compromise heading towards shock, adrenaline should be the first option. Intravenous adrenaline at a strength of 1:10,000 tends to be reserved for those with no pulse or in extremis; furthermore, when time is of the essence and venous access is not yet secured, the intramuscular route of adrenaline is preferable. Options 1 and 2 are the correct doses of drugs given in conjunction with adrenaline, but their effects are not so immediate and they are therefore not your absolute priority, but should be administered as soon as possible.

**Q.122 - Part 2 - Answer: 2**
Roshan had a clear anaphylactic response to the bee sting. It may be difficult to avoid future exposure to the allergen (unlike some food allergies) and if encountered again, the response is likely to be even more severe. For that reason, an injectable adrenaline, e.g. Epipen ® with instructions, is an important agent to carry with him. Options 5 and 3 can be useful for those with minor skin reactions to allergens. Similarly options 1 and 4 are useful for those with a systemic response, including hayfever.

**Q.123 - Answer: 2**
The incidental finding of a high lymphocytosis with mild or rubbery lymphadenopathy, with a mild anaemia in an older man, is typical of chronic lymphocytic leukaemia (CLL). Philip may live for a long time and die of other causes than the CLL. CLL can lead to progressive anaemia and hepatosplenomegaly. Options 1 and 3 refer to pathology of the myeloid cell lines (neutrophils, erythrocytes and platelets), to which lymphocytes do not

belong. Acute lymphoblastic leukaemia tends to be a paediatric condition. Lymphocytosis can occur in acute viral or chronic bacterial infections, however this does not fit so well with the clinical picture described.

**Q.124 - Answer: 1**

The key to answering this question is to understand the two types of bleeding patterns attributed to reduction or dysfunction in either platelets or clotting factors. Problems affecting platelets will lead to prolonged bleeding from mucous membranes and skin wounds that then develop into bruises. Clotting factor dysfunction or deficiency tends to cause delayed bleeding following trauma, e.g. bleeding into joints and muscle. Haemolytic uraemic syndrome (HUS) involves acute renal failure, thrombocytopenia and microangiopathic haemolytic anaemia (which can cause mild jaundice). HUS can be triggered by drugs or infection with organisms such as E.Coli 0157 or Shigella. HUS forms a spectrum with thrombotic thrombocytopenic purpura (TTP) and disseminated intravascular coagulation (DIC). All of the other options in some way or another can lead to clotting abnormalities by interfering with the production of clotting factors. Options 4 and 5 interfere with the enterohepatic circulation of the fat soluble vitamin K.

**Q.125 - Answer: 3**

Options 1, 2 and 4 are all antithrombotic agents, i.e. deficiency leads to thrombosis. Anticardiolipin antibody, also known as the lupus anticoagulant, are antibodies associated with the antiphospholipid syndrome, which involves arterial and venous thrombosis and recurrent miscarriage. The cleavage of factor V is one of the physiological controls of thrombosis. The Factor V Leiden mutation leads to loss of this control and thence to thrombophilia.

**Q.126 - Answer: 3**

The high normal mean cell volume and low iron binding capacity make iron deficiency unlikely. Furthermore, the dark stools are more likely due to iron tablets than melaena. Options 2 and 4 cause a macrocytic anaemia, and option 5 is associated with microcytosis. This leave hypothyroidism, which can give a normal or high mean cell volume, and can explain Mary's lethargy as well as her bowel and menstrual irregularities.

**Q.127 - Answer: 3**

The diagnosis of myeloma requires 1 major and 1 minor criterion or 3 minor criteria from the following.

- Major criteria include: plasmacytoma on bone marrow biopsy; high level monoclonal bands on electrophoresis (of urine or plasma); or >30% plasma cells on bone marrow biopsy.
- Minor criteria include: lytic bone lesions; 10-30% plasma cells on marrow biopsy; <50% immunoglobulins, or abnormal but low level monoclonal bands on urine or plasma electrophoresis. Hypercalcaemia is a feature but not a diagnostic criterion of myeloma. Reed-Sternberg cells are a feature of Hodgkin's lymphoma. Auer rods are cellular elements found in acute myeloid leukaemia. Teardrop cells are found in a peripheral blood film in those with myelofibrosis.

**Q.128 - Answer: 2**
Male sex, age <1 year or over 10 years at diagnosis, a white cell count over 100 billion/L and B-cell type are also indicators of poor prognosis. Lymphadenopathy and bruising are just common features of the condition.

**Q.129 - Answer: 2**
Reticulocytes are young red blood cells which are larger than mature ones and still possess genetic material. Their levels are raised in peripheral blood during haemolysis as the bone marrow 'churns' them out to meet increased demand. Rouleaux, which have the appearance of a fallen stack of coins, suggest a high ESR. Haemoglobin electrophoresis can help to diagnose haemoglobinopathies such as sickle cell disease and thalassaemias. Bence-Jones protein is found when excess light chains spill out of the kidneys and is detected in the urine of patients with myeloma. Howell-Jolly bodies are red blood cells containing nuclear remnants. They would otherwise be eliminated from the circulation by the spleen and so are detected in cases of hyposplenism or splenectomy.

**Q.130 - Answer: 1**
Mild neutropenia is a relatively common finding in black and Middle Eastern populations with no pathological consequences. Instead of a neutropenia, steroids give a relative neutrophilia (due to neutrophil disaggregation rather than a rise in actual numbers of cells). Chemotherapy does lead to neutropenia but there is no clinical information that indicates that this is the case. HIV infection can lead to a lymphopenia rather than neutropenia in particular. Sickle cell disease would cause a microcytic anaemia.

**Q.131 - Answer: 3**
Opiate analgesia should not be restricted for those with crises. Some staff can be unsympathetic to the degree of pain suffered by those with sickle cell

disease, and they can be suspicious of the motives of frequent attenders with such crises, and there is a tendency to undertreat such patients in terms of analgesia. All the other statements are correct.

## MUSCULOSKELETAL

**Q.132 - Answer: 2**

Sciatica is pain due to sciatic nerve compression which is felt in the buttock and thigh (as in option 5). A prolapsed intravertebral disc is a common cause of unilateral sciatica; however, bilateral sciatica suggests an alternative and possibly sinister pathology, since a prolapsed disc is unlikely to protrude bilaterally to encroach on both sciatic nerve roots. Pain in multiple directions of movement would also be a worrying feature. Pain after a period of rest may be suggestive of an inflammatory rather than a mechanical arthrosis.

**Q.133 - Answer: 3**

In addition to erosions, the joint space is normal and soft tissue swelling may also be seen in gout.

**Q.134 - Part 1 - Answer: 3**

Insidious polyarticular onset has a worse prognosis. All the other factors are inter-related since early active and erosive disease with extra-articular manifestations all suggest poor prognosis.

**Q.134 - Part 2 - Answer: 2**

Rheumatoid nodules affect about a fifth of patients, but tend to be located over pressure sites such as the extensor surface of the forearms or the Achilles tendon, and would not commonly be seen in the hands. The other manifestations may all be seen in established disease.

**Q.135 - Answer: 1**

Arthritis mutilans is one of the manifestations of psoriatic arthritis, which is by classification 'rheumatoid negative'. Other seronegative spondyloarthopathies include ankylosing spondylitis, Reiter's syndrome / reactive arthritis and other enteropathic arthritides. Although the rheumatoid factor is certainly not positive in all cases of the other options, it is positive in over 75% of those with Sjögren's syndrome and in 20-40% of those with SLE. Furthermore, it is present in 4% of the general population and 25% of the elderly. Rheumatoid factor is immunoglobulin that is targeted to the Fc portion of human IgG. There is a long list of other conditions where rheumatoid factor may be found, including autoimmune hepatitis, pulmonary tuberculosis, infective endocarditis and even transiently during acute infection.

**Q.136 - Answer: 3**

The presence of crystals is the give-away here, indicating that it has to be either option 2 or 3. One way to remember which is that Positive birifringence is for Pseudogout and Negative if for Normal gout. Additional clues are that gout tends to affect the small joints, e.g. first meta-tarsal, whereas pseudogout tends to affect larger joints such as the wrist, hip or knee. Pseudogout is due to accumulation of calcium pyrophosphate, which when seen alone, can be termed chondrocalcinosis. It can be caused by hyperparathyroidism (or other causes of hypercalcaemia), Bartter's syndome (or other causes of hypomagnesaemia), hypophosphatasia, ochronosis (the black discoloration of tissues seen in alkaptonuria), Wilson's disease, haemochromatosis, hypothyroidism, acromegaly, dehydration or intercurrent illnesses.

**Q.137 - Answer: 4**

Non-steroidal anti-inflammatory drugs (NSAIDs) are the first option in gout attacks unless a contraindication is already known. Diclofenac would not be used in this example, firstly because Ted had already used a potent NSAID, so giving another may not be of much use but also would incur a risk of side effects, and secondly, Ted has had gout for some time and underlying renal impairment is a possibility. Further NSAIDs would not then be the best choice, especially since good alternatives exist. Allopurinol is contraindicated during acute attacks as it can make matters worse. Steroids can be used in gout, but much further down the line, and with specialist guidance. Dihydrocodeine, as an opiate rather than an anti-inflammatory does not formally feature in the treatment schedule for gout, and would certainly not come before colchicine which is the therapy of choice following failure of resolution with NSAIDs.

**Q.138 - Answer: 3**

Options 1 and 2, although less suggestive of RA, certainly do not rule it out nor strongly indicate a spondyloarthropathy as the cause. Enthesitis is the inflammation of soft tissue insertion sites into bone (e.g. ligaments, tendons and joint capsules). This is a characteristic feature of the seronegative spondyloarthropathies and does not typically occur in RA. Eye and skin manifestations may differ between these two diagnoses but they do present in both types of condition.

**Q.139 - Answer: 5**

This is a description of ankylosing spondylitis, for which active and intense physiotherapy early on is known to reduce disease progression. This may be facilitated by taking NSAIDs, but NSAIDs alone or with rest may just allow progression of the inflammatory process. Disease modifying agents from option 3 are used, but later on in the condition. Their benefits appear to be restricted to peripheral joint disease. Osteotomy is an uncommon approach to treating severe joint disease once it has occurred rather than as prevention.

**Q.140 - Part 1 - Answer: 4**

This case is long and complicated, so once again it helps to list the clinical features that are being described: Raynaud's phenomenon (hand symptoms), gastro-oesophageal reflux (wheeze when supine especially after eating), hypertension, microstomia or small oral orifice (unable to fit lips around the peak flow meter) and mild anaemia with renal impairment (blood results). It should now appear clearer that these are features of systemic sclerosis (scleroderma), in particular the limited cutaneous or the CREST syndrome. In full, this includes calcinosis, Raynaud's phenomenon, oesophageal dysmotility, sclerodactyly and telangectasia. Associated features include: renal impairment, anaemia and pulmonary hypertension. The limited auto-antibody screen is unhelpful in this instance, but is a good example of how such tests can be misleading since RhF and ANA are not specific to any of the conditions listed above. At best the dual positivity would make mixed connective tissue disease least likely.

**Q.140 - Part 2 - Answer: 1**

ENA is a useful term when ordering an auto-antibody screen since it includes all of the following antigens and would help to distinguish between their associated disease:

- Anti-Scl70 :Diffuse scleroderma with limited involvement
- Anti-centromere: Limited scleroderma with systemic involvement - CREST
- Anti-Ro or Anti-La: Sjögren's syndrome
- Anti-Sm (or Smith): SLE
- Anti-histone: Drug-induced lupus
- Anti-Jo1: Polymyositis
- Anti-RNP (or ribonuclear protein): Mixed connective tissue disease or SLE

Option 2 is positive in Wegener's granulomatosis and other vasculitides. Options 4 and 5 may be useful for assessing nephropathy associated with connective tissue diseases.

**Q.141 - Answer: 4**

The triad of arthritis, conjunctivitis and urethritis points towards Reiter's disease or a reactive arthritis. It is one of the spondyloarthropathies and is associated with HLA-B27, not HLA-DR4, which is associated with rheumatoid arthritis. Recurrent or chronic disease can occur in up to 25% of cases, particularly in those who are HLA-B27 positive. This syndrome is triggered by infective agents, including Chlamydia trachomatis. Paul's exposure to a sexually transmitted infection is entirely speculative, since we do not know what he did on his travels with or without his partner; nor do we know whether she has been carrying Chlamydia or not herself. What we can say is that they did have reasonable exposure to enteric illnesses and since Yersinia, Shigella, Salmonella and Campylobacter are all associated with a reactive arthritis, Chlamydia is not the most likely to be the underlying cause. In reactive arthritis, joint aspirates are typically sterile and antibiotics do not lead to resolution of the condition. Steroids and other disease-modifying agents are used in some cases.

**Q.142 - Answer: 2**

In a patient with SLE, a raised CRP with other options being normal is suggestive of an intercurrent illness other than an SLE flare. Conversely, options 1, 2, 4 and 5 are all good indicators of a flare in SLE, even when the CRP remains normal.

**Q.143 - Answer: 1**

This combination of recurrent miscarriages, migraine either with neurological symptoms or possible cerebrovascular events and livedo reticularis (the 'net-like' rash) is suggestive of antiphospholipid syndrome. This condition occurs in association with or independently of SLE and involves the presence of autoantibodies and a tendency to recurrent arterial or venous thrombosis. As such, other manifestations of thrombosis, including myocardial infarction, stroke or deep vein thrombosis, can occur. Option 1 is likely to be the best to provide long-term prevention of serious complications.

**Q.144 - Answer: 3**

Pericardial or pleural effusions are examples of serositis, which are recognised features of other conditions, including rheumatoid arthritis. The malar or 'butterfly' rash is characteristic of SLE; however the nasolabial region is not involved. Option 3, also known as Jaccoud's arthropathy, is characteristic of SLE which, unlike rheumatoid arthritis, is a non-erosive arthropathy rather than arthritis per se. Uveitis is more commonly associated with seronegative spondyloarthropathies.

**Q.145 - Part 1 - Answer: 2**

The description is of proximal myalgia, a heliotrope rash on the face and Gottron's papules on the phalangeal extensors. This, along with a raised CK, is virtually diagnostic of dermatomyositis. While it is true that statins are associated with rhabdomyolysis, a cause of myalgia and a raised CK, the incidence is around 1 per 100,000 treatment years. Statin therapy would not account for all the other features that Mrs Goodman displays. Drugs can cause skin manifestations of lupus, although they tend to be different than here, and may also be secondary to drugs such as hydralazine or isoniazid. Hypothyroidism can cause a proximal myopathy but not the other features here. PMR also gives proximal myalgia; however the CK tends to be normal and again the other skin features do not occur.

**Q.145 - Part 2 - Answer: 1**

As already established, this is likely to be dermatomyositis, in which case a search for an underlying neoplasia is important. From the drug history, it is likely that she has chronic lung disease secondary to smoking and therefore a chest x-ray is an appropriate starting point for further investigation. Option 3 refers to the management of suspected giant cell arteritis. Physiotherapy may be a useful adjunctive treatment and one would consider dapsone rather than hydrocortisone cream for the skin lesions.

**Q.146 - Part 1 - Answer: 5**

The combination of abnormal bone growth (frontal bossing and iliac crest) and increasing chronic bone pain is consistent with Paget's disease. This is further supported by the warmth over the bone but even more by the laboratory and radiological findings. Normal electrolytes with a greatly raised ALP and abnormal trabecular pattern with bony expansion is practically pathognomic of Paget's disease. The joint space narrowing and osteophytes are an unsurprising incidental finding of osteoarthric changes in this person.

**Q.146 - Part 2 - Answer: 3**

Option 3 refers to the intra-epithelial spread of a ductal breast carcinoma also known as Paget's disease of the nipple. High output heart failure can result as high vascular flow through bone acts like arterio-venous shunting. Bony overgrowth of the skull can cause nerve compression and deafness. Osteosarcomas and pathological fractures are also recognised complications.

**Q.147 - Answer: 5**

The combinations of facial pain, worsened by mastication and touch and accompanied by visual symptoms, makes giant cell arteritis the most likely diagnosis here. Unilateral facial-head pain is a feature of all of the other options. Herpes zoster in immunocompetent patients is usually confined to one dermatome; however a wider distribution is described here. Furthermore, neither option 1 or 3 would involve visual disturbance.

**Q.148 - Part 1 - Answer: 4**

It is a relative reduction in oestrogen exposure (late menarche and early menopause) that increases the risk of osteoporosis. All the others are valid risk factors for osteopenia and osteoporosis.

**Q.148 - Part 2 - Answer: 3**

The BMD result can be considered in two different ways and these are called the T-score and Z-score. The BMD is compared against values for young normal adults of the same sex, to give a 'T-score', which in fact equates to the number of standard deviations (s.d.) from the mean for a 'young normal'. In other words, a T-score of 1 is 1 s.d. above the mean, and a T-score of 0 lies on the mean. This determines the fracture risk, which is higher the further BMD falls below 'young normal' levels.

The interpretation is as follows:

| | |
|---|---|
| T- score > 0 | BMD above the reference range - treatment not required |
| T- score 0 to -1 | BMD in the top quartile for females, no evidence of osteoporosis - treatment not required |
| T- score -1 to -2.5 | BMD is diagnostic of osteopenia - preventative measures should be considered |
| T- score <-2.5 | BMD is diagnostic of osteoporosis - treatment should be considered |

The Z-score compares the subject's BMD with that of an age- and size-matched population, but can be a little misleading in terms of actual fracture risk, as low BMD is common with increasing age.

**Q.149 - Answer: 1**

Musculoskeletal shoulder problems may appear fairly subspecialised to you as a junior doctor, but this is an area that you will face more frequently in primary care. For that reason, the options have been chosen to illustrate key learning points in alternative shoulder pathologies. The story of moderate trauma, with a gradual onset of pain on active or passive movement and even to pressure (in bed), points towards an adhesive capsulitis, also known as a frozen shoulder. A serratus anterior injury or long thoracic nerve palsy tends to give a painless winging of the scapula. The long head of biceps rupture results in retraction of the muscle bulk, forming a rounded subcutaneous mass that would obscure the contour of the upper arm and would not be associated with this type of pain on both active and passive shoulder abduction. The time-course and pain at rest is inconsistent with osteoarthritis. Supraspinatus is responsible for the first 15 degrees of abduction, beyond which active movement is achieved by other muscles. Pain on passive movement is unlikely in that case.

**Q.150 - Answer: 3**

As always, no presentation will be exactly 'textbook'; however the combination of features makes a meniscal or semilunar cartilage tear the most likely. Particular to this type of injury is trauma following adduction and internal rotation followed by lack of extension and poor function. All the other injuries tend to occur from blows or traction to or from that particular side (ant, post, med or lat) with resulting lack of joint stability from that side. Furthermore, ligament tears tend to give significant swelling and haemarthrosis with pain specifically over the region of that ligament. Meniscal tears classically give pain all around the joint margin.

**Q.151 - Answer: 2**

Spinal shock is the initial clinical phase after acute spinal cord injury. It is characterised by a flaccid paralysis, hypotension with no tachycardia and urinary retention. This is then followed by several stages where urinary and faecal continence are lost and a spastic paralysis, i.e. upper motor neurone pattern of damage, manifests.

**Q.152 - Answer: 4**

Firstly, the combination of a claw hand and loss of medial sensation in the hand should suggest ulnar nerve injury. Next, you have to remember the route of the ulnar nerve. It arises from the lower roots (C8 and T1) of the brachial plexus then passes by the medial epicondyle of the humerus, travels on the ulnar aspect of the forearm and passes through the ulnar tunnel (by the hamate and pisiform bones). This should clearly eliminate options 3 and 5. Finally you have to decide if this is a 'low' or distal nerve injury, i.e. below the elbow, or a 'high' proximal injury, at or above the level of the elbow. Low lesions damage the ulnar nerve after branches to the deep flexor muscles (Flexor digitorum profundus) have been given off. The result for the ring and little finger is flexion at the DIP joints from intact FDP unopposed by the paralysed lumbricals, leading to hyperextension at the MCP joints. In high lesions, the FDP is also paralysed and flexion at the DIP is lost, so marked clawing is not seen. Since options 1 and 2 are high lesions, 4 is the only possible answer.

## PAEDIATRICS

**Q.153 - Answer: 5**
Research evidence exists to support options 1, 2, 3, and 4. The government recommends vitamin D supplementation for those infants who are exclusively breastfed beyond 6 months of age. Vitamin D deficiency can occur prior to this in infants whose mothers are themselves vitamin D deficient. The infant usually has sufficient stores of vitamin D from fetal life to last for the first 8 weeks postnatally. Very brief exposure to sunlight is thought to help most babies generate adequate stores themselves. The BabyFriendly website (www.babyfriendly.org.uk) and La Leche League (www.llli.org) provide useful information about breastfeeding for parents and professionals.

**Q.154 - Answer: 3**
The baby is, in fact, relatively large-for-dates, the average weight at this gestation being 1.7kg. The other four conditions would be more likely to produce a small-for-dates or normal baby. Premature labour is more likely for women with any of the above conditions.

**Q.155 - Part 1 - Answer: 2**
This is a classic description of 'colic'. The cause is unknown and the most popular theory is that the crying behaviour is caused by abdominal discomfort due to trapped flatus, but this has not been definitively proven to be the cause. Around 20% of babies suffer with colic. Other causes of crying should be eliminated, such as the baby being overheated, in pain or suffering from an infection, or having nappy rash. Most parents will have searched for any such cause or explanation very thoroughly before bringing the problem to your attention. Less experienced or poorly-supported mothers

are likely to become more anxious about this problem and may require a great deal of reassurance. It is vital that serious conditions are excluded on the history and examination, but unless there is something unusual about the presentation, involvement of a paediatrician is the least appropriate action at this stage.

**Q.155 - Part 2 - Answer: 2**

The majority of cases of 'colic' can be alleviated by simple measures. These include carefully winding or 'burping' the baby after each feed, wrapping and comforting the baby, using sound or motion (e.g. a drive in the car) to soothe the baby, or considering adjusting the feeding position and type of equipment used to bottlefeed so that less air is gulped down with feeds. Bottlefed babies may do better on a different infant formula so it would be worth trying this as a next step if the above fails. There is no good evidence in favour of changing to soya milk nor for eliminating cow's milk from the mother's diet unless there genuine cow's milk allergy is very likely. In other words, a strong family history, or other features suggestive of an allergy. Stopping breastfeeding may well make colic worse as well as removing the benefits that the baby is receiving from this. Many parents will try non-prescription remedies such as 'gripe water' or homeopathic remedies. These are unlikely to be harmful to the baby but equally there is not much evidence to suggest that they are effective. Infacol® can be prescribed but the use of medication for colic is not the first-line approach.

**Q.156 - Answer: 4**

Harvey is likely to have pyloric stenosis. This typically presents at around 4 weeks and is commoner in male and first-born infants. There is usually a history of worsening vomiting, closely related to feed times, which becomes 'projectile' in nature. As the condition progresses, although the baby classically remains hungry, he tends to lose weight rapidly and become dehydrated, as less and less of the feed is absorbed. Babies can develop a hypochloraemic, hypokalaemic metabolic alkalosis if vomiting continues and this can be indicated from a blood gas measurement. The pyloric mass can usually be palpated in the right upper quadrant, particularly during a feed. A 'test feed' is carried out as this allows the clinician not only to palpate the abdomen for an olive-shaped mass (the pylorus) but also to witness whether the vomiting is genuinely projectile. However, the diagnosis must still be considered even if the test feed is negative and if necessary an ultrasound can be used to confirm the diagnosis. Barium studies are occasionally useful but an abdominal radiograph is not indicated in this case.

**Q.157 - Answer: 3**

Severe nappy rash should not spread beyond the margins of the nappy unless hygiene is very poor or there is superadded infection. Candidal superinfection will typically give an angry rash with small satellite lesions that are starting to spread beyond the nappy area. The classically-described whitish appearance to the lesions is often not seen, and the lesions can be eroded. It is important to check for Candida infection at other sites. Staphylococci and Streptococci can lead to superadded infection, which again would appear severe compared to normal nappy rash, with pronounced erythema, and often pustules or crusting will be seen. Acrodermatitis enteropathica is very rare indeed, and is caused by an autosomal recessive genetic defect in zinc absorption. There would typically be perioral involvement and the appearances are often very severe. The presentation given does not indicate specific flexural involvement and flexural psoriasis would tend to create large confluent areas of involvement rather than numerous small lesions. For eczema herpeticum, one would expect to see vesicular lesions. This can be a very serious condition and it is important to be aware of it, but the appearances here do not fit with it.

**Q.158 - Part 1 - Answer: 5**

Cystic fibrosis is included on neonatal screening, but there are so many possible mutations in the gene that plenty of children still go undetected. Cystic fibrosis could be considered in this case, but is not very likely, given that it affects >1:2000 children, the majority of whom would now be identified on neonatal heelprick screening tests. Affected children also tend to show failure-to-thrive and malabsorption from birth.

Glucose-galactose malabsorption causes severe and life-threatening diarrhoea from the time of introduction of milk feeds, and fructose is the only suitable carbohydrate for such children. This child is presenting too late to have this condition. Threadworm is unlikely to have taken hold by this early age, especially in a child who has little exposure to potential sources of infection in the form of other children. The symptoms would usually be less severe and furthermore offensive bulky stools are not typical for it. Late-onset lactase deficiency is very common in those from ethnic groups other than Northern Europeans. Lactase is not expressed beyond early childhood in these populations. However, the symptoms would not usually be so severe, and they would reveal themselves at 2 or 3 years of age or later, rather than in infancy. Coeliac disease is the best option. It is common in the UK, especially amongst those of Irish descent, and may occur in around 1 in 500 people. It typically presents in the under-twos following the introduction of the cereals which are a source of gluten. Gastrointestinal symptoms are not necessarily predominant and anaemia and buttock wasting are other clues to the diagnosis. Jejunal biopsy showing a flat mucosa, followed by symptomatic improvement on a gluten-free diet are diagnostic. A gluten rechallenge in later childhood is recommended for those diagnosed below 2 years of age.

**Q.158 - Part 2 - Answer: 4**

Buckwheat, corn, potatoes, tapioca and rice are some of the cereals considered safe for a gluten-free diet. Oats may be tolerated by some, but others do seem to react to them. Oats can also be cross-contaminated with other cereal products, so the advice is that for someone just starting out on a gluten-free diet, oats should initially be eliminated. Wheat, rye and barley should be excluded on a permanent basis. These cereals can lurk in all sorts of places where they are least expected, and are often used to thicken gravies, soups and sauces, coat meat and fish, and to add bulk to products such as sausages and reformed ham.

**Q.159 - Answer: 1**

There is a 90% chance that Shania's sample was a genuine urinary tract infection, providing it was collected correctly. Although it would be appropriate to ensure that a second clean-catch specimen is obtained and that this is done under optimal conditions, Shania will require investigation nonetheless, not only because there is as much as a 50% chance that she will have a structural abnormality, but also because the UTI itself may damage her kidneys, leading to scarring and hypertension in later life. All children with a proven first UTI should have a renal ultrasound to exclude structural abnormalities and hydronephrosis. The need for other scans is determined by the child's age, family history, recurrence of UTI, and whether any abnormalities are detected on the ultrasound. Local protocols will vary somewhat but the basic principles are the same. An abdominal radiograph can be appropriate in cases where renal stones or occult spinal abnormalities are suggested by the history or family history. A DMSA scan (static radioisotope scanning) shows renal scars and renal function, and is recommended for most cases, but is deferred for 3 months post-UTI for two reasons: firstly, scars (functional defects as a result of damaged renal tissue) often do not show up immediately; secondly, there can be false-positive results due to inflammation and temporary reflux when the DMSA scan is performed around the time of an infection. Micturating cystourethrograms and MAG-3 scans are used to identify reflux. MAG-3 is the investigation of choice in older children who are capable of passing urine on request, but an MCUG is necessary in those who are too young to do so.

**Q.160** - **Answer: 3**

Hypothyroidism can cause precocious puberty, not hyperthyroidism, which tends to delay puberty and menstruation. Short stature would be more likely but this would of course depend on how tall Fawzia was prior to the onset of the hypothyroidism, so actual height is not as useful as growth velocity in assessing this. Familial precocious puberty is the most likely cause. Fawzia's mother is of relatively short stature so it would be sensible to enquire as to her age at menarche, as despite Fawzia currently appearing tall for her age group, she is likely to be short as an adult, due to premature epiphyseal closure induced by the sex steroids.

A variety of intracranial pathologies can lead to central or gonadotrophin-dependent precocious puberty (LH and FSH both increased, LH greater than FSH). This usually leads to puberty occurring in the normal sequence. Gonadotrophin-independent causes are rare, and LH and FSH are low. For such cases, sex steroids are generated from a source other than through usual route of the hypothalamo-pituitary-adrenal axis e.g.: adrenal disorders, ovarian or testicular tumours, or intake of exogenous sex steroids. Pubertal changes can occur out-of-sequence in these cases, particularly with isolated pubic hair development and virilisation of the genitalia.

**Q.161** - **Answer: 3**

When you are seeing a person under 16 for contraceptive advice and the parents or guardians are not aware of the consultation, you need to follow the Fraser Guidelines to protect the child, but also yourself from a medico-legal viewpoint, should the young person or their family subsequently become dissatisfied with your actions and challenge them. The guidelines are that prior to contraceptive advice you must be sure that:

1. the young person has the capacity to understand the advice you are giving
2. they cannot be persuaded to involve their parents or guardians in the decision, nor to allow you to liaise with them on their behalf
3. the young person is likely to commence or continue intercourse even if you do not prescribe contraception
4. the young person's physical or mental health would be likely to suffer if you do not prescribe contraception
5. it is in the young person's best interests to receive contraceptive advice and/or treatment without parental consent

In essence it amounts to: capacity to understand risks and benefits, encouragement at least to ask parent-guardian involvement, and best interests of the patient i.e. prevent likely risk of unwanted pregnancy or physical-mental health by refusal to consult. For this reason option 3 is definitely a clause to opt out prescribing her the OCP since she is adamant that sexual activity is not imminent. You may still prescribe in anticipation of sexual activity but it is also defensible not to.

**Q.162 - Answer: 5**

All options can affect cystic fibrosis patients, including meconium ileus. However, this occurs within the first couple of days of life, so if Brandon were going to be affected, this would already have occurred. Around 10% of cases are detected when the child presents neonatally with bowel obstruction from meconium ileus. People with CF do remain vulnerable to distal intestinal obstruction due to thick secretions, but this is considered a 'meconium ileus equivalent'. Pneumothorax and diabetes are unfortunately common, and liver dysfunction is also significant in many patients, and can require liver transplantation. Infertility is essentially universal in male patients due to vas deferens defects. Standard IVF would not be appropriate but successful pregnancies have arisen from newer technologies whereby individual spermatozoa can be extracted from the testes and used for intra-cytoplasmic sperm injection (ICSI). Successful pregnancies are also increasing amongst young women with CF, though subfertility is the norm, and pregnancy and labour is hazardous for most, due to the cardiorespiratory strain involved.

**Q.163 - Answer: 4**

The onset of Hyperkinetic Disorder, according to the ICD-10 criteria, should be prior to 6 years of age, and although affected individuals may present to services much later than this, there should be evidence of difficulties stemming back to pre-school age.

Both impaired attention and overactivity are required for diagnosis. The disorder must manifest itself in more than one setting. Jordan's mother may tolerate a different type of behaviour or not realise what is age-inappropriate behaviour if she is, for example, under considerable strain for other reasons, has some impairments herself, or has little contact with or experience of other children. Schools and after-school activities find it easy to compare behaviour between peers and are often best-placed to detect these problems. The disorder is also most clearly manifest in situations where there are strict rules and standards of behaviour, even if these are carefully explained to the child, as the gulf between them and other children becomes more clearly accentuated.

Clumsiness, learning disability, and specific motor or language impairments or delays are relatively common in affected children. Other diagnoses must be considered, especially if there are any atypical features to the presentation; alternative diagnoses include agitated depression, organic causes, mania or psychosis if the onset is sudden in an older child, conduct disorder, or autistic spectrum disorder.

**Q.164 - Answer: 2**

DTP, killed polio, and HIB should be given at 2, 3 and 4 months. Men C is given at 3 and 4 months. Pneumococcal conjugate vaccine is given at 2 and 4 months. MMR is not due until 12-15 months. Marie should have been given BCG at birth, as the vaccination programme is now 'targeted' so that those in high-risk groups are immunised shortly after birth. These groups include those living in high prevalence areas, or whose parents come from a high-risk country. Very clear information is provided on the website www.immunisation.nhs.uk and it is important to keep up-to-date with the current guidelines, as there have been a number of changes recently (including to the BCG, polio, and pneumococcal vaccine recommendations), and the guidelines are constantly evolving.

**Q.165 - Answer: 4**

The pattern of rash described is typical of measles. There may be desquamation in the second week. Cases of measles are on the rise as herd immunity has fallen below critical levels in some areas of the country following adverse reports about the MMR vaccine. You are unlikely to have seen measles yourself, but it is vital to familiarise yourself with the clinical features through your reading and through clinical images, as it is a notifiable disease and you will need to have a high index of suspicion to identify a case from amongst numerous other presentations of viral illnesses. The rubella rash also starts on the head and spreads, but is described as pink dots under the skin that can spread and also desquamate. The rash of parvovirus B19 or fifth disease is often described as "slapped cheeks," with erythema across the cheeks and sparing the nasolabial folds, mouth and forehead. Parvovirus B19 can also give 'lace-like' rashes on the limbs and trunk. Scarlet fever tends to give multiple individual red macules that blanche with finger pressure rather than a confluent rash as seen with measles. Coxsackie virus can cause blistering as well as itchy painful rashes.

**Q.166 - Answer: 1**

Although only 8 in 1000 children have congenital cardiac abnormalities, around 1 in 3 children have a murmur at some point during their lives, so the vast majority are innocent murmurs. Innocent murmurs should have the following features:

1. The child is otherwise well and growing and feeding appropriately (both the total volume and the time taken to feed are important in infants – 40 minutes would be a long time for a 6-week-old bottlefed infant, and could suggest the infant is tired and needing to rest during the feed, which inexperienced parents may not necessarily identify as a problem)
2. localised to the left sternal edge
3. heard only in systole
4. no radiation, no heaves or thrills
5. undisplaced apex beat (4th-5th intercostal space in the midclavicular line)
6. no added heart sounds, normal character of heart sounds

There are two main types of innocent murmur: ejection mumurs and venous hum. Ejection murmurs are generated by turbulent flow but there is no structural abnormality. These may be heard as soft, blowing systolic murmurs in the 2nd left intercostal space when generated by the right side of the heart (pulmonary flow), or as in option 1, a short buzzing murmurs in the 4th left intercostal space when generated by the left side of the heart (aortic flow). A venous hum results from turbulent flow as well, but originates from the veins of the head and neck. It is a rumbling, low-pitched murmur that is heard beneath the clavicle on either side. It is accentuated by exercise and by inspiration, and disappears with ipsilateral jugular compression or on lying flat. Innocent murmurs may be picked up for the first time during a febrile illness, as cadiac output increases. Although option 5 suggests increasing intensity on exercise, this is true of pathological and innocent murmurs alike and cannot exclude the possibility of pathology.

**Q.167 - Answer: 3**

Most cases of congenital heart disease are non-cyanotic, for example, ventricular septal defects represent a third of the total cases. The most common cyanotic heart conditions are Tetralogy of Fallot (6%) and transposition of the great arteries (5%). These can both cause neonatal cyanosis, as can pulmonary atresia, tricuspid atresia, and total anomalous pulmonary venous drainage (TAPVD). Cyanosis can occur as a result of reduced or duct-dependent pulmonary circulation (Fallot's, and pulmonary and tricuspid atresias), or as a result of abnormal mixing of circulations, with blood that has already circulated around the lungs mostly recirculating rather than being diverted to the body (transposition of the great arteries and TAPVD). Abnormal mixing also occurs in septal defects but the proportion of deoxygenated blood returning to the systemic circulation is less and is not sufficient to cause cyanosis, as enough oxygenated blood is still passing to the systemic circulation. Pulmonary stenosis does reduce the blood flow to the lungs but not completely as in pulmonary atresia which is a cyanotic heart condition. It can seem very daunting to learn about the above, but in fact it is not difficult to work out from first principles whether or not a particular condition will cause cyanosis, as long as you understand the direction of flow in the defect, and therefore how much chance there is of the blood being successfully oxygenated before being returned to the systemic circulation. With a little practice, you'll be pleasantly surprised how you nearly always get it right without having to learn anything by rote!

**Q.168 - Answer: 3**

Abdul should receive fluid resuscitation and antibiotics as a priority before you consider performing a lumbar puncture (LP), as although this investigation is important in guiding his treatment, it will not make an immediate contribution to reducing his morbidity and mortality, and in fact could increase it if not carried out at an appropriate point in his care pathway. Abdul may remain relatively hypotensive due to sepsis, and of course this must be optimally managed in an ITU setting if severe, but if mild and stable then it is not in itself an absolute contraindication to LP. Options 4, 5 and 1 (a low heart rate in the context of sepsis at this age) are suggestive of raised intracranial pressure, which of course is an absolute contraindication to LP. The AVPU scale for assessing consciousness (Alert, responds to Voice, responds to Pain, Unresponsive) is used in pre-verbal children instead of the Glasgow Coma Scale. If Abdul has thrombocytopenia or a coagulopathy, then a LP will again serve to increase his risk of morbidity and mortality rather than reduce it. It is important to ensure that clotting function is normal or corrected before performing this investigation. Note that useful information can still be obtained from the LP even if it is taken a considerable time after administering antibiotics.

**Q.169 - Answer: 1**

The others are compatible with mild-moderate dehydration, though would also be present and more pronounced in more severe dehydration. The fontanelle and eyes appearing more than very slightly sunken are relatively late signs in dehydration, and usually by this stage the child is too drowsy and weak for oral rehydration to be successful. Oral rehydration does require understanding, patience and persistence on the part of the attending parent, who may themselves be exhausted or unwell. However, it is the safest and least traumatic option for a mildly dehydrated child (5% or less), and parents should be encouraged to persist and given an appropriate explanation as to why a 'drip' is not being used, as they often see this as a better treatment option. Most moderately dehydrated children can also attempt oral rehydration initially, but require careful monitoring to ensure that there is improvement in their fluid status, and consideration of the use of intravenous fluid if the clinical picture is not soon changing for the better. Children who are severely dehydrated (>10%) require intravenous rehydration with careful and regular reassessment of fluid status and monitoring of the urea and electrolytes and urine output.

**Q.170 - Answer: 5**

There is considerable variation in the 'normal' timing of achievement of developmental milestones. The standard times we all learn carefully are medians, and are all very well in theory, but in fact 50% of all children will acquire the skill after the standard age, and of course very few of these have genuinely delayed development. This is why it can be more helpful, as a practising doctor, to think in terms of warning signs that represent a cut-off point by which the significant majority of normal children could be expected to have acquired a particular skill. These warning times can be used to determine when referral to a developmental specialist is appropriate. Some children will be 'normal' even if they go beyond the warning times, as periods of illness, separation from a caregiver, unsettled domestic environment, or different patterns of development (eg bottom-shufflers and commando crawlers walk later but are not 'slow developers' overall), can all lead to a temporary delay in skill acquisition. Bola should be sitting unsupported by 9 months of age, the median age being 6 months. All the other options suggest a delay in development.

You probably had enough trouble learning the milestones in the first place so will not relish the prospect of being expected to remember warning times as well. Fortunately, most of them are exactly 50% longer than the 'expected' times, so this gives you a fair shot at a correct answer. You can memorise the few that do not quite fit this pattern, e.g. no social smiling by 8 weeks, easily enough.

**Q.171 - Answer: 2**

Yee Sook is performing at approximately the 8-month level in all areas. It may seem difficult to identify this precisely, as some rather less common measures of development have been used to describe her progress, but you can eliminate the other options easily enough. She would normally cruise at around 10 months, and would sit for prolonged periods by 9 months – these are quite well-known markers, so you can identify that her gross motor is less than this. Pincer grip also emerges at 9 months, and she cannot yet do this. She is beyond the six-month stage as she would not normally use consonants in her babble at that stage, and she would not long have started solid food, so would not be finger-feeding yet.

## PHARMACOLOGY / THERAPEUTICS

**Q.172 - Answer: 2**

Constipation is a common side effect of opioid analgesia especially in the elderly and, while some laxatives work well for some, they can themselves be troublesome in others. Ispaghula husk, also known as Fybogel ®, is used by many to increase fibre, but can increase bowel gas and bloating, which are problems she has already raised. Besides, she has already had little luck with increasing fibre in the diet. Senna is a stimulant laxative and her complaints of cramping pains are well-recognised. Lactulose® and Movicol® are osmotic laxatives that act by drawing fluid into the bowel and which can help to bulk out and ease the passage of stool. Out of the two, lactulose is particularly associated with excess flatus and bloating and so Movicol ® would be the preferred option. Glycerine suppositories are gentler than the more powerful enemas; however, their action tends to be limited to the rectum and there is evidence here of constipation higher up. Sodium picosulfate, also known as Picolax®, produces a strong irritant reaction and is used as a pre-procedure bowel 'prep'. This may be an unwise first choice given that there are other more suitable options available at this stage.

**Q.173 - Answer: 4**

Although not the most common side effect, angioedema is a well-recognised complication of angiotensin converting enzyme (ACE) inhibitor therapy. Vertigo refers to the abnormal sensation of movement, which suggests vestibular pathology rather than the dizziness from postural hypotension that is commonly experienced with ACE inhibitors. The cough of ramipril is dry, not productive.

**Q.174 - Answer: 5**

It is likely that she has a urinary tract infection (UTI) Metronidazole treats anaerobic infections and is less useful against the range of possible UTI organisms. Cephalexin does have good activity against the likely causes of a UTI and is the only other drug that is safe to use in pregnancy.

**Q.175 - Answer: 2**

All of the agents have some activity against upper respiratory tract pathogens. Ampicillin is absolutely contraindicated in someone with a penicillin allergy. Cephalexin is a cephalosporin and therefore has a 10% chance of causing a reaction in those who have a known penicillin allergy. However, in some circumstances, a cephalosporin may be given – if there were no other feasible alternatives, the history of allergy was weak, premedication with an antihistamine is given, and the patient is in a controlled environment such as being an inpatient where emergency drugs are at hand. Doxycycline is absolutely contraindicated since it can enter breast milk and will interfere with bone and teeth growth. Erythromycin, if taken by the mother, will be present in small quantities in breast milk, but is not known to be harmful in the context of breastfeeding. Likewise, clarithromycin will also transfer into breast milk and has been used in children; the manufacturers instructions indicate that it should only be used when no other better option is at hand and the benefits outweigh the potential risks. This therefore makes erythromycin the best option.

**Q.176 - Answer: 1**

Other indications include: poliomyelitis, severe pelvic injury, spinal cord injury, spina bifida, dialysis for renal failure, prostatectomy/radical prostate surgery, kidney transplant and severe distress. This distress has to be assessed by a specialist and includes features such as severe disruption to work, social or personal relationships.

**Q.177 - Answer: 3**

Bisphophonates must be taken on an empty stomach and definitely separated in time from the ingestion of any calcium or iron-containing products. They can cause oesophageal irritation and so taking the tablets with a full glass of water then remaining upright for 30 minutes afterwards is advised.

**Q.178 - Answer: 1**

Carbimazole is associated with agranulocytosis and neutropenia with sepsis and so clinicians are advised to look out for warning signs such as described in the case. If there is any possibility of neutropenia, the drug should be stopped immediately and an urgent white cell count performed.

**Q.179 - Answer: 5**

Interactions with alcohol vary according to which antibiotic is taken. Some clinicians express concerns over alcohol affecting the liver metabolism of antibiotics thereby affecting efficacy or toxicity of the drug. A small amount of alcohol may have very little problem with some regimens. Other clinicans claim that abstinence is the best policy since the patient may have a clearer mind to adhere to the treatment course. All that said and done, even a small amount of alcohol can produce a very unpleasant 'disulfiram-like' reaction when metronidazole is taken and a kind doctor may do well to warn their patients of it.

**Q.180 - Answer: 5**

Aminoglycosides are associated with damage to the vestibulo-cochlear system i.e. giving deafness, vertigo and/or tinnitus. The effects tend to be dose-related, and hence vary depending on which aminoglycoside is given, its dose and duration of therapy. In the UK this patient would be unlikely to have been given streptomycin unless he was extremely unwell, or isoniazid resistance had been established prior to the initial phase of treatment (usual initial phase is 2 months of isoniazid, rifampicin, ethambutol and pyrazinamide; continuation phase is 4 months of isoniazid and rifampicin).

**Q.181 - Answer: 1**

Buproprion can be given on the NHS to those who show a commitment to stop smoking. They must have a target stop date in mind before they can commence therapy. Failure to give up on therapy is not a complete contraindication to recommence at a later date, although practice is usually not to fund a further attempt until 6 months after the first trial and with evidence of continuing commitment to give up. Medical contraindications to buproprion include a history of eating disorder, CNS tumour, seizures, or drugs or conditions that lower the seizure threshold (ciprofloxacin can do this). It is also contraindicated in pregnancy and breast feeding.

**Q.182 - Answer: 2**

All of the choices above can be used for treating nausea. Options 3 and 4 tend to be reserved for drug-induced or particularly cytotoxic drug-induced nausea and vomiting. Nausea and vomiting during diabetic ketoacidosis is partly related to the metabolic acidosis but also to gastroparesis. Metoclopramide is a prokinetic agent and is thereby thought to be of benefit not only by a direct action on the gut but additionally by enhancing gastric emptying.

**Q.183** - **Answer: 3**

All of the options are recognised side effects whilst a patient is taking steroids, except option 3, which is a feature of adrenal suppression and can occur during steroid withdrawal. Steroids would commonly cause hypertension.

**Q.184 - Part 1** - **Answer: 5**

For artificial valves and other indications for warfarin therapy, there are subtle variations between clinicians on target INRs depending on age and risk of stroke, as well as the type of valve in situ. Generally around 3.0 is recommended for aortic valves and 3.5 for mitral valves, but specific guidance is available if the valve type is known.

**Q.184 - Part 2** - **Answer: 2**

Ciprofloxacin can cause inhibition of the liver p450 enzyme system leading to reduced metabolism of warfarin and hence enhanced anticoagulant effect. Rifampacin is a p450 enzyme inducer and so leads to increased metabolism of warfarin and hence a reduced anticoagulant effect. Macrolides such as clarythromycin have also been listed as p450 inhibitors but data on azythromycin is scarce.

**Q.185** - **Answer: 3**

With an INR under 8 and no signs or symptoms of bleeding, the next warfarin dose can be omitted or discontinued until an INR < 5 is reached. With an INR>8, in addition to stopping the warfarin, oral vitamin K is given if there are indications of possible risks of bleeding. Vitamin K may also be administered if there were particular risks of bleeding with an INR less than 8. If there are features of major bleeding at any level of abnormally elevated INR, then fresh frozen plasma or Factor VII and IX concentrates and intravenous vitamin K (5mg) is indicated, and urgent liaison with the haematologist would be appropriate.

**Q.186** - **Answer: 4**

This may be a controversial question since no doubt local practices vary, partly by protocol and partly by anecdote, but the reasoning behind the choice given here should at least teach several lessons about opioid analgesics. A clear and comprehensive summary can be found in British National Formulary and is worth a read. The reasoning here is to give this patient an effective step up in pain control whilst minimising side effects. Co-proxamol is dextropropoxyphene in combination with paracetamol which has been reported to give minimal extra benefit than paracetamol itself and has as such been removed from many formularies. Co-codamol is paracetamol with codeine phosphate. (8/500) refers to 8 mg of codeine per 500g of paracetamol, hence maximum of 64mg a day, which gives little extra analgesia for noticeble side effects of nausea and constipation. Options 3 and 5 are opioids of comparable grade, although co-dydramol is by weight more potent. Tramadol offers as good efficacy as these drugs; however it is known to have less opioid side effects including less respiratory depression. Finally non-co-formulated drugs may prove a better option since they can be dose titrated independently of the paracetamol component, thereby avoiding paracetamol overdose and allowing for higher doses than the paracetamol would otherwise restrict them to.

**Q.187 - Answer: 2**

Spacer devices remove the need for co-ordination between actuation of a metered-dose inhaler and inhalation of the drug and so are useful for children and adults. They allow dispersal of the propellant together with the drug and extra time for the patient to be able to inhale as much as possible of the drug dose delivered by the inhaler. This reduces the risk that the drug just hits the back of the oropharynx, which, in the case of steroids, can lead to oral candidiasis. Spacer devices should be cleaned approximately monthly and changed every 6 to 12 months. After cleaning with a simple detergent, they should be rinsed then left to air dry. They should never be wiped dry since it can create an electrostatic charge that will then attract drug particles, reducing effective drug delivery to the patient.

**Q.188 - Answer: 4**

Microgynon® is a very common combined oral contraceptive. Carbamazepine is a potent inducer of the p450 liver enzyme system that can reduce the effect of this contraceptive.

**Q.189 - Answer: 4**

Amiodarone contains iodine and can cause hyper or hypothyroidism. Like many antiarrhythmics it can induce an arrythmia. Yellow vision is a side effect of digoxin therapy.

**Q.190 - Answer: 1**

Digoxin is a cardiac glycoside acting via the sodium-potassium ATPase. It competes with potassium on this enzyme and so hypokalaemia can lead to toxic effects of the drug. Bumetanide is a loop diuretic that can lead to potassium wasting and so affect digoxin in this way. Spironolactone is a potassium-sparing diuretic, therefore, if anything, it would reduce the effects of digoxin. Quinine and calcium antagonists can interfere with tubular elimination of digoxin and amiodarone is known to displace digoxin from tissue binding sites thereby leading to toxicity.

**Q.191 - Answer: 5**

One approach to hypertension is the 'ABCD' rule, i.e. ACE inhibitor, beta blocker, calcium channel antagonist and diuretic. Start on one drug from dual group A-B if young, or if older, start with a drug from dual group C-D. If this fails after long enough follow-up, then add one from the other dual group. The exception is that black people tend to react better if starting with the C-D group, regardless of age. This leaves options 4 or 5 open to Charles. Since nifedipine, a calcium channel antagonist, is associated with ankle oedema, the best option of those above is bumetanide in the first instance.

**Q.192 - Answer: 2**

Psychosis is an effect of toxicity, typically when lithium levels exceed 2 mmol/L. The safe therapeutic range of lithium is between 0.4 and 1.0 mmol/L. In this range, all of the other options are commonly-noted side-effects. The polydipsia is accompanied by polyuria and is due to lithium competition with ADH at the collecting ducts, creating a mild nephrogenic diabetes insipidus.

**Q.193 - Answer: 2**

Hyoscine is used for muscle spasms in IBS, but it is hyoscine butylbromide or Buscopan ®. Hyoscine hydrobromide is the type of hyoscine that often accompanies morphine in a syringe driver to reduce respiratory secretions in palliative care patients. Ispaghula is also known as Fybogel ® and can help with constipation. Peppermint oil and mebeverine also help with abdominal cramps.

**Q.194 - Answer: 4**

All the options are correct except number 4. This information must be stated but, like options 2 to 5, it must be in the prescriber's handwriting.

**Q.195 - Answer: 3**

Levels are not taken to monitor olanzapine, although it is very important to monitor potential metabolic side effects of olanzapine, and patients taking this drug should have regular checks of their blood pressure, blood glucose, cholesterol and weight. There isn't much robust evidence indicating what levels of sodium valproate should be regarded as therapeutic for treatment for, or prophylaxis of, bipolar relapses. However sodium valproate levels are monitored at times in psychiatry when there are concerns about dose adequacy or compliance. The accepted therapeutic levels may vary slightly between clinicians.

**Q.196 - Answer: 3**

This is likely to be a case of neuroleptic malignant syndrome, characterised by hyperpyrexia, confusions, muscle rigidity and deranged white cell count and biochemistry; transaminases are typically raised, and a grossly elevated Creatine Kinase is highly suggestive of this diagnosis. Myoglobinuria is also seen and 'coca-cola urine' can be observed. NMS has a high mortality (up to 20%) and patients generally require at least High Dependency Unit care, and often intensive care. Dantrolene has been shown to reduce temperature in cases of hyperpyrexia (often anaesthesic-associated). Dothiepin is a tricyclic antidepressant and so may make sedation and neurocardiac side-effects worse. Likewise, diazepam, despite being useful for any convulsions, would be inferior to dantrolene in treating the underlying problem, but it can be a useful adjunct in managing the patient's agitation whilst antipsychotics have to be withheld. Donepezil is a drug used in dementia care and has no role here. Doxapram is a respiratory stimulant used in those with respiratory failure and is not appropriate at this point.

**Q.197 - Answer: 3**

Co-amoxiclav or Augmentin® is a well-recognised cause of cholestasis, and since it is such a commonly prescribed drug, this side effect is worth remembering. Pyrazinamide does cause liver dysfunction but this is more of a hepatitis than cholestasis. Erythromycin is also associated with an idiosyncratic hepatitis that can lead to cholestasis.

**Q.198 - Answer: 5**

The specific alterations in drug dose can be fairly individualised in renal impairment; however, general principles can be found in the British National Formulary. Many drugs may be affected to some degree in renal impairment. The clearance of metronidazole is not dependent on renal function, unlike the other drugs listed here. In particular, accumulation of these other drugs can occur in renal failure, leading to signs of toxicity.

**Q.199 - Part 1 - Answer: 3**

Diagnoses in psychiatry may not be as clear cut as we would like them to be. Despite classification systems, many patients with psychiatric conditions may exhibit features of more than one disease. For example, a patient with severe depression may have hallucinations or delusions which are psychotic symptoms. In an attempt to clarify the diagnosis of schizophrenia, the 'first rank' symptoms were listed by Schneider, but are not the actual diagnostic criteria for the condition. In actual fact, a quarter of patients believed to have schizophrenia may not have first-rank symptoms and furthermore at least 10% of manic patients may also exhibit these features. Option 1 is a grandiose delusion that is most suggestive of mania. Option 2 is an aspect of any confusional state, and those with schizophrenia should not be disorientated in time or place unless there is some other concurrent pathology. Option 4 is an aspect of frontal lobe pathology, and although there is some mild frontal impairment in schizophrenia, if this were prominent it would be suggestive of alternative diagnoses. Option 5 is a visual hallucination which can occur in many states including organic delirium, and these are much less common than auditory hallucinations in schizophrenia, although hallucinatory experiences can occur in any modality. Option 3 can also be termed a third person auditory hallucination which is a first-rank symptom.

**Q.199 - Part 2 - Answer: 3**

Features of poor prognosis include male sex, social isolation, insidious onset, substance misuse, premorbid personality disorder, onset under age 25 and absence of mood disturbance. The last point involves absent affective response (flat or blunted affect) or inappropriate (incongruent) response to the situation e.g. laughing when being told bad news.

**Q.200 - Answer: 1**

Olanzapine is an atypical antipsychotic. There is some evidence to suggest particular efficacy over the negative symptoms of schizophrenia as described in this case, but this area does remain controversial.

**Q.201 - Answer: 2**

Many of the features of anorexia nervosa (AN) are shared with bulimia nervosa (BN), including preoccupation with weight - whether that be a distorted body image (AN) or the need to purge after food binges (BN), weight reducing strategies such as laxative abuse, vomiting or excessive exercise. Menstrual disturbance is also common. With BN however, there is a craving for food, which leads to binges, after which a feeling of disgust is followed by actions to counteract the calorie intake. As a result, the weight may fluctuate and the sufferer may be underweight, overweight or of normal weight. With AN, the preoccupation is with weight loss, and an abnormally low BMI is required for diagnosis – the criteria are < 85% of normal body weight or having a BMI < 17.5 kg/m$^2$.

**Q.202 - Answer: 3**
In some cases, it may at first be difficult to distinguish dementia from delirium. However, the key is that delirium is an acute confusional state and there is clouding of consciousness. Options 1, 2 and 5 may be seen in delirium but can also occur in dementia. The combination of drowsiness, poor attention, disorientation with abnormal perceptions is more suggestive of delirium.

**Q.203 - Answer: 4**
Alzheimer's dementia can be thought of as a global progressive dementia in comparison to a vascular or multi-infarct cause which is characterised by step-by-step patchy loss of cognitive function on the background of cardio- or cerebro-vascular disease. Insight is typically lost earlier in Alzheimer's disease compared to vascular dementia. All the other options are more typical features of vascular dementia.

**Q.204 - Answer: 2**
Acute intermittent porphyria can give acute episodes of delirium and psychosis which would alter cognitive function. However, this isn't a long-term cognitive deficit. All the other options have cognitive impairment as a more prominent feature.

**Q.205 - Answer: 3**
The onset of an acute confusional state, with vivid visual and/or tactile hallucinations, pyrexia and tremors three days after admission is suggestive of delirium tremens. This is a syndrome of autonomic overactivity and psychosis that presents up to 4 days after alcohol withdrawal. A GABAergic sedative such as chlordiazepoxide is a good therapeutic option. Phenothiazines e.g. chlorpromazine should be avoided since they may precipitate seizures. Haloperidol could be used if required, but the symptoms are usually best managed with reducing dose regimen of chlordiazepoxide or diazepam titrated carefully against the response.

**Q.206 - Answer: 4**

Option 4 is the 'G' of the CAGE screening assessment that also includes: feeling a need to Cut down, Annoyance when someone mentions their need to reduce alcohol and the need for an Eye-opener or an early morning drink. Incidentally this overlaps with option 1 which refers to relief drinking. CAGE is a screening questionnaire only and does not have diagnostic value – the ICD-10 criteria for alcohol dependence are used. The alcohol dependence syndrome is characterised by those other options as well as a compulsion to drink alcohol, alcohol consumption taking precedence over other activities, and the developed of a narrow repertoire and stereotyped pattern of drinking.

**Q.207 - Part 1 - Answer: 4**

Confabulation is the phenomenon whereby a patient with poor memory attempts to cover up the memory deficit by inventing answers to questions (they are not necessarily aware that these answers are untrue). For example if asked what they had for breakfast, they would say "cornflakes and milk" rather than admitting that they couldn't remember. It is a feature that goes along with the memory loss that forms Korsakoff syndrome. This syndrome is a chronic state, usually evolving from a state of acute thiamine deficiency as in Wernicke's encephalopathy. The precise subcellular pathology remains to be elucidated but there is evidence of brainstem and cerebellar damage. All the other options are the true features of Wernicke's.

**Q.207 - Part 2 - Answer: 3**

Persistent vomiting in pregnancy is a rare but well-recognised association with thiamine deficiency and Wernicke's encephalopathy. A gastrinoma leads to peptic ulceration. Pancreatitis can lead to malabsorption but thiamine deficiency is not significant enough to lead to Wernicke's. Pernicious anaemia involves failure to absorb B12, not thiamine (B1).

**Q.208 - Answer: 3**

It can be difficult to distinguish mania from hypomania, since they lie on a spectrum. Hypomania is characterised by someone who has an elevated mood, extra energy and 'zest'. They can have poor concentration and be irritable at times, they may be a little reckless but in contrast to mania, they may have some degree of insight or restraint and may be able to continue with work and social relationships despite some difficulties being evident. Mania, however, goes one step further and refers to patients whose actions or behaviours are too extreme to be compatible with daily living. So option 1 refers to an overvalued idea rather than a delusion. Option 2 relates to elevated mood. Option 4 relates to increased energy. Option 5 would not necessarily be of any significance. However the overspending is a sign that things have got out of proportion, the patient is manic and is very likely to lack insight into their behaviours and the consequences of their actions. It is also a sign that she is unwell enough to put her well-being at risk and there is a strong possibility that she would take other risks, such as driving hazardously, or engaging in sexual relationships she would not normally engage in.

**Q.209 - Answer: 4**

A delusional perception is a false belief that a particular experience which has been observed or sensed signifies the advent of a particular consequence. There should be no logical or culturally-accepted link between the perception and the anticipated consequence, or broader meaning attached to the perception, in order for it to be a true delusional perception.

It is important to understand Liam's cultural, social and religious background in order to be able to assess his beliefs and perceptions and whether they represent genuine psychotic experiences. 1 and 2 are superstitions and are not outside the bounds of British culture, although they are not logical beliefs. 3 and 5 are also culturally-acceptable beliefs which are widely held in Britain amongst persons of a variety of religions.

**Q.210 - Answer: 1**

Option 1 is a guilt-based cognition held with delusional intensity. This therefore signifies a psychotic depression has developed, which would move depression into the 'severe' category. Options 2, 3 and 4 are biological features which can occur at any stage of the spectrum from mild to severe depression. The degree and number of biological and cognitive features determine where the episode should be classified along this spectrum. Option 5 is an example of anhedonia or inability to derive pleasure from previously pleasurable experiences or activities. This feature can occur in depression of any degree of severity.

**Q.211 - Answer: 3**

Option 3 reflects some of the lack of insight that patients with dementia exhibit. All the other options are features more typical of cognitive impairment related to depression or 'pseudo dementia'. However, it is important to bear in mind that depressive features are common in the early stages of dementing illnesses, and although it is of course important to treat the depression, one must ensure that there has been a corresponding improvement on cognitive testing and that this improvement is sustained over the following months.

**Q.212 - Answer: 2**

Catatonia can be an indication for ECT rather than being a consequence. NICE guidelines agree that it may also be used in severe mania, patients with ongoing very high suicide risk, and patients refusing food and fluids. All the other options have been reported, although fractures and dislocations are rare nowadays as muscle relaxants are used and the actual physical manifestations of the brain's seizure activity are actually minimal.Short-term memory problems (anterograde and retrograde) around the time of administration are common, but it seems likely that a minority of patients are also affected by the loss of some specific episodes and information from long-term semantic memory, and patients should be advised of this before undergoing the treatment.

**Q.213 - Answer: 1**

This patient is experiencing specific physical symptoms with no medical explanation for more than 6 months. Dissociative disorder or conversion disorder involves an abnormality (usually loss) of a specific bodily function e.g. movement of a limb. The patient may exhibit an absence of concern for this loss of function. Somatisation is partly a diagnosis of exclusion, but the symptoms should be in several different bodily systems to meet the diagnostic criteria. Hypochondriasis is also a somatoform disorder, however the patient will be fixated on the idea that they have a disease in particular (usually serious and potentially life-threatening e.g. a cancer) rather than just a set of symptoms, and they will not be reassured by investigations. A factitious disorder or malingering involves the presentation of symptoms with the aim by the patient to gain something by it e.g. attention, support or financial assistance.This man has apparently little to gain by persisting in 'making up' symptoms since he loses out financially and personally with his wife. Patients with hypochondriasis, somatisation and factitious disorder will typically 'shop around' for different opinions and investigations. Post-traumatic stress disorder could certainly have arisen after an event such as witnessing a bank robbery, but the patient would be expected to have at least some symptoms from hypervigilance, emotional numbing, avoidance of reminders of the situation, flashbacks, nightmares and often anxiety and depressive features.

**Q.214 - Answer: 3**

All options except number 3 are characteristics of an obsession. To be true, option 3 should state that to the patient it is thought of as absurd and as a product of their own mind. This is important because it is what defines it as being a neurosis, i.e. insight is preserved, rather than a delusion, which is a symptom of psychosis.

**Q.215 - Answer: 1**

Agoraphobia is not the fear of open spaces per se. It is the anxiety associated with situations where there are lots of people and the subject feels it may be difficult to escape. This may manifest as a panic attack, and agoraphobia is often co-existent with panic disorder. However, Jemima has not suffered panic attacks at home or in other contexts as far as we can tell. Panic disorder on its own is characterised by recurrent panic attacks or episodes of severe anxiety which are triggered by fear of the attacks themselves rather than any situational trigger. Social phobia is an extreme shyness related to lack of self-esteem that leads to social withdrawal. It is more often the case of someone who avoids socialising with others because of fear of negative judgements of others rather than being trapped with no escape. Generalised anxiety as the name implies is a persistent state of free-floating anxiety that is not closely associated with a specific situation, although it will be worse in some contexts than others.

**Q.216 - Part 1 - Answer: 4**

Homonymous means that both eyes are seeing the same hemianopia. Left eye blindness broadly implies a problem from the eye and the optic nerve anterior to the optic chiasm. Option 2 refers to a lesion at the chiasm e.g. from a pituitary tumour. Option 5 would occur mainly with a retinal vascular occlusion or retinal pathology affecting only part of one field of vision.

**Q.216 - Part 2 - Answer: 3**

Two vertebral arteries join to form the basilar artery, which gives off branches to the cerebellum before the two posterior cerebral arteries, which anastamose with the anterior portion of the circle of Willis. The posterior cerebral arteries supply the occipital lobes. This is the site of the visual cortex which, when damaged, leads to homonymous hemianopias. Although options 1 and 2 feed into this posterior supply, if they were occluded one would have expected far more wide-ranging deficits, in particular in the cerebellum. The anterior cerebral artery supplies the anterior portion of the medial aspect of the cerebral hemisphere, whereas the middle cerebral

artery feeds the lateral aspect. Both of these arteries are derived from the internal carotid arteries and form the anterior portion of the circle of Willis.

**Q.217 - Answer: 4**
The presence of delusions make this a clear-cut case of puerperal psychosis rather than post natal depression. Psychotic depression can develop postnatally but this would not be a typical time-course. Puerperal psychosis usually occurs between a few days and 4 weeks after the baby's birth. Treatment with antipsychotics, mood-stabilisers and benzodiazepines can be very successful, and ideally the mother should be admitted with her child to a mother-and-baby unit, though spaces are scarce. Management at home as in the first two options would involve unacceptable risks to the health and safety of the mother and baby.

**Q.218 - Answer: 5**
This scenario describes apraxias and acalculia which are features of a lesion in the dominant parietal lobes. The dominant parietal lobe lesions also lead to agraphia, inability to read, visiospatial neglect and inferior visual quadrantanopias. The frontal lobe lesions cause abnormal behaviours due to disinhibition, failure to plan and 'execute' activities, expressive dysphasia and anosmia. Temporal lobe lesions lead to: receptive dysphasia, auditory agnosia, emotional disturbances, memory impairment and cortical deafness as well as superior visual quadrantanopias.

**Q.219 - Part 1 - Answer: 4**
The patient exhibits a combination of a flaccid paralysis, urinary retention and upgoing plantar responses with an upper lumbar sensory level. This translates to mixed upper and lower motor neuron, bladder and sensory deficit. This should eliminate options 1, 2 and 3 because of the symmetry and the extensive lower motor neuron involvement. In fact, this mixed pattern is typical of a conus medullaris lesion. This is the region in which the caudal spinal cord tapers off into the distal lower motor neurone roots of the cauda equina. So, at any point in this upturned 'cone', you have upper and lower motor nerves. A lesion to the cauda would behave like a lesion to a bundle of lower motor and sensory nerves; therefore no upgoing plantars would be seen and a more distal loss would be exhibited.

**Q.219 - Part 2 - Answer: 3**
As previously discussed, this is not a cerebral lesion and so options 1 and 2 are futile. The question asked for the best investigation rather than the most appropriate or readily available option. That being the case an MRI is the

best imaging modality here. Although we discussed the site of the lesion earlier, this may also have been 'academic' since, ultimately, a whole spine MRI is likely to be the best choice, allowing to search for other occult lesions which would help determine future treatment and prognosis.

**Q.219 - Part 3 - Answer: 3**

Whatever the site of the lesion, acute neurological signs or cord compression due to a likely neoplasm is an emergency and rapid administration of intravenous dexamethasone (4mg then 16mg daily in divided doses) should not be delayed. It will buy time to reduce swelling of the lesion while the imaging can be discussed. The case can then be discussed as to whether neurosurgery or radiotherapy may be the best option. Relief of urinary retention is very important, however setting up a trolley and passing the catheter may waste valuable time if this delays giving steroids. On the other hand the dexamethasone can be arranged with the nurse quickly before you attend to the catheter. In real life, if the patient had an acutely distended bladder, you would probably do both these options simultaneously with the help of the nursing staff.

**Q.220 - Answer: 3**

This is the description of an antalgic or painful gait which arthritis or trauma can cause. The base is normal, excluding option 1, i.e. an ataxic gait. Cerebro-vascular disease would suggest previous stroke with a spastic gait which presents with a spastic or stiff limb that one can't lift during the normal gait cycle; so either the foot scuffs the ground or swings outwards (circumduction) to avoid the scuffing. Extra-pyramidal gaits are those characteristic of parkinsonism, i.e. hesitant, shuffling with stooped posture etc. A proximal myopathy would give weakness of the hip girdle which leads to poor hip abduction, overcome by a waddling movement at the pelvis to avoid foot scuffing.

**Q.221 - Answer: 1**

Although options 2 to 5 can occur in epileptic seizures, they are not specific to them. For instance, Stokes-Adams attacks, which are caused by transient arrhythmias, can cause sudden-onset loss of consciousness during which a few limb jerks are seen. Urinary incontinence is also seen, albeit less commonly in these cases and in vaso-vagal syncope. Tongue biting is the most specific feature of an epileptic seizure from the list. A sudden onset and muscle twitching are also seen in pseudoseizures, and urinary incontinence is rare but occasionally noted. Tongue-biting would be most unusual in the context of pseudo-seizures.

**Q.222 - Answer: 3**

A unilateral throbbing headache lasting more than several minutes with no visual disturbance, makes options 1, 4 and 5 less likely. However, in practice this is a difficult case, since both migraine or cluster headaches could be possible diagnoses here. However in the world of MCQs there are some classical features of cluster headaches which, although they do not exclude migraine, are described to paint a classical description of cluster headaches. These are: several episodes occurring over a short space of time, intense throbbing pain with eye watering and nasal congestion.

**Q.223 - Answer: 2**

Friedreich's ataxia is an autosomal recessive disorder affecting the spinocerebellar and corticospinal tracts. Features include a cerebellar ataxia, hence there is intention rather than either resting or postural tremor as in this case. All the other options can cause a fine tremor at rest, but the story of tremor more apparent on held posture and relieved by alcohol is typical of benign essential tremor, and it is usually found to be familial. The onset is typically in early adulthood with a worsening in later years.

**Q.224 - Answer: 3**

Option 3 is potentially dangerous since hypotension due to antihypertensive administration can cause extra harm in this situation. Most of the time, hypertension is just monitored rather than actively controlled. All the other options are essential considerations.

**Q.225 - Answer: 2**

The decision to perform an endarterectomy would lie with the surgeon, however general considerations include likelihood of benefit over operative risk, as for any operation. Operative risk is increased in those over 75, hypertensive and with bilateral stenosis. A TIA in the occipital lobe implies ischaemia via the posterior circulation, i.e. vertebro-basilar arteries, and not the carotids. Therefore carotid endarterectomy is unlikely to be particularly indicated for that presentation in isolation. However, finding evidence of at least 75% stenosis of one internal carotid alone is a good indicator for referral.

**Q.226 - Answer: 2**

A CT of the head can miss between 2-10% of SAH, either due to poor visualisation of the posterior fossa, a small leak or headache due to vasospasm prior to an impending major bleed. Meningism is in fact a key feature due to meningeal irritation from blood. Tachycardia would be typical due to the severe pain, and is not necessarily indicative of sepsis. Although decreasing red blood cells may suggest a bloody tap, it can't exclude a background of blood in the CSF. Furthermore, option 5 is false, since a lumbar puncture should be taken after 12 hours to best identify xanthochromia (caused by red cell breakdown products).

**Q.227 - Answer: 5**

The subacute history of fluctuating consciousness and confusion with this crescent or moon shaped mass on CT is typical of a subdural haematoma. It is caused by subdural venous rupture, hence relatively slow accumulation of blood with a concave surface against the cerebral hemisphere. It is an important diagnosis to reach early on, since referral for neurosurgical treatment is highly successful. Normal pressure hydrocephalus (NPH) presents with dementia, gait disturbance and urinary incontinence. CT findings show enlarged ventricles with normal pressure on lumbar puncture. NPH is caused by a defect in CSF reabsorption and CSF shunting is a useful therapy. Fronto-temporal dementia or 'Pick's disease' manifests as dementia with signs of frontal dysfunction such as disinhibition, inability to plan and other behavioural and personality changes. One would not expect such a short history nor radiological changes such as in this case. A subarachnoid haemorrhage is caused by an arterial bleed and as such has a much more acute and painful onset. Extradural haematomas can have a fluctuating course of change in consciousness but generally follow a more memorable episode of head trauma. The typical history would be far shorter than the one given in this scenario, and a lucid interval after a head injury followed by deterioration would be classical. One would see a biconcave higher-attenuation lesion on CT head, due to fresh blood from a small artery in the extradural space pressing inwards against the cerebral hemisphere.

**Q.228 - Answer: 2**

If intravenous access is secure, then lorazepam is the first option, since its kinetics are more reliable than diazepam. Option 1 is used when venous access is difficult. Options 3 and 4 are subsequent options if the first fails. Dextrose is given if you suspect or confirm hypoglycaemia.

**Q.229 - Part 1 - Answer: 3**

A partial seizure refers to focal features with consciousness maintained. Partial complex is again localized but consciousness is lost, i.e. as if Kyle had the seizure here described, but up to and including losing consciousness. Partial with secondary generalization as described here is a focal onset, followed by loss of consciousness, then spread to both hemispheres with visible bilateral involvement. Primary generalized or generalized is where consciousness may be lost from the start and includes option 5, which is the typical 'grand mal' seizure, where a period of limb stiffening occurs before jerking.

**Q.229 - Part 2 - Answer: 2**

It is good to understand some common management principles. Carbamazepine is currently the first choice in those with partial seizures with or without secondary generalisation and sodium valproate is second-line. Sodium valproate is often the first choice for primary generalized seizures, with lamotrigine as second line. Due to its many interactions, need for therapeutic drug monitoring, and often troublesome side-effects, phenytoin is not commonly used as a first option.

**Q.230 - Part 1 - Answer: 4**

Typical neuroleptics give such 'extrapyramidal' effects and these can be attenuated with procyclidine. Encephalitis rather than meningitis can, in rare cases, give late sequelae of parkinsonism. Multiple system atrophy has three main manifestations, and one of these aspects tends to predominate in each case. These include the Shy-Drager syndrome (autonomic failure) that involves autonomic features of postural hypotension and poor bladder control; Parkinsonism which does not respond to treatments for Parkinson's disease (striatonigral degeneration); and olivopontocerebellar atrophy manifesting as cerebellar ataxia.

**Q.230 - Part 2 - Answer: 1**

Since the effectiveness of medications is limited to a short timescale, it is usually best to save treatment until symptoms interfere with the patient's life. In young patients it is thought best to start with ropinirole and a new dopamine agonist. They are thought to give a reduced risk of dyskinesias.

**Q.231 - Answer: 1**

Two questions in one! First, what is the diagnosis? - Carpal tunnel syndrome. Second, what are its associations? Others beyond those listed above include trauma, amyloidosis (associated with dialysis) and acromegaly. Incidentally, it is hypothyroidism for carpal tunnel syndrome above, but options 1, 2, 3 and hyperthyroidism are the common associations with palmar erythema!

**Q.232 - Part 1 - Answer: 3**

This 'harlequin' distribution is classical of Brown-Sequard syndrome, in which a lesion affects only one side of the cord. It therefore disrupts pain sensation fibres crossing at that level from the other body side as well as those ascending from that side. It affects already crossed upper motor neurones descending further on that side and dorsal column proprioceptive and vibration sense fibres ascending on that side (which are due to cross over in the brainstem). Syringomyelia is due to a fluid-filled central spinal lesion covering several levels. It therefore begins with a (cape-like) anaesthesia to pain, affecting several cord levels, by interfering with decussating spinothalamic fibres at the level of the lesion. Spinal muscular atrophy is an inherited group of disorders usually presenting in childhood with muscular weakness, but no sensory component. The Arnold-Chiari malformation is an anatomical defect whereby an extension of the cerebellum protrudes through the foramen magnum. It is associated with syringomyelia. A transverse myelitis is inflammation of the spinal cord, usually around one level, and usually doesn't limit to one side, though the symptoms may be of unequal severity on both sides. It may be related to an infective agent or to multiple sclerosis, though it can be the presenting event in what will later become clear-cut multiple sclerosis.

**Q.232 - Part 2 - Answer: 2**

If we establish that this is due to a lesion in one part of the spinal cord with both motor and sensory features, and then discover that there are additional lesions, then multiple sclerosis has to be the best possible answer. Motor neurone disease does NOT give sensory features and neither does poliomyelitis, which affects the anterior horn cells. Herpes infections can cause transverse myeliltis but are unlikely to give the MRI appearances described in the scenario. Likewise, HTLV-1 infection or tropical spastic paraplegia gives bilateral spastic paresis with sensory symptoms, but we would not expect multiple discrete lesions in the cord.

**Q.232 - Part 3 - Answer: 2**

Female sex, relapsing-remitting progression, early age of onset and presence of sensory symptoms are all indicators of a good prognosis.

**Q.233 - Part 1 - Answer: 4**

Think systematically and list the features in this case: unilateral partial ptosis, normal pupils, normal eye position, complex ophthalmoplegia. Now either list the features found in each diagnosis of the list or (maybe easier) cross compare each of the 4 features of the case at a time against the options to eliminate them. Unilateral disease – this eliminates option 5, since that is bilateral. Partial ptosis - this eliminates option 2, in which the lid is usually firmly closed. Normal pupils - eliminates 1 (pupils are small) and 2 (pupils are large). Pupil constriction is carried by parasympathetic fibres around the third nerve; these remain intact in partial palsies. Normal eye - eliminates 2 and 3. Complex ophthalmoplegia - implicates and now confirms option 4. Furthermore, these symptoms fluctuate and the ophthalmoplegia is worsened on repeat testing (fatigue).

**Q.233 - Part 2 - Answer: 3**

An alternative test is the Tensilon® test when test doses of edrophonium are given. Options 1 and 2 are used to assess lesions to the third nerve and the cervical sympathetics respectively.

## REPRODUCTIVE

**Q.234 - Answer: 5**

Clinically speaking, a wise approach to such a case would be to rule out common causes of PCB, such as a sexually transmitted infection and hormonal medications, visualise the cervix and review cytology. Chlamydia is common in this age group and causes a cervicitis leading to PCB; however, the recent negative test is reassuring in this case. Despite being an important cause of PCB and a diagnosis not to miss, cervical cancer is rare in this age group. But what about the report? Well, a good cervical smear has to sample the transformation zone which is the interface between columnar and squamous epithelium of the cervix. Nowadays, liquid-based cytology apparatus for taking smears involves a 'broom' style spatula that sweeps the cervix. However, if the patient has an ectropion (which is where the squamo-columnar junction lies very lateral to the cervical os), the broom will not cover the junction and only columnar cells are 'swept up', as in this case. The epithelium of an ectropion (also called ectopy) is fragile, leading to PCB. Breakthrough bleeding is a common cause of PCB in young women on combined hormonal contraception, and can be due to taking the pill continuously without a pill free interval ('back–to-back packets'), when there is a drug interaction due to concomitant antibiotic therapy, or just due to irregularity in taking the pill on time. Mandy however is on depot and in fact progestogen therapy often leads to amenorrhoea, which most women on 'depot' experience by 6 months of usage. Atrophic vaginitis does lead to bleeding after intercourse, but is due to a fragile or even painfully inflamed vaginal epithelium that is thinned, due to low oestrogen levels that typically occurs perimenopausally.

**Q.235 - Answer: 2**

Minimal bleeding that is confined to the middle of the cycle is often physiological, occurring in response to fluctuations in oestrogen levels around the time of ovulation. Cervicitis is unlikely, as the pattern of bleeding would not be so clear-cut as here, but also since she would have been screened and thoroughly treated around the time of her Chlamydia episode. Endometrial neoplasia is less likely in the age group and would not usually present quite like this. Endometriosis tends to present with discomfort due to ectopic endometrial tissue that peaks just before and during early menstruation and is then relieved. A foreign body can inflame the vagina and cause bleeding, but this would tend to be in the form of a worsening, blood-stained, offensive discharge.

**Q.236 - Answer: 1**

The combined oral contraceptive pill is very good at regulating the menstrual cycle thereby masking any underlying 'normal' oligomenorrhoea. When stopped, the irregular bleeding pattern is revealed and this can often be a cause for patient concern. In fact, Tracy is not fully amenorrheic now since she had a subtle bleed which might just be her irregularity. The fact that she has had bleeding in the past excludes option 2 since this causes primary amenorrhoea. Low weight can disrupt menstruation; however, her BMI is too high to be classified as anorexia nervosa. One should always consider that pregnancy is possible until proven otherwise but with a negative test today, the time-course of her symptoms is too long for pregnancy to be a cause. PCOS can cause secondary amenorrhoea and acne, and not all patients are obese (some authorities describe an 'athletic' type of PCOS who can have relatively low BMI). However, the normal TVUS 2 months ago makes this diagnosis unlikely.

**Q.237 - Answer: 3**

DUB is a diagnosis of exclusion, and describes heavy and or irregular bleeding with or without pain. An IUD is associated with worsening of such bleeding disturbances; however an intrauterine system (IUS) or Mirena®, which is a device with progestogen, can be useful here, as it reduces menstrual loss by a local action. The other 4 options are reasonable treatment options for DUB, but in different types of cases. Danazol is an ovulatory inhibitor and would be given by a specialist, not as first line. Likewise, endometrial ablation is not appropriate, particularly since this is a young woman who may still wish for future children. This would tend to be used for older patients. Tranexamic acid is an antifibrinolytic agent that can reduce the menorrhagia very successfully, but mefanamic acid (an antiprostaglandin) has the additional benefit of helping with the pain (dysmenorrhoea).

**Q.238 - Answer: 3**

The definition depends on how much of the foetal products have been passed and whether the os is closed or not. In a primigravida, an os at 1cm counts as openand indicates that fetal loss is either impending or that some products have already been passed, and usually more are still to be passed. Option 2 refers to some bleeding or pain which passes, and the os has remained closed, but the outcome in terms of fetal viability is still uncertain. An incomplete abortion arises with an open os; a lot of products have passed but more is still to come. A missed abortion refers to the death of a foetus which is subsequently retained.

**Q.239 - Answer: 1**

This question refers to recurrent spontaneous miscarriage which is defines as 3 or more recurrent miscarriages. While all of the options are associated with miscarriage, the last two are least likely to lead to such recurrence, since they would often have been identified as causative factors and steps would normally have been taken to address them by this stage. Cervical incompetence is not unusual following termination of pregnancy or other operations requiring cervical dilatation, or procedures related to cervical neoplasia. Out of the first three options, number one is just the most common since it covers over half the cases of recurrent miscarriage with an identifiable cause and encompasses conditions such as diabetes, thyroid disease and polycystic ovarian syndrome. Overall, however, it must be remembered that there are many women who suffer three miscarriages simply due to bad luck, with around a 1 in 4 chance that it will happen to any woman for each pregnancy, three in a row is sadly not rare occurrence. Fortunately, if there is no identified cause, many women will go on to have successful term pregnancies.

**Q.240 - Part 1 - Answer: 4**

It is conceivable that a patient with any of the first four options can present with these symptoms. However, a bulky uterus that has a snow storm appearance is synonymous with a hydatidiform mole. Large ovarian cysts also occur in this condition. It is also a recognised cause of hyperemesis gravidarum, along with multiple pregnancy. While it is true that options 4 and

5 both represent forms of gestational trophoblast disease, the latter would occur subsequent to the former.

**Q.240 - Part 2 - Answer: 1**
HCG levels will indicate ongoing disease resulting either from incompletely excised tissue from the original focus, or from metastatic spread if it has progressed to for a choriocarcinoma. Since these conditions can persist and develop over longer time periods, long-term follow up is necessary. Pregnancy is indeed hazardous and should be avoided for up to a year, but since these tissues are hormonally responsive, the contraceptive pill is contraindicated. Option 3 is true of choriocarcinoma. Options 4 and 5 are just irrelevant to this case.

**Q.241 - Answer: 3**
This is a harmless nabothian cyst which is caused by retention of secretions and can give a cloudy appearance, but tends to be firmer that a vesicle or herpes virus. They do not give symptoms but also tend not to clear spontaneously, but may be easily removed by electrocauterisation. Herpes simplex cervicitis tends to give groups of painful, easy-to-break vesicles, which rupture to leave erosions. A sebaceous cyst is a retention of sebum on hair-forming skin. A Bartholin's cyst results from fluid retention of a blocked Bartholin's duct and would be lower down towards the entrance to the vagina and larger than this.

**Q.242 - Answer: 1**
While it is true that the combined contraceptive is a treatment for some women with menorrhagia or dysmenorrhoea, it in actually known to increase the size of fibroids. All the other options, although not common, are indeed true. Infertility is thought to be due to interference with implantation.

**Q.243 - Answer: 5**
The tumour is driven by excessive exposure to oestrogens unopposed by progestogens. The first options 4 relate to this, but option five is a localised progestogen-only hormonal contraception method.

**Q.244 - Part 1 - Answer: 5**
A copious, offensive discharge with a raised pH (>4.5) means either TV or BV. Thrush tends to give a thicker, whiter and itchier discharge with a faint yeasty odour, rather than a very strong odour. Options 1 and 2 typically affect predominantly the cervix rather than the vagina itself, and discharge is less marked, or may not be noted at all. TV can cause a vulvitis (hence the

itch) even in the absence of significant vaginal discharge. TV can also cause a cervicitis and even, as depicted here, a strawberry cervix which is swollen red (which is not seen in BV).

**Q.244 - Part 2 - Answer: 2**
TV is a sexually transmitted infection (STI), and as such, current and past partners should be notified (as far as practically possible) and the current partner should also have completed treatment before sex is resumed to prevent re-infection. Metronidazole treats TV and BV. BV is not an STI, it is rather an imbalance in vaginal flora associated with a rise in vaginal pH triggered by a variety of factors including cosmetics and soaps, menstrual flow or unprotected sex (semen is alkaline and raises vaginal pH). Option 3 is a good treatment for thrush (Candida). Option 4 is a treatment for Chlamydia trachomatis. Option 5 is a treatment for gonorrhoea.

**Q.245 - Answer: 1**
You can decipher the diagnosis by excluding the others. Primary syphilis just involves the site of inoculation (usually genitals) with a solitary painless ulcer and none of the other features mentioned. For psoriasis, one would expect to see skin or nail manifestations and ulcers would not be anticipated. Herpes simplex virus tends to cause small crops of tiny vesicles that evolve and resolve over one to two weeks. Finally, a fixed drug eruption can occur with non-steroidal anti-inflammatories, but it is characterised as a rash or ulcer (usually shallow) in any particular location, that recurs in that same place with rechallenge with that drug at a later date. This leaves Behçet's as the best choice. It is an autoimmune connective tissue disease associated with HLA-B5. The skin manifestation of a lesion developing after the blood tests were taken is known as the pathergy reaction to skin trauma.

**Q.246 - Part 1 - Answer: 5**
Figures vary depending on populations studied; however, over a quarter of cases of subfertility remain unexplained. There is a reasonable possibility of spontaneous conception eventually in such cases. Just under a quarter are due to male factors. About a fifth are due to anovulation, about 1 in 7 is due to tubular causes and around 1 in 20 due to endometriosis.

**Q.246 - Part 2 - Answer: 2**
Basal body temperature rise for a few days following ovulation is a well known biological phenomenon, but it is fraught with problems, not only due to variation of cycle length, practicalities of measurement, but also other factors that can alter the woman's temperature. The serum progestogen rise

seven days before expected menstruation is a standard to indicate ovulation. One would expect a fall in FSH due to normal functioning ovarian feedback; however FSH is pulsatile and single measurement may be misleading. LH does rise at different parts of the cycle but is not specific to ovulation since a high serum LH forms part of the investigations for polycystic ovarian syndrome. Oestrogen levels do rise and fall as part of a healthy menstrual cycle, but yet again they are not a reliable and practical measure of ovulation compared to option 2.

**Q.247 - Answer: 5**

The emergency contraceptive (EC) pill is now given as a single dose of Levonelle 1500mg, i.e. a progestogen-only method. It can be given by doctors, but also by some nurses and pharmacists. Patients must be warned that the bleeding pattern will be disrupted. Patients can take EC more than once in a cycle. The EC is around 95% effective up to 24 hours after unprotected sexual intercourse, 85% effective between 24-48 hours, and 58% 48-72 hrs later, hence it is best referred to as EC and not the 'morning after pill'. It still has some effect after 3 days but this is low, so it is not licensed for that time, and only doctors can prescribe it at that stage. The copper IUD is effective at preventing pregnancy from any episode of sex during one menstrual cycle if placed up to 5 days from likely ovulation, i.e. day 19 in a regular 28-day cycle. It is not considered by most people to be a form of termination, since its effects are primarily toxic to sperm and preventing implantation. The copper is also embryotoxic, however. It must be left in place at least until the next period comes.

**Q.248 - Answer: 2**

It might be easier to tackle this question by looking at the obvious contraindications and eliminating the options. Firstly, she is going to be on her travels soon; for that reason, NFP is unsuitable, since it takes some training and regular measurements of temperature and other physiological features to get right, which would be difficult when travelling. Furthermore, it is the least effective option from the list. Also, although effective and less user-dependent, the depot injection is prescribed on a 12-weekly basis, and would only be helpful for a relatively short trip.. IUDs do not give of themselves give increased rates of ectopic pregnancies. They should obviously give lower pregnancy rates than without the IUD; however if a woman becomes pregnant with an IUD in situ, a higher proportion of these pregnancies will be ectopic than in women without an IUD. Having a previous ectopic pregnancy or being primiparous are not absolute contraindications to an IUD; however, there may be other more suitable

options in such a patient. The heavy menstrual loss is another additive factor against offering an IUD. The choice is therefore between the POP and COCP. The migraines are here as a distraction to you. Migraines with aura are an absolute contraindication to the COCP; however, if she has no other vascular risk factor, and the migraines have no features other than a headache, then COCP may be acceptable. The problem with the standard POP is that you have to be sure to take it within 3 hours every day, which will be difficult if travelling in general and particularly when crossing time zones. Furthermore, standard POPs do not act by suppressing ovulation and so are less desirable in a patient with a history of ectopic pregnancy. An additional learning point is regarding Cerazette®, a new-generation POP that is different in that it acts primarily by ovulation suppression and has a dosing window of freedom of up to 12 hours, i.e. you can be up to 12 hours late with it and it won't fail.

**Q.249 - Part 1 - Answer: 1**

Smoking is associated with a lower risk of pre-eclampsia. Pre-eclampsia is more common in primigravidae and those whose pregnancies have resulted from a new relationship. The risk of pre-eclampsia is increased by a positive medical history of it; however this risk is decreased in subsequent pregnancies with the same partner. It increases again following conception from a new male partner. While maternal epilepsy means that she has a lowered seizure threshold compared to other women and although seizures are the consequence of pre-eclampsia evolving into overt eclampsia, epilepsy is not a risk factor per se for pre-eclampsia. Obesity and high pregnancy weight gain also increase the risk somewhat.

**Q.249 - Part 2 - Answer: 4**

Pre-eclampsia is also termed pregnancy-induced hypertension with proteinuria and hence option four is a requisite for diagnosis, though of course can occur for other reasons, but these are far rarer than pre-eclampsia. Option 1 is a consequence of pre-eclampsia but also a common finding in pregnancy in general. Options 2, 3 and 5 are found in severe pre-eclampsia, but again not specific to it since they occur in other conditions.

**Q.250 - Answer: 3**

Options 1 and 2 are false since the natural history of this condition can be unpredictable, these markers may fluctuate and the patient can deteriorate suddenly. Delivery is the only ultimate cure, but the mother remains at risk of complications for over a week after delivery, and a considerable proportion of the mortality from this condition actually occurs within the first few days post-partum. Magnesium sulphate is most useful in established seizures, but there is some evidence that it also has prophylactic value in reducing the risk of severe pre-eclampsia developing into eclampsia. Unfortunately this does not seem to reduce the perinatal mortality risk to the foetus.

**Q.251 - Answer: 2**

A placental abruption involves detachment of the placenta from the uterus. The detachment and bleeding can therefore be concealed yet disturb the uterus, causing pain and contraction, or a 'wooden' uterus on palpation. The foetus loses blood and would become compromised or distressed, which would be reflected in its heart rate. In contrast, a placenta praevia that is disturbed would cause overt vaginal bleeding that would predominantly affect the maternal circulation; initially the foetal heart rate would be normal, but significant maternal circulatory compromise would of course rapidly lead to fetal compromise. A history of smoking does not aid clinical assessment, although it is thought to be associated with placental abruption.

**Q.252 - Answer: 5**

Although many people find the TENS gives little or no pain relief, there are some who use it successfully as their sole agent for pain relief during labour. Pethidine given within 2 or 3 hours of likely delivery risks neonatal respiratory depression, and is avoided if possible, but is not absolutely contraindicated. Entonox ® can commonly cause nausea and vomiting as well as light-headedness, both of which can make the drug intolerable for a small proportion of women.

**Q.253 - Answer: 2**

Anti-D immunoglobulin is given to counteract the immunogenic potential of any Rhesus D positive foetal blood cells that may have entered the maternal blood stream in a foeto-maternal haemorrhage, FMH). This is done to cover the antigenic sites with preformed antibody and thus prevent their recognition by the mother's immune system, which would otherwise become sensitised and generate maternal immunoglobulin. If this happens, IgG is eventually formed which can cross the placenta and cause haemolytic disease (foetal hydrops) in this or, more typically, in future pregnancies. Anti-D is given for events that risk FMH. These include: invasive prenatal diagnosis (foetal blood sampling, amniocentesis, chorionic villus sampling); antepartum haemorrhage; and external cephalic version of the foetus. A threatened abortion that is resolved with no foetal harm before 12 weeks' gestation does not require Anti-D (according to Royal College of Obstetrics and Gynaecology guidelines), unless bleeding is heavy, or there is associated abdominal pain. Although it may seem specialist to know the condition for option 2, the other options should be known and one could therefore work this out by elimination.

**Q.254 - Answer: 4**

Polyhydramnios rather than oligohydramnios is more common in multiple than single pregnancies. All other options are more common in multiple pregnancies.

**Q.255 - Answer: 3**

2 out of 5 babies are breech at 20 weeks, 1 out of 5 at 28 weeks and around 3 percent by term. ECV is contraindicated in certain situations, some of which are those predisposing to the breech in the first place. These include: multiple pregnancy, placenta praevia, pre-eclampsia, uterine scars and babies that are 'small for dates'.

**Q.256 - Answer: 3**

All options except option 3 are part of the management of retained placenta, although they obviously do not fall in this order. A full bladder interferes with uterine contractions and breast stimulation leads to oxytocin release. The cord should be pulled firmly yet gently as to avoiding snapping or inversion of the uterus (which is rare, but can lead to collapse and death). If this fails, then manual separation is attempted and, if this does not work, a hysterectomy may be the last resort.

**Q.257 - Answer: 2**

The fluctuant swelling confined to the bone margin is typical of the cephalhaematoma, since it is a subperiosteal collection of blood. It may take a few weeks to resolve and can contribute to neonatal jaundice. Moulding is the movement of the cranial bones, which can approximate or override each other during delivery. The caput succedaneum is soft tissue oedema that is exterior to the periosteum and is therefore not confined to it. A large version of this due to Ventouse-assisted delivery is called a chignon. Chignon is french for 'bun' and is another name for having the hair in a bun shape. The fifth option is a collection of blood but, again, is not determined by bony boundaries.

**Q.258 - Answer: 1**

The risk of Down's syndrome according to maternal age is approximately: 1 in 1500 at age 20, 1 in 800 at age 30, 1 in 270 at age 35, 1 in 100 at age 40 and >1 in 50 in those over 45 years. There are several types of antenatal screening tests which can be combined in different ways, depending on the time of presentation and local access to resources. The UK National Screening Committee (UKNSC) has set out guidelines to assist and direct the decision-making process. To understand this guidance, you must first understand a little about the tests. First trimester testing includes:

1) Nuchal Translucency (NT) - an ultrasound scan that has up to 85% sensitivity for detecting Down's syndrome with around 20% false positive rate. It tends only to be performed between 11 and 14 weeks' gestation.
2) Serum testing at 10 weeks comprises pregnancy-associated plasma protein A (PAPP-A) and human chorionic gonadotropin (HCG).
3) The combined test of the first 2 just listed. Second trimester screening involves the 'quadruple test' (alpha feto-protein, HCG, inhibin-A and unconjugated oestriol).

Where not currently available, the triple test (without the inhibin) is used. Uptake of first trimester screening varies due to patient choice but also since some women, like Carole, present too late. However, the UKNSC has recommended that all pregnant women should at least be offered second trimester serum screening, irrespective of their age. Carole is 42 and would benefit from chorionic villus sampling; however, now being over 20 weeks, this is too hazardous and is not recommended. There is no upper time limit for a termination of pregnancy as long as there is thought to be serious physical/mental harm to the mother or serious handicap to the child if born, though clearly most parents and most clinicians would aim for the procedure to be performed at the earliest possible stage to lessen distress and maternal risks.

## RENAL / UROLOGY

**Q.259 - Answer: 1**

This is a picture of bilateral ureteric obstruction which would not be typical of amyloidosis or myeloma. One would expect a glomerulonephritis with these , but the dipstick is negative for protein or blood. Amyloidosis typically gives enlarged and echobright kidneys. A urethral stricture does give bilateral obstruction but one would expect a change in urine flow. Likewise, with prostatic hypertrophy, one would expect increased urine frequency and flow changes. All this aside, the pattern of medial shift in ureters and bilateral hydronephrosis is a classical picture for retroperitoneal fibrosis.

**Q.260 - Part 1 - Answer: 5**

The results show renal impairment which, in this situation, may well be acute. A raised CK can infer rhabdomyolysis, a cause of acute renal failure. An MSU, urine dipstick and ultrasound are all reasonable investigations for acute renal failure; however the results also show a very high potassium. The blood test is going to be repeated, which is always important in case the first sample was decayed or haemolysed, giving a falsely high potassium, ,but in the meantime one must take this result seriously as a potential emergency and consider corrective measures to protect the heart against high potassium. An ECG would be the best and quickest indicator of myocardial danger. Calcium gluconate can stabilise and protect the myocardium. Serial ECGs will reflect this and indicate the need for further calcium gloconate.

**Q.260 - Part 2 - Answer: 2**

Ask yourself what is happening: normal saturations, but pleuritic chest pain worse when flat and pericardial rub signifies pericarditis, which is caused by uraemia. This is one of the main indications for haemodialysis besides persistent hyperkalaemia, severe or worsening acidosis, pulmonary oedema refractory to treatment, and uraemic encephalopathy. The other options suggest other common complications; however, on the whole, the key features of pericarditis make option 2 the best. Clinically significant pulmonary embolus is unlikely here because the saturations are normal. Sodium bicarbonate can be used for some cases of acidosis. Diuretics can be used in pulmonary oedema but this is not clinically significant here.

**Q.261 - Answer: 1**

The creatinine clearance is the best guide to determine the time for renal replacement therapy and this cannot be determined by spot values of creatinine alone. Calculations take into account serum creatinine but also factor in the patient's muscle mass, sex and age. The glomerular filtration rate is also a measure of renal function and is particularly useful in directing alterations in drug doses. It does not, however, account for tubular creatinine excretion, and therefore underestimates renal handling of creatinine in comparison to creatinine clearance.

The Cockcroft-Gault formula is a method for calculating creatinine clearance using age, weight and sex, but does not adjust for body surface area.

**Q.262 - Answer: 2**

Dialysate is changed about 3 to 5 times per day. Peritonitis associated with CAPD is not uncommon, though estimates of its frequency vary – around once every 1-2 years is found in most studies. Raised intra-abdominal pressure due to the dialysate can, in some patients with respiratory illness, compromise their breathing, by limiting chest expansion.

**Q.263 - Part 1 - Answer: 3**

Diabetes mellitus is the most common cause, with hypertension, glomerulonephritis and vascular disease in the top 4.

**Q.263 - Part 2 - Answer: 5**

Uncontrolled ischaemic heart disease and peripheral vascular disease are contraindications. Up until recently, no HIV seropositive patients were considered for transplant; however, given the advances in the management of HIV, patients who were otherwise reasonably well with good CD4 counts could now be considered. Chronic glomerulonephritis may recur in the transplanted kidney, but the rate of development may be rather slow and it is not therefore an absolute contraindication for renal transplantation. Hepatic insufficiency, active peptic ulceration, septicaemia and incurable cancers are also absolute contraindications to renal transplantation. It is also advisable to delay a transplant for up to five years after the resolution of most cancers because of the risk of recurrence when immunosuppressant medication is administered.

**Q.263 - Part 3 - Answer: 5**

Ischaemic heart disease is extremely prevalent in those with ESRF and is exacerbated post-transplant.

**Q.264 - Answer: 2**

Hyperacute rejection occurs around the time of the transplant surgery and is related to tissue incompatibilities. Acute rejection occurs between 3 to 6 months after grafting and its features are as described in this case. It is an immune-modulated complication that is responsive to immunosuppressive therapy. Chronic rejection occurs after 6 months and biopsies show atrophy, fibrosis and vascular damage. Immunosuppression is of limited value in these cases. The original disease could recur; however, this is rather soon for it to do so, and the biopsy shows tubular damage, which is not a feature of the original condition.

**Q.265 - Answer: 4**

You should be able to work this out by elimination, even if the answer is not instinctive at first. Reflux nephropathy can lead to clubbed calyces but one might expect either a history of obstruction in an older person or, if due to vesico-ureteric reflux, a story of earlier onset. IgA nephropathy is a form of glomerulonephritis, and therefore the histology is likely to be confined to glomerular features. Urate nephropathy (gout) would tend to produce crystals in the urine. Balkan nephropathy does indeed give interstitial fibrosis, but is a rather enigmatic disease localised to certain rural communities living along a stretch of the Danube, and is now thought to be caused by wheat contamination with the seeds of a weed that can cause kidney failure in animals. This leaves option 4 as the best, since this is an analgesic nephropathy which has led to a chronic interstitial nephritis.

**Q.266 - Answer: 5**

Ramipril is an angiotensin converting enzyme inhibitor (ACEI). ACEIs act on the renin-angiotensin system that autoregulates salt and water homeostasis. In those with renal artery stenosis, the reduced blood flow to the juxtaglomerular apparatus alters the feedback of this hormone system, which can lead - as in this case - to accelerated fluid retention and overload. The story of 'flash' pulmonary oedema given here is typical of this phenomenon. ACEIs do cause the first two options but the case doesn't depict the histories one would expect. Renal vein thrombosis tends to present differently, with loin pain, proteinuria, haematuria and deteriorating renal function.

**Q.267 - Answer: 1**

Diabetic reviews should include a 24-hour urine collection for protein that will test for microscopic proteinuria, i.e. 25 - 250 mg/24hrs. This implies early nephropathy and is an indication to introduce an angiotensin-converting enzyme inhibitor. Standard urine dipsticks cannot detect below 250mg of protein. Diabetes can lead to type 4 renal tubular acidosis.

**Q.268 - Answer: 4**

Red cell casts indicate bleeding from the glomerular or tubular systems. Glomerulonephritis is the best example of this from the available options.

**Q.269 - Answer: 5**

Bence-Jones protein, i.e. light chains from myeloma, doesn't typically show on a urine dipstick, but all the other options can cause a dipstick to be positive for protein.

**Q.270 - Answer: 2**

Nephrotic syndrome comprises hypoalbuminaemia (albumin<30g/L), oedema and proteinuria (>3g/24hr) and is related to the leakage of proteins in the glomerulus. Protein loss includes loss of immunoglobulin and thrombotic inhibitors, leading to increased tendency to infection and thrombosis respectively. The liver upregulates cholesterol output at the same time as it tries to compensate for decreased plasma proteins. Loss of protein also means loss of plasma oncotic pressure, which results in oedema, and eventually pleural effusions and ascites. The problem tends to be glomerular and not tubular. Hence, the sodium that is freely filtered is reabsorbed and manipulated as normal, and hyponatraemia is not a likely eventuality.

**Q.271 - Answer: 4**

Urethral discharge can be associated with several of the options. However, painful ejaculation and discharge on passing stool are classical features of prostatitis.

**Q.272 - Answer: 3**

Dysuria in a man of this age is much more likely to be due to a sexually transmitted disease than a urinary tract infection or anomaly. For that reason, it would be best to take a urethral smear to Gram stain for pus cells and gonococci, as well as performing a nucleic acid amplification test for Chlamydia and gonorrhoea. If these are both negative, then investigations 1 and 2 may be of use.

**Q.273 - Answer: 1**

Three early morning samples on consecutive days are often requested to help evaluate and/or exclude urinary tract tuberculosis. Terminal stream urine sampling is used to test for schistosomiasis. The Stamey procedure assesses for prostatitis and involves digital rectal examination with prostatic massage while urethral secretions are collected.

**Q.274 - Answer: 2**

Vasectomy can be related to the production of antisperm antibodies due to the exposure of semen antigens to the peripheral blood stream during the procedure. This is a proposed cause of poor return to feritility after vasectomy reversal. All the other options are commonly recognised as leading to an elevated PSA.

**Q.275 - Answer: 1**

Renal cell carcinomas arise from renal tubular epithelium. They can therefore cause an increase in erythropoietin and hence a polycythemia. Infiltration of the left renal vein can lead to obstruction of left-sided scrotal drainage and hence a varicocele on that side. Transitional cell carcinomas arise from the renal pelvis distally down the urinary tract. Wilms' tumours or nephroblastomas are childhood neoplasias. The kidneys would tend to be palpable bilaterally in adult polycystic kidney disease, and the patient would not feel so generally unwell until there was renal failure, which is not the case in the blood tests given.

**Q.276 - Part 1 - Answer: 5**

Staghorn calculi are 'struvite' or triple phospate stones composed of magnesium ammonium phosphate (occasionally with a little calcium). They are associated with Proteus spp. infection and so antibiotics are indicated to reduce further occurrence of infection and may reduce growth, and can lead to a degree of reduction in stone size, rather than resolution.. Only stones less than 5mm are able to pass spontaneously. Chocolate and tea contain oxalate which in high quantities contribute to oxalate stones, but not triple phosphate stones. An alkalinised urine will help to rid uric acid stones, which, incidently, are radiolucent; an alkaline urine tends to contribute to the formation of staghorn calculi. Manipulation of dietary calcium is not usually helpful and can have its own adverse effects.

**Q.276 - Part 2 - Answer: 3**

Large staghorn calculi such as this one may well be resistant to lithotripsy alone. Therefore an operative procedure such as the minimally invasive percutaneous nephro-lithotripsy (PCNL) is a worthwhile consideration. Since PCNL has a stone clearance rate of up to 95%, this makes open stone removal procedures increasingly unnecessary nowadays.

Note: a J-J stent is a stent with a curl at either end that can be placed along the course of a ureter to maintain patency and allow calculi debris to easily pass without obstruction. Large stones however would tend to produce more debris with the risk of obstruction.

**Q.277 - Answer: 2**

Classification of the glomerulonephritides (GN) is complex and can easily become confusing, given with overlaps in aetiology and presentations, with one condition causing several types of GN, and several types of GN causing variable combinations of haematuria, proteinuria and renal failure. However, rather than attempting to learn all the changing classes, it is probably of more help to learn a few key associations and principles. Firstly, membranous, minimal change and diabetic GN lead to nephrotic rather than nephritic (no haematuria or hypertension) pictures. Rapidly progressive (or cresentic) and IgA (Bergers' disease) commonly give a nephritic picture, with the latter being the most common cause of nephritic syndrome. Minimal change disease is more common in children than adults. Membranous GN is the most common cause of nephrotic syndrome in adults and has many associations, including malignancy (particularly haematological). Diffuse proliferative GN tends to present as a nephritic syndrome in children or young adults following a streptococcal infection. This is a case of nephrotic syndrome in an elderly man with CLL, so 2 is the best option.

## RESPIRATORY

**Q.278 - Answer: 3**

Cavitation on a chest x-ray due to infections is limited to a number of conditions including tuberculosis, Staphylococcus, Klebsiella, Legionella (rare), Pseudomonas aeruginosa and anaerobic infections. The latter two options, cytomegalovirus and Pneumocystis jirovecii, are far more common in the immunosuppressed, and would tend to give an interstitial pneumonitis rather than airspace consolidation. Non-infective conditions such as Wegener's granulomatosis and carcinomas can also lead to cavitation.

**Q.279 - Part 1 - Answer: 5**

Protein < 30g/L is suggestive of a transudate rather than an exudate. Mesothelial cells can be present in exudates and transudates. Options 1 and 4 refer to an exudate. Low glucose levels in pleural fluid compared to serum is consistent with infection or rheumatoid arthritis.

**Q.279 - Part 2 - Answer: 3**

Pulmonary emboli most often cause an exudate, although they can sometimes cause a transudate. Myxoedema, nephrotic syndrome, acute glomerulonephritis, left ventricular heart failure, liver cirrhosis and other protein-losing states are all causes of a transudate pleural effusion. The other options are associated with an exudative pleural effusion.

**Q.280 - Answer: 1**

This is a case of primary pneumothorax with no underlying chest disease. A recurrent pneumothorax or one secondary to an underlying pathology is managed a little differently. The British Thoracic Society (BTS) suggest that if there is no respiratory distress and the air space is <2cm wide, discharge can be considered. If however there is any respiratory compromise or the space is > 2cm wide, one would work through options 2 to 4, stopping once success is achieved.

**Q.281 - Part 1 - Answer: 3**

The picture of daytime sleepiness with lack of concentration in someone who snores and appears to stop breathing during the night fits with OSA. Patients are often overweight and during the night, loss of tone in pharyngeal muscles allows collapse and obstruction of the airway by soft tissue, causing the picture depicted in this case. Whilst absences can appear to give episodes of poor concentration, they do not account for the snoring and breathing pattern at night. Sinusitis can give bad head pains and disturb sleep, but yet again do not fit with the whole story here. Morning headaches are a sign of raised intracranial pressure and could be caused by a space-occupying lesion (SOL), but the rest of the story doesn't fit with an SOL. Narcolepsy is characterised by altered night time sleep but also by falling asleep spontaneously and involuntarily during the day.

**Q.281 - Part 2 - Answer: 3**

As already described, this is OSA. The symptoms often resolve if the patient reduces their weight. If, weight loss does not resolve the issue or cannot be achieved to an adequate degree to produce improvement within a reasonable time-frame, many patients attain good sleep with a CPAP (continuous positive airway pressure) device, which they use at home. This maintains open airways throughout the night and prevents obstruction from occurring. OSA can be secondary to other causes such as acromegaly and thyroid disease. Treating the underlying cause would of course also be necessary in those situations, but the CPAP option would tend to be required in addition.

**Q.282 - Answer: 2**

If you extract the basic features, we have a chronic respiratory deficit with upper lobe fibrosis in a smoker who worked in a glass factory. Conditions causing upper-lobe fibrosis include: EAA, silicosis, sarcoidosis and coal workers' pneumoconiosis. Beryllium exposure causes fibrosis throughout the lungs, and asbestosis affects the lower lobes. Glass is formed from ingredients including silicon dioxide and hence, without proper breathing apparatus, factory dusts are likely to have caused this patient's problem. Neither occupational asthma nor EAA would present in the way that this patient has, and one would expect a presentation of exacerbations and relative resolution rather than a chronic decline.

**Q.283 - Answer: 2**

The pattern of flu-like symptoms with aches, pains, fevers and respiratory features that occur in the presence of an allergen but clear completely after a few days separation is typical of EAA. The birds are the most likely culprit here, with proteinaceous allergen from their excreta. It is an IgG-mediated hypersensitivity, so repeat exposure perpetuates the symptoms. Asthma is an example of the immediate or IgE mediated (atopic) type of hypersensitivity and would tend to give bronchospasm, tightness and wheeze that is more tightly temporally-related to allergen exposure. ABPA has many similarities to EAA. It is a type I and II hypersensitivity to the fungus Aspergillus fumigatus and so symptoms will have a relation to allergen exposure. However, one would expect symptoms of cough and bronchospasm to predominate. Brucellosis is an infective illness caused by the bacterium Brucella abortus that is acquired from handling livestock. It can give very similar clinical features as described in this case, but the clinical picture would be progressive until treatment is initiated, rather than intermittent according to repeated exposure. Psittacosis is a bacterial infection. It is caused by Chlamydia psittaci, which is spread by domestic and wild birds. It causes an atypical pneumonia and again would not fit the chronology as described in this case.

**Q.284 - Answer: 1**

Options 2 to 4 are combined to give a CURB score (confusion, serum urea, respiratory rate and blood pressure) which is now recognised as a useful prognostic indicator in patients presenting with pneumonia. Oxygen saturation is a useful observation but may change transiently and will also be dependent on the amount of oxygen being administered.

**Q.285 - Part 1 - Answer: 5**

Features of a severe attack include options 2, 3 and 4 plus PER < 50% of normal. Life-threatening episodes are characterised by hypotension, bradycardia, exhaustion/confusion or coma, cyanosis, a silent chest, low oxygen, raised carbon dioxide or lowered pH on arterial blood gas, and PEF<33% of normal. Patients may deteriorate suddenly and both should be treated as an emergency with a low threshold for anaesthetic input.

**Q.285 - Part 2 - Answer: 4**

All the drugs listed here are used in the management of acute severe asthma. Options 1, 2 and 5 tend to be given immediately. Options 3 and 4 are given later on if the patient does not impove. This patient is already taking oral aminophylline and therefore is at increased risk of toxicity if an aminophylline infusion is given.

**Q.286 - Answer: 5**

Squamous cell carcinoma accounts for a slightly larger proportion of lung cancers than adenocarcinoma. These types are followed by small cell, then large cell, and finally bronchio-alveolar cell carcinomas, which are fairly rare (<1%).

**Q.287 - Answer: 3**

Pleural plaques are a relatively benign finding. They are caused by exposure to asbestos but they appear at least 20 years after asbestos exposure. They may co-exist with mesothelioma or asbestosis but they can also occur by themselves. Diffuse pleural thickening is a different pathology from pleural plaques but does indeed lead to a restrictive lung deficit.

**Q.288 - Part 1 - Answer: 3**

This is a case of bronchiectasis. If there is an element of bronchospasm, then options 1 and 2 may be appropriate; however, core therapy involves postural drainage and sputum expectoration, either self-administered or aided by others. Nebulised (not intravenous) antibiotics can be used for long periods at a time to offer reduction in deterioration with fewer acute episodes.

**Q.288 - Part 2 - Answer: 5**

The majority of cases are idiopathic, but in fact any condition that can distort or obstruct the airways may lead to abnormal dilatation and mucus accumulation. The list also includes bronchial tumours, pulmonary fibrosis/sarcoidosis, chemical or irritant pneumonitis and Kartagener's syndrome. Emphysema is a histological diagnosis typified by abnormal and permanently enlarged air spaces distal to the terminal bronchioles and hence the condition is not related to dilatation of the bronchi.

**Q.289 - Answer: 5**

Option 1 should be an obvious inclusion since smoking is dangerous with oxygen therapy. Options 2 to 4 complete the inclusion criteria if one also notes that patients should also be established on optimal medical therapy.

The development of LTOT has arisen from several studies in which long-term survival improved in the trial groups who received a minimum of 15 hours' daily oxygen. Reduction of hypoxic stress is likely to reduce pulmonary hypertension and compensatory cardiac changes that lead to morbidity and mortality.

**Q.290 - Part 1 - Answer: 2**

MDR-TB is a serious personal and public health concern that is on the rise due to a combination of several factors including incomplete and erratic TB therapy, imported infections, and HIV infection. With no previous exposure to anti-TB drugs, HIV infection or a source of likely MDR-TB, there is no particular reason to suspect MDR-TB in this case. If he has had two weeks of standard quadruple anti-TB treatment as an inpatient (i.e. observed), he has passed the openly infectious state and any further AFB noted in sputum are likely to be non-viable organisms. Since he is apparently well-educated and in a supportive environment there should not be an obvious need for DOT. For these reasons, option 2 is the most appropriate.

**Q.290 - Part 2 - Answer: 4**

All household contacts should be assessed for active or latent TB. Only if infection is detected in household contacts would casual contacts then be screened. Screening for TB in the household contacts involves either a Mantoux test or chest x-ray as a first step, depending on previous BCG vaccination status and age. Further steps involve newer interferon-based tests which also suggest contact with TB. The full guide to TB diagnosis and management can be downloaded from the Royal College of Physicians' website. Contact tracing is undertaken with the help of local TB specialist nurses and the local consultant in communicable diseases should be informed of positive index cases.

**Q.291 - Answer: 1**

Asthma and COPD have similar clinical presentations and at times it may be difficult to distinguish between the two, due to the shared benefit of various therapeutic options. Some authorities describe COPD as a group of diagnoses including chronic bronchitis, bronchiectasis, variants of bronchial asthma and so on. Asthma is characterised by a reversible airway obstruction, whereas in COPD there is a progressive airway obstruction with minimal or no reversibility to steroids. A hallmark of asthma is a diurnal variation in PEFR beyond the normal diurnal pattern that one expects to see in a normal individual. Option 2 is true of both and since some COPD patients do benefit from steroids, option 3 doesn't absolutely exclude COPD.

Asthma tends to be more likely in the young and COPD in the old. However adult-onset asthma is recognised, and COPD due to agents other than tobacco smoke, or related to an predisposition such as alpha-1 antitrypsin deficiency, would typically present before the age of 40. Cough with mucus is common to both diagnoses.

**Q.292 - Answer: 3**

The question is really asking you which chest factors can cause the syndrome of inappropriate anti-diuretic hormone production (SIADH). Regarding tumours, it is mainly the small cell type that tends to lead to SIADH as well as other forms of ectopic hormone production including that of ACTH, osteoclastic activating factor or PTH, to name but a few. Pancoast's tumour is just a term describing the unusual location of a tumour in the apical position, as this site accounts for only around 5% of lung malignancies. Pancoast's tumours can cause compression neuropathy of nerve roots from the lower brachial plexus (C8 & T1). However, pneumonias do also lead to SIADH (especially atypical pneumonias and TB). Given the short history of these symptoms, the radiological pattern and the absence of other signs suggestive of malignancy, a pneumonia is the most likely option. One could argue that a small cell carcinoma could lead to a pneumonia by bronchial obstruction and hence give this presentation; however a lot of small cell tumours tend to be more peripheral than to cause a whole lobar obstruction as here. If they were so large and central, one would also expect more widespread foci, which is often the case with small cell tumours, as they present later than solitary squamous cell lesions for instance. An empyema refers to pus in the pleural space, and this is not commonly associated with SIADH.

**Q.293 - Answer: 4**

Adult respiratory distress syndrome (ARDS) is a condition of acute lung injury. It arises following severe systemic or pulmonary illness where inflammatory mediators are released. This increases pulmonary vascular permeability (leaky capillaries), which hinders gas transfer and reduces lung compliance (stiff lungs), thus causing both respiratory and ventilatory failure. It is characterised by acute onset, 'fluffy interstitial infiltrates' on chest x-ray, refractory hypoxia and a low pulmonary artery wedge pressure. This may sound specialist, but essentially it really means that the increased interstitial oedema is NOT due to congestive cardiac failure. For that reason we fulfil the criteria for ARDS in this case. In particular, option 2 is eliminated as well as option 3. Pulmonary emboli are most unlikely given the deranged clotting, as disseminated intravascular coagulation is not suggested in the scenario

described. Pulmonary haemorrhage would cause airspace opacities and not infiltrates on chest x-ray.

**Q.294 - Part 1 - Answer: 2**

RAST is a test which involves taking patients' serum and assessing the amount of IgE antibody that reacts to specific allergens. It is useful in determining the presence of specific allergies, including allergic bronchopulmonary aspergillosis (ABPA), in which type I (IgE) and type III hypersensitivity exists towards Aspergillus fungi. This, however, is a case of a mycetoma or aspergilloma, in which a fungal ball accumulates in a pre-existing lung cavity and does not involve an allergic syndrome. Likewise, skin prick tests also show hypersensitivity and would be unreliable as a marker of Aspergillus in the lung. c-ANCA is associated with Wegener's granulomatosis. p-ANCA is associated with other vasculitides, including microscopic polyangitis and Churg-Strauss syndrome (which does give an asthma-like eosinphilic lung disease). Although not 100% sensitive, the serum precipitins test is the best test here to indicate the presence of Aspergillus exposure.

**Q.294 - Part 2 - Answer: 2**

An aspergilloma or mycetoma can persist asymptomatically; however it can instead lead to chronic cough, haemorrhage and, particularly in the immunosuppressed, spread to become an invasive lung disease. Aspergillus per se, if inducing a longstanding allergic response, can cause chronic inflammation and a degree of fibrosis in the long term; however, in this instance, the patient has an incidental aspergilloma rather than a history of allergic bronchopulmonary aspergillosis (ABPA).

**Q.295 - Part 1 - Answer: 1**

All of the options are associated respiratory complications of rheumatoid arthritis. Bronchiolitis obliterans is relatively rare, but more so would be Caplan's syndrome, which we all read about in books, but this massive lung fibrosis is indeed very rare. Caplan's syndrome involves rheumatoid arthritis on the background of chronic coal dust exposure, which is not the case for this lady.

**Q.295 - Part 2 - Answer: 2**

Methotrexate is associated with the development or enlargement of rheumatoid nodules in the chest and elsewhere. It is useful to note however that gold, methotrexate and cyclophosphamide can also lead to lung fibrosis in their own right.

**Q.296 - Answer: 3**
Out of all the options, a CTPA is the best test to confirm a PE, partly because it can specifically look for a PE where the other tests are just suggestive of, rather than specific to this diagnosis. Furthermore the other tests may be difficult to interpret in this case, given the other aspects of the scenario. For example, a V/Q nuclear medicine scan will identify areas of ventilation-perfusion mismatch, however if there are other lung diseases, including the likely pneumonia, the result will be difficult to interpret. The D-Dimer identifies thrombosis per se and is not specific to a PE; furthermore it may be raised in sepsis. The chest x-ray can show 'wedge-shaped' areas of lung change after established infarction from a PE; but again, the changes may be difficult to distinguish from infection or other pathologies. An ECG is supposed to show a typical '$S_I Q_{III} T_{III}$' pattern but this is often not present. A sinus tachycardia and signs of right heart strain (right axis deviation, right ventricular hypertrophy) can suggest pulmonary hypertension; however, yet again, this just indicates chest disease but cannot specify further.

**Q.297 - Answer: 4**
Pulse oximetry calculates oxygen saturation of Haemoglobin (Hb) by comparing the amount of light absorbed at two wavelengths. One wavelength targets $HbO_2$ (value a), the other targets Hb (value b). So a/(a+b) gives the saturation of Hb by $O_2$. The trouble is that a small percentage of Hb is bound to other particles. Normally, this doesn't interfere with this calculation; however, in carbon monoxide poisoning, oxygen is displaced by CO, thus decreasing the 'b' value and so more of the Hb appears to be saturated by $O_2$, as is the case here.
Methaemoglobin, on the other hand, is the oxidation of Hb from the $Fe^{2+}$ to $Fe^{3+}$ state. This also affects absorption, but in both wavelengths. The result is that the true $PaO_2$ is also very low compared to the pulse oximeter saturation reading; however, the oximeter saturation is also reduced (usually to around 85%). A venous blood gas sample can give a lower $PaO_2$ than expected by pulse oximetry; however, one would expect a higher $PaCO_2$ from a venous sample. Poor peripheral perfusion and nail varnish would, if anything, give lower readings by pulse oximeter than those found on arterial blood gas analysis, which would be normal.

**Q.298 - Answer: 3**
The arterial blood gases show a hypoxia $< 8$ kPa and hypercapnia $> 6$ kPa, i.e. type II respiratory failure, also known as ventilatory failure. Pulmonary oedema is associated with oxygenation failure alone, i.e. type I respiratory failure. All the other conditions can impair ventilation either by anatomical

restriction in ventilation or by neuromuscular means, thereby limiting carbon dioxide evacuation as well as reducing oxygenation.

**Q.299 - Answer: 4**

A flow volume loop is a functional test that can help identify the degree of airways obstruction but, unlike PEFR and spirometry, it can indicate the contribution from both extra- and intrathoracic disease. In other words, co-existent COPD would contribute to the deficit in the other tests, whereas the contribution from the thyroid compression can be best identified by a flow volume loop. PEFR measures the expiratory phase, but stridor (i.e. extrathoracic obstructions) predominantly affects the inspiratory phase of respiration. A functional test such as this may prove to be more useful than static CT imaging, which may not objectively infrom you of the postoperative benefit from partial resection of the mass. Gas transfer is of limited use in assessing obstruction in this case.

**Q.300 - Answer: 3**

This is a case of sarcoidosis, presenting with bilateral hilar lymphadenopathy, pulmonary fibrosis, erythema nodosum and anterior uveitis. Although calcium can be raised in sarcoidosis, it is of course not specific to this condition and a low or high value is not a useful diagnostic test. Options 1, 4 and 5 aid diagnosis of Wegener's granulomatosis, alpha-1 antitrypsin deficiency (emphysema) and other connective tissue diseases respectively. Serum ACE is the best marker from the options to support a diagnosis of sarcoidosis. However, it is not highly sensitive for sarcoidosis and a negative result does not exclude the condition. In one study of 110 patients with sarcoidosis, serum ACE was elevated in 59% of cases, yet the serum lysosyme was even more sensitive, being raised in 79% of cases [Tomita et al. *Lung* 1999].